Tangled Up in School:
Politics, Space, Bodies, and Signs
in the Educational Process

Sociocultural, Political, and Historical Studies in Education
Joel Spring, Editor

Tangled Up in School:
Politics, Space, Bodies, and Signs in the Educational Process

Jan Nespor

Places of Memory:
Whiteman's Schools and Native American Communities

Alan Peshkin

Political Agendas for Education:
From the Christian Coalition to the Green Party

Joel Spring

Non-Western Educational Traditions:
Alternative Approaches to Educational Thought and Practice

Timothy Reagan

The Cultural Transformation
of a Native American Family and Its Tribe 1763–1995
A Basket of Apples

Joel Spring

Tangled Up in School: Politics, Space, Bodies, and Signs in the Educational Process

Jan Nespor
Virginia Polytechnic Institute and State University

Routledge
Taylor & Francis Group
New York   London

First published by Lawrence Erlbaum Associates, Inc., Publishers

10 Industrial Avenue
Mahwah, New Jersey 07430

Reprinted 2010 by Routledge

Routledge

270 Madison Avenue
New York, NY 10016

2 Park Square, Milton Park
Abingdon, Oxon OX14 4RN, UK

Library of Congress Cataloging-in-Publication-Data

Nespor, Jan.
      Tangled up in school : politics, space, bodies,
and signs in the educational process / Jan Nespor.
           p. cm.
      Includes bibliographic references and index.
      ISBN 0-8058-2652-1 (cloth : alk. paper). —
ISBN 0-8058-2653-X (paper : alk. paper)
      1. Elementary school environment—Vir-
ginia—Roanoke—Case Studies. 2. Community
and school—Virginia—Roanoke—Case studies.
3.   Politics   and   education—Virginia—Roanoke—Case studies. 4. Educational
sociology—Virginia—Roanoke—Case studies. 5.
Thurber Elementary School (Roanoke, Va.) I. Title.
      LC210.6.V8N47 1996
      306.43'2'09755791—dc21   97-1959
                                                       CIP

For Liz Barber

Contents

Preface

Educational discourse usually treats the school as a bounded system, a container of classroom processes and curricular texts, an institutional shell waiting to be filled up by the actions of teachers, students, and administrators. But looking at schools as somehow separate from cities, politics, neighborhoods, businesses, and popular culture obscures how these are all inextricably connected to one another, how they jointly produce educational effects.

When groups and processes are analytically detached from each other in this fashion and treated as independent agents, it becomes easy to slide into the bleak loops of contemporary educational debate, where politicians blame teachers, teachers blame parents and kids, parents blame politicians and teachers, then join with them to blame the media, and kids are excluded altogether from the conversation.

The debate becomes less simple, but more constructive, when we focus on the dense interconnections among various actors and processes. Instead of looking at the school as a container, we have to peel back its walls and inspect the strings and rhizomes linking it to the outside world (which is no longer "outside"). We have to examine the crumpled spacetime topography that brings some institutions and neighborhoods close and pushes others away. We need to map the material trajectories of bodies to and from school, and weigh the densities of symbolic forms imported, created, and appropriated by students. The question then becomes, What do we talk about when we talk about schools?

The answer is not simple. This book takes a particular elementary school as its starting point and examines the local politics, regional economics, community–school conflicts, corporate influences, body discourses, neighborhood histories, and streams of popular culture that coursed through it over a 2-year period. The first chapter looks at how administrators, teachers, and parents struggled, often with one another, to define the school. The second chapter examines efforts by administrators, city politicians, and business representatives to define the school as an adjunct to the corporate economy—and kids' responses to that effort. The third chapter explores the place of the school as a neighborhood institution, examining the intersections of city planners' efforts to regulate city space, and kids' experiences carving out lived spaces in their neighborhoods. The fourth chapter queries the meaning of school as a site for bodily experience. It examines how organizations of space and patterns of control in the school shape kids' bodies, and how kids use body-based languages to construct maturity, gender, and race. The fifth chapter examines the school as a space for the deployment of symbolic resources, where kids learn and construct identities through engagments with television, comic books, movies, and sports.

All of these topics are knotted up in the single school. What I hope to show is how the meaning of "schooling" gets contested, negotiated, and re-invented across multiple, loosely connected streams of practice. The chapters, which slice the school into different planes, are connected, but not seamlessly so. This text itself can be thought of as a kind of discontinuous space revealing different facets of the school, focusing attention on the relationships of those facets, and reminding readers that a book like this one is made of partial, incomplete perspectives. My hope is that researchers, teachers, parents, and policy makers can move through those perspectives to get richer understandings of schools, leaving with questions better than their initial answers.

A number of people helped me produce this book. The excerpts from the oral history interviews quoted in chapter 3 are from a project entitled "Hidden History: The Black Experience in the Roanoke Valley," and are used with the kind permission of the Special Collections Department, University Libraries, Virginia Tech, Blacksburg, Virginia, and the Harrison Museum of African American Culture, Roanoke, Virginia.

At Thurber, Mr. Watts and Mrs. Court (sorry for the pseudonyms) not only put up with me during the fieldwork but read and responded to sections of the manuscript dealing with them. Liz Barber, who inspired my interest in elementary schools, gave me encouragement and advice, helped me throughout the fieldwork, and read and responded to the manuscript. I also had the critical help of several graduate students who worked with me in a writing group as I drafted this text. Stephanie Kimball, Karin Hauger, Linda Pacifici, and Randall Ward tried to keep my writing intelligible and brought their own wisdom and teaching experiences to bear in critiques of earlier manuscripts. Susie Murphy responded to an early version of chapter 1. Naomi Silverman, editor at Lawrence Erlbaum Associates, and Joel Spring, the editor of the series this book appears in, gave me much needed encouragement along with some key suggestions for reorganizing the chapters. Along with two reviewers whom I would also like to thank, Pamela Bettis and JoAnn Danelo Barbour, they encouraged me to squeeze out as much of the jargon as possible and make this a more reader-friendly text.

Introduction

School ethnography is a familiar genre, but what I do with it in this book is a little unusual. Instead of treating the school as a container filled with teacher cultures, student subgroups, classroom instruction, and administrative micropolitics, I look at one school, Thurber Elementary,[1] in Roanoke, Virginia, as an intersection in social space, a knot in a web of practices that stretch into complex systems beginning and ending outside the school. Instead of looking at educational settings—schools, classrooms, and so forth—as having clear boundaries and identifiable contents, I look at them as extensive in space and time, fluid in form and content; as intersections of multiple networks shaping cities, communities, schools, pedagogies, and teacher and student practices.

Part of my aim is to subvert the common focus on schools and classrooms as privileged sites of educational work. As Meyer (1977) pointed out, "Educational systems are, in fact, theories of socialization institutionalized as rules at the collective level" (p. 65), and the primacy of schools in creating educational effects is a key facet of such theories. Focusing on schools or classrooms as autonomous systems makes sense as a strategic moment in educational research—teachers, and to a lesser extent students, have to construct a lot of their everyday school life within these premises. But such a focus obscures how political, cultural, and economic forces shape school practices and are articulated with them and ignores the many critical strands of activity that connect schools to life outside schools.

In this book I want to explore the contrary notion that the key to understanding education isn't to be found in what happens *in* classrooms or schools but in the relations that bind them to networks of practice extending beyond. I want to give school its due, but not on its own terms—to treat it not as the focus of study but as a point of entry (Smith, 1987) to the study of economic, cultural, and political relations shaping curriculum, teaching, and kids' experiences.

---

[1]The principal, his school, and the teachers, parents, and other public schools mentioned have been given pseudonyms. Because I drew on newspaper articles and public oral history archives, however, I used the real names of the city and of public officials.

Looking at a school as an "array of intersections" (Rosaldo, 1989, p. 20), as an "articulated moment in networks of relations and understandings" (Massey, 1993, pp. 65–66) means questioning conventionally defined boundaries, looking for flows rather than states, focusing on networks and the layered connections that knot them together rather than on simple linear histories of circumscribed events or settings. It means asking which parents from which communities get involved in a school, where their opinions and beliefs about education come from, how they're situated in their communities, and how these communities are themselves created and situated in larger cityscapes. It means asking how the meanings of teaching get shaped within school system bureaucracies and particular schools; and how certain kids end up with certain teachers. It means asking where the curriculum comes from and what happens to it as it moves through the school; how the school is connected to other schools and to the business world; and how kids understand their neighborhoods as well as the things they read and watch on television. It means, I suspect, asking more questions that I can begin to answer.

I came to understand these questions through two years of ethnographic research at Thurber, from September 1992 to July 1994. The school had a diverse student body: About 54% of the kids were European American, 39% African American (bused in from outside the neighborhood), and 7% Asian American or Latin American. The school was situated in a working class neighborhood of the city, and most students' families were blue collar. In one class I worked in, for example, out of 25 kids, parents of 5 worked as domestics or custodians; 5 kids' parents were manual laborers for local factories or for construction and landscaping firms; parents of 2 were delivery drivers, and parents of 2 others were in appliance or auto repair; parents of 4 did some form of clerical work; a parent of 1 was disabled, and 4 kids' parents gave no information about their occupations. Only 2 seemed "middle class": One kid's parent managed a small firm, and the other's parent was "self-employed."

As I describe my fieldwork in this setting in some detail in the final chapter, I give only the barest outline here. When I say "ethnographic," I mean that most of my fieldwork consisted of participant observation and note writing. At first I sat in the teachers' lounge or in the school office and got to know the faculty. Then I gradually moved into classrooms and spent the second half of the first year of fieldwork with fifth graders and the second year in a fourth-grade class. I attended teachers' meetings and teacher in-service workshops (and even helped put on an in-service workshop for teachers). At the invitation of teachers, I made presentations to students (e.g., on Native Americans), helped students with their classwork, and worked with them in small groups. I went along on field trips, sometimes riding with parents and other times sitting on the bus with students. I attended parent–teacher association

(PTA) meetings (and joined the PTA, where I was invited to its executive committee meetings) and served with parents and teachers on the school's site-based management and report card revision committees. I organized and managed (not very well) a class newsletter with fourth graders and led a group of student researchers who were studying their classroom and the school. I took hundreds of pictures of the kids and let them use my camera to take pictures of the school; I always gave them copies of the pictures, regardless of who'd taken them. I made photocopies of the writing portfolios of 40 kids and collected copies of all the memos sent from the school to parents. For a stretch of one month at the end of my first year of fieldwork, and with a fifth-grade teacher's cooperation, each day I gave a different student a tape recorder and one hour's worth of tape so they could record their experiences.

I audiotaped meetings and events when I could, but sometimes taping was not appropriate or possible. I did have 11 formal, sit-down interviews with parents, but most of the parent-generated data I draw on comes from public meetings of parents and school staff or from notes of informal conversations in parking lots, on fieldtrips, and at PTA meetings. At a meeting where I got a certificate for my volunteer work in the school, I met a group of about 12 retired community members, former teachers at Thurber or parents of now-adult children who had attended the school, and later interviewed them about the history of the school's relation to the community.

I had about half a dozen taped interviews with the fourth-grade teacher I worked with during my second year of fieldwork, and I taped several interviews with two other teachers, and four interviews with the principal. Again, however, most of the teacher- and principal-generated data I use comes from field notes and from the 2 years of audiotaped staff meetings, in-service workshops, and parent–teacher meetings.

I did formal interviews in varying formats with 26 kids ("formal" meaning I sat down with kids for the exclusive purpose of interviewing them. I probably have as much or more recorded kid speech from tapes of everyday activities, which I don't consider "interviews"). I interviewed fifth graders in groups but did many of the interviews with fourth graders in one-on-one situations in which I asked them to draw maps of their neighborhoods and to talk about what they did around their homes or to go through the contents of their portfolios and talk about their school work. In all, my fieldnotes mentioned 67 children with whom I interacted and talked informally during the school days, along with 16 staff, the principal, and about 15 parents. As a *sample,* the major omission in the data is the lack of representation by parents of African American children. As I explain in chapter 1, African American parents were spatially and socially separated from the school, and this separation is reflected in my fieldnotes. I did, however, work with a representative number of African American students.

Outside the school, I attended, audiotaped, and transcribed public meetings on creating a new strategic plan for the city, meetings arranged by the school superintendent to gather input from community members about the school system, city council meetings on the selection of school board members, school board meetings, public radio programs, meetings for the revision of the state public school curriculum, and so on. For background on the school system, I interviewed faculty members and graduate students from my university who had worked with the Roanoke schools in the past. I hunted through the local history section of the library and went through 15 years of clippings from the local newspaper. All told, my files hold about three quarters of a million words and thousands of pages of material.

I've spun some of these data into this book. Thurber was an innovative school and had adopted among other things, literature-based approaches to reading and writing instruction, heterogeneous grouping practices, portfolio assessments, and a nontraditional grading scale. In chapter 1, I explore how these innovations came about and how, over the course of my 2 years of fieldwork, they became points of dispute among administrators, teachers, and parents. Parents were puzzled and frustrated by the innovations and ultimately organized a public protest at the school. The resulting confrontations, complaints, and meetings forced participants to articulate assumptions about teaching, learning, and parental involvement. Instead of just reporting this debate, however, I treat it as an intersection, a knot to be unraveled. I construct a history of city and school system politics to show how it was possible for the school to innovate in the first place; then I look at how teachers were (or were not) enrolled in the innovative schemes. Finally, I describe how parents found the political will to publicly challenge those schemes, and I situate the roots of the conflict in the different logics parents and teachers used to explain and evaluate school practice.

One way educators defended their innovations was to link them to the changing demands of work in the postindustrial United States. In chapter 2 I examine a manifestation of this logic in an intersection of business ideology and educational reform. I first trace the recent political and economic history of Roanoke to show how a discourse that privileged education as the solution to economic ills emerged locally and dovetailed with nationally circulating discourses emphasizing the importance of learning "in context" through "realistic" activities. I then discuss how Mr. Watts, the principal, and the school's "business partner," the local branch of a large multinational corporation, invoked elements of these discourses to legitimize a plan to refashion classrooms into business enterprises where teams of students would form companies to produce, market, and sell goods. I trace this effort from beginning to end, examine the misgivings of the teachers who were asked to implement it, and look closely at the students' reactions to it. I look at the enterprise-based classroom as an attempt to move students into a "space of finance" in which everything from personal characteristics to the objects of everyday life were to be treated purely as commodities for exchange; where actions would be measured in abstract units of value, and in which activity would be motivated by the discovery, creation, or exploitation of "needs." I examine the students' reactions to this effort and explore the sources of its failure.

The third chapter begins with short histories of the neighborhoods where students lived, to show how the relations of schools and neighborhoods were shaped by the sociopolitical histories of cities, in particular, spatial organizations of race and class. The focus of the chapter then shifts to the question of how the kids moved through these neighborhoods. I show that kids living in the same neigborhood can experience their spaces of activity differently. Some had lived in the same house for most or all of their lives and were embedded in neighborhood routines and city-based activities. Others had recently moved to the area around Thurber from cities where they'd spent most of their lives. These "displaced" kids, at the time I talked to them, still felt they belonged to their former neighborhoods and were struggling to re-establish spatial routines. Other, mobile students had moved so frequently that they seemed to feel no great attachment to any neighborhoods. The categories of *embeddedness, displacement,* and *mobility* are analytical conveniences that denote *relationships* between children and neighborhood spaces at particular points in the kids' lives. I use them not to label internal attributes of the kids, but to suggest that communities are themselves intersections of various and complex trajectories, not well-bounded and self-contained entities.

Chapter 4 moves from the neighborhood to the school, focusing on how children interacted with the world through their bodies. One of the key roles of schooling is to shape kids' bodies in particular ways and to attach these re-formed bodies to particular practices (such as reading and writing). I look at the spatial organization of Thurber and the practices of its teachers in shaping bodily practices; and at regionalizing and functionally defining school space to allow adults to monitor kids' bodies. Desks, for example, were arranged to regulate conduct, avenues of communication, and lines of sight. I try to put these patterns of regulation in the context of historical changes in assumptions about the meanings of bodies and bodily activity in Western society and suggest that the school was organized to create a particular body—silent, motionless, masculine. I also show that kids continued to articulate alternative meanings, to make sense of age, gender, and race in terms of languages grounded in the body. I describe, for example, the body-based boundary work that kids engaged in to distinguish genders, to articulate varied meanings for gendered activity, and to construct racial difference.

Bodies, of course, are not isolated systems of meaning; they intersect with flows of representations and systems of images. The issue I explore in chapter 5—really a bundle of issues—is what occupied the kids' attention most of the time I was with them: not school-sanctioned representations such as books, but representations taken from television, comic books, and video games. These media allowed kids to interact with their worlds in ways that extended experience beyond the body—by consuming, using, and reshaping representations from print, music, film, or video. I show how the kids used commodities, images, and meaning systems borrowed from popular culture to structure their interactions with one another and to give meaning to these encounters. I talk about their engagements with the economies of signs that constitute pop culture as participation in "kid-based funds of knowledge" (cf. Moll, Tapia, & Whitmore, 1993)—spatially and temporally distributed networks of exchange and identity construction. I examine articulations of these networks and focus on the kids' constructions of gendered and mature identities.

Rather than a conventional summary or conclusion, chapter 6 sketches questions raised by the preceding chapters. I suggest that the text be read generatively, as a point of departure rather than an end point. To that end, I formulate some issues I was left with at the end of my work, in the hope that others might take them up or formulate issues of their own.

Instead of hiding it in a methodological appendix, a final chapter, in the guise of a fieldwork chronicle, contains my attempts to contruct a collaborative research relationship with teachers, and describes how they ignored or resisted my efforts or tried to fit them into their routines. My ideas for collaboration clashed with the teachers' already overloaded schedules, and more pressing issues—parents and kids, for example—distracted those who *were* interested in collaborating. I also analyze my fieldwork relations with kids in this chapter. Whereas my work with the principal and the teachers involved ongoing negotiations about my role and the meaning of my work, my interactions with kids involved less negotiation than appropriation: They often treated me not as a friend or an adult but as a manipulable context they could exploit for their own interactional ends. One consequence of my struggles to define a "research" frame for our interactions was that I was able to explore how the children understood research in general, my project in particular, and our interactional formats that shaped the data in different ways.

These chapters don't flow together smoothly to reveal a single picture of the school. Rather, they wind their way through layers of intersections that sometimes spread out independently and sometimes cascaded into dense knots. Although the text is not, I think, hard to read or overly technical or academic, its structure is intentionally baroque and shifts in style from chapter to chapter; a picture of the school builds not through a continuous narrative but through a layering of narratives and analyses on top of one another. In chapter 1, for example, narrative strands—dealing with school division politics and history, with teachers' mutual interactions, with school–community relations, and with parent resistances to school change—loop in and out of each other and across a 15-year time frame. Chapter 2, by contrast, opens with a section that frames the economic history of the city and follows that with accounts of three chronologically linked events spanning only a few months. Chapter 3 contains mini-case studies of 5 kids' neighborhood routines, and chapters 4 and 5 are dense conversations between data and theory about bodies and popular culture.

I want readers to remember that the text, and the act of reading it, are intersections too. The style shifts are meant to draw attention to the book's artifice, its constructed quality. "Show that you are showing!" Brecht (1976) admonished. Some ethnographers do this by writing about themselves and showing themselves in the text (cf. Latour, 1988; Nespor & Barber, 1991). My strategy, by contrast, is to make the *work* of the text visible by shifting across issues and moving from a broad to a narrow focus and back—from explicating city politics to analyzing teacher conversations, and on and on. The idea of moving through multiple, partial perspectives while crafting knowledge, an idea I take from Donna Haraway (1988), doesn't mean just vicariously wearing the shoes of different actors; it means looking at different events, practices, and structures, contextualizing them in multiple spaces and times, and talking about them with different theoretical languages. This last sentence notwithstanding, I do not intend the text to be difficult or obscure. I merely want to disrupt the rhythm of the reading, to put the emphasis off the beat, to preserve in the reading some of the confusion and cacaphony of the intersections of school and everyday life.

A final point: Treating a school as an intersection makes it difficult to keep the setting anonymous. Methodological, ethical, and theoretical issues collapse on each other as the effort to situate activity in space and time requires that people, events, and settings be located with increasing specificity. Community studies are notoriously difficult to keep anonymous (Orlans, 1967), and because I drew on newspaper and local history accounts, the city, at any rate, is openly identified. I have, however, changed the names of streets and neighborhoods associated with the school and I've given the kids, parents, teachers, and principal pseudonyms and omitted or slightly altered information that might have identified them. Readers would gain nothing by trying to find out exactly which school I'm talking about or who the people I'm quoting are. Intersections aren't static, and the people and situations I've described have changed since my fieldwork. Students and faculty come and go (more than one third of the Thurber staff, as of 1995, consisted of new teachers with whom I had no contact at all), the administrative structure of the school changes, and teachers change what they do.

So although this book at times focuses in great detail on what was in the intersections at Thurber Elementary between 1992 and 1994, the *particulars* of the story are valuable mainly insofar as they allow readers to generate questions about their own experiences with schools and the processes that swirl through them. To borrow a metaphor from Walter Benjamin, my aim is to create part of a "stereoscopic" picture, "to educate the image-creating medium within us to see dimsionally, stereoscopically, into the depths of the historical shade" (quoted in Buck-Morss, 1989, p. 292). The particulars of this or any case study are only a flat surface until a reader provides "the other half of the picture from the fleeting images of his or her lived experience" (Buck-Morss, 1989, p. 292). Teachers, parents, researchers, and others who work in schools or with children can find much here with which to reexamine their own lived experience—however distant events at Thurber may be, however different from that experience.

But I claim more for the book than that. Along with Dorothy Smith (1987), I argue that:

> The relation of the local and particular to generalized social relations is not a conceptual or methodological issue, it is a property of social organization. The particular "case" is not particular in the aspects that are of concern to the inquirer. Indeed, it is not a "case" for it presents itself to us rather as a point of entry, the locus of an experiencing subject or subjects, into a larger social and economic process. (p. 157)

Thurber was a particular, unique articulation of flows and networks, but these flows and networks were themselves not merely local; they were extensive in space and time. This study, although it only partially reveals the shape of the networks and the motion of the flows, and traces them only a short distance from my particular standpoint, explicates an aspect of a social relations framework in which many U.S. schools are situated. The book is a challenge to think about schools as elements of systems spread across space and time, as well as an argument about the institutional shape of U.S. education, the latter considered not as what happens in school but as the processes that intersect there. Either way, the book tells a complicated story, one I delay telling no longer.

1 Adults at Elementary School

During my two years at Thurber Elementary School, the principal, Mr. Watts, embraced, with varying levels of passion, a host of innovations: portfolio assessment, outcomes-based education, cognitive coaching, performance assessment, business–school partnerships, business-in-the-school programs, computer simulation curricula, volunteer mentoring programs, site-based management, whole language and writing process pedagogies, cross-age grouping, the integration of special education students into regular education classrooms, and nontraditional report cards. This barrage of innovations, unique among Roanoke schools, produced a good deal of opposition from the community.

The parents of children at the school were especially critical of the novel-based curriculum, the heterogeneous grouping of students, and the nontraditional grading scale. They often asked me, as an education professor, what I thought about such things and listened politely while I explained their value. But they remained skeptical; they conceded that such practices might work in an ideal world but not in the real world of the Roanoke city schools. By 1993–1994 their skepticism had developed into the organized protest described in this chapter. A breakdown in the usual silence between parents and teachers on matters of curriculum, the dispute forced both parties to articulate fundamental assumptions about the functions of schooling, in particular about the role of the school in representing, ranking, and categorizing students.

To understand the protest we have to unravel a historical–political–pedagogical knot in which subtle, complex, deeply layered flows of practice came together. First I examine how city and school system politics created a space for attempting innovations. Then I try to make sense of the Thurber innovations by looking at Mr. Watts's educational ideas and the teachers' struggles to understand and implement the innovations. Next I put the parents' relations to the school in context by reconstructing the history of Thurber's ties to the neighborhoods from which its students came—a history that had recently included a turnover of the school's staff along with major changes in the boundaries of its attendence zone. Finally I turn to the protest itself and look at the perspectives that gave parents and educators their different understandings of the purposes of instruction and assessment.

POLITICS AND POWER SHAPE THE SPACES OF CURRICULUM

At the time of this study, many school boards in Virginia were still appointed rather than elected. In Roanoke a city council decided on board membership, and for decades prior to the 1980s their decisions had been influenced by a small elite of millionaire businessmen and corporate officers. When I asked an informant, who'd been politically active in the city for decades, how politicized the selection of the school board had been back in the 1960s, he replied:

> It's much more political *now*, I think. It used to be pretty cut and dried. [*Laughs*] A lot of people served forever on the school board....They just used the same people over and over and over. It was just this group that served on everything. But it's much more political now. *Much* more political.

In the old days, he explained: "People, like the group of millionaires, they'd say 'I think so and so ought to be on the school board' when a vacancy occured, and so and so would be put on the school board."

This situation began to change around 1980, when political interests other than those of the dominant business class gained influence in city politics. In particular, middle-class White property owners, feeling pinched by the declining regional economy, began a "tax revolt." My informant explained that, in 1980 and 1982 respectively, the city council (and through it, the school board) began to change with the elections of a couple of "populist" councilmen:

> They rode the wave of "gettin' the people"—"We're gonna serve the people"; "We need people on the council that's gonna look after the citizens, lower taxes," la-di-da....It was a tax revolt kind of thing [*Laughs*]. That was funny....They were the candidates of Concerned Taxpayers....I'm very fond of both of them. But about their first two or three years on Council, they weren't going to put a rubber stamp on *anything*, not on anything! Didn't make any difference. And that was when the school board began to change. 'Cause whatever the incumbents were for, they were against [*Laughs*].

Even before the city council shift, the school board was becoming increasingly antagonistic toward the entrenched administrative leadership of the school system. When mistakes were discovered in the district budget in 1980, the board made the first break with tradition by firing the superintendent (Pack: "Severed relations," 1980). After a year-long search, the board made a second break by bringing in an outsider from New York, Frank Tota, to serve as the new superintendent. According to the school board chairman, Tota's mandate was to provide "the highest quality of instruction for the least possible cost" (Chamberlin, 1982a, p. A14). According to my informant:

> [Tota was] hired with that understanding, that he would clean house. And he did. And a lot of people blamed him. But it was understood before he came that he *would* do this. I mean, names were named. When he came he knew he had to get rid of certain people. [The school board had decided that? I asked. He nodded.]
>
> So he had an uphill battle. A lot of people here absolutely hated him when he came and did what he did. Because it was not known for a number of years that when he came, he knew he had to do this....You really couldn't blame him directly for the things that happened. But I guess with him came the advent of the modern school system that we have today in Roanoke City.

In the first 6 months of his tenure, in a system with 2 high schools, 6 junior high schools, and 21 elementary schools, Tota changed the principals of 10 schools, moved 9 assistant principals from 6 other schools, and reassigned or demoted 16 central office administrators. He began this process his first week on the job, with a series of lateral transfers and promotions that moved 9 principals or assistant principals and 11 central office administrators. There was no great public reaction to these moves, but things were different 6 months later when Tota demoted 16 veteran principals, assistant principals, and central administrators to lower-paying, lower-status positions. Given no warning or opportunity to defend themselves before the decision, the demoted administrators received form letters that varied only in the reasons given for their demotion. One junior high principal was told: "You have failed to demonstrate sensitivity toward students from lower socio-economic groups and have not responded in a satisfactory manner to their educational and sociological needs" (Chamberlin, 1982b, p. A1). One principal of an elementary school was reassigned with this explanation: "You have not indicated superior knowledge of elementary curriculum and program development" (Chamberlin, 1982b, p. A1). Because the administrators were merely "reassigned" rather than fired, they had few due process rights in the matter. Their fates, however, triggered widespread criticism of Tota among educators. Tense relations between central office administrators and teachers persisted for years.

Reshaping School–Community Ties

Along with cutting costs and reducing the number of administrators, the reassignments signaled a break with past practice. A newspaper editorial of the period described Tota's moves as a necessary shake-up of the system ("Upheaval," 1982):

> There *is* a rough consensus...on why Tota was hired. The city school system for years has limped along with deadwood in the ranks. The Peter Principle operated freely. A dozen or so administrators were elevated to their levels of incompetence and they stayed put.
>
> The new superintendent was told to clean out the deadwood. In a series of moves, he has shaken up both the central administration and at least half of the system's schools. (p. A8)

But if most people seemed to agree there was "deadwood" in the school system, others questioned some of the demotions. The elementary school principal mentioned earlier was a 30-year veteran of the system who had strong ties to the community served by his school and seemed to have been well liked and respected by teachers, parents, and pupils. When his demotion was announced, teachers and parents rallied to his support and submitted petitions to the school board asking that he not be reassigned; the parent teacher association's petition contained the signatures of 80% of the school's families (Chamberlin, 1982c). Nevertheless, the school board endorsed his demotion along with the others recommended by Tota.

My point is not to defend the principal or the Roanoke schools as they were before Tota's arrival but to suggest that in addition to trimming "deadwood," the reassignments fractured whatever collegial and communal ties might have existed between school personnel and the parents of the kids attending their schools. This kind of break in relations between parents and schools had begun to affect most of the city's African American communities a decade or more earlier, as urban renewal and desegregation undercut neighborhood schooling and community involvement (see chapter 3). Tota merely extended the process to the European American communities. In contrast to previous regimes, his administration marked a period in which principals and teachers were frequently reassigned from one school to another. These transfers made it more difficult for educators to develop close relationships with the communities served by their schools, to define clear roles for community members in school activities, or to develop bases of support among parents. In some cases, this loosening of community ties might have made it possible to innovate, to change neighborhood schools into magnet schools, for example. But, as we'll see was the case at Thurber, the weakening of community attachments could also make it difficult to implement and maintain support for innovations over the long term.

Centralizing Control

Within Tota's new administration, schools and teachers were placed under increased scrutiny from the central office. Teachers were pressured to adopt routinized, textbook-driven teaching methods—a kind of technical control (Edwards, 1979) buttressed by frequent administrator observations. Elementary teachers, for example, were expected to use an "instructional management systems" approach involving weekly, chapter by chapter, pre- and post-test measures of student achievement. At the high schools teachers were drilled in "effective teaching" methods. A year after the demotions, a feature article in the local newspaper, based on more than 50 interviews with teachers and administrators, painted a dismal scene (Chamberlin, 1983):

> Few of those interviewed were willing to speak up and be identified....Several teachers and administrators said they have been told at staff meetings or individually that teachers and administrators who don't conform to prescribed methods and who don't measure up to the new standards can be replaced. They said they have been told that public criticism of the system will not be tolerated. "Tota said, 'You play on my team or you don't,'" an administrator said [paragraphing suppressed]. (p. A12)

Not surprisingly, morale plummeted and remained low for years. Teachers reported increased stress and illness and a vastly diminished sense of control over their practice (Chamberlin, 1983; Jones, 1985). High school teachers were warned that they would be expected to do better, regardless of how well they'd done in the past:

> An assistant principal at [one of the high schools] sent this memo to his teachers in November regarding their evaluations: "If you are doing no more than you have done in previous years, your progress will certainly be considered wanting, and the assessments will reflect a need for improvement" [paragraphing surpressed]. (Chamberlin, 1983, p. A12)

These policies suggest a change strategy designed to produce quick and highly visible results. Instead of, say, bringing together groups of teachers, parents, and students to talk about the state of the schools, to study or analyze the system, and then to systematically experiment with different reforms, reform was accomplished through the adoption of visible markers of innovation (e.g., effective teaching strategies), and intrusive evaluations were used to enforce at least token compliance. Internally, the routinized teacher evaluations strengthened central administration power by translating pedagogy into stable, standardized, mobile representations that could be accumulated at the central office and there used to compare, rank, reward, and punish (cf. Latour, 1987). Externally, the high visiblity of the control strategies seemed designed to address the concerns of an increasingly conservative public audience being told by media and government reports that the nation was "at risk" because of its inadequate schools.

Standardized testing became a major emphasis in the schools for similar reasons. Testing reduced students to scores, numbers on paper that could be collected and combined to produce comparisons across schools and judgments about the performances of particular schools. Although Superintendent Tota insisted he did not want teachers "teaching to the test," teachers consistently complained that they were being directed to do so (e.g., Jones, 1985). Even at the time of my fieldwork, more than a decade after these events, the district was still known for its preoccupation with testing. When I talked to my Virginia Tech colleagues who supervised student teachers in Roanoke city elementary schools, they told stories like the following:

> I have one student teacher that I'm very—the placement I had her, I don't know that I got to see her do hardly any teaching at all, because of the fact that every time I would go, they were preparing for a standardized test. And this was a fourth-grade classroom. And it was constant....There was a lot of emphasis on preparing for the tests. Iowa Test of Basic Skills (ITBS)....They were doing a lot of worksheet type things. They were doing some pre-tests; they were doing situations set up as testing situations. And actually then—it was a format; some of it was standardized it looked like, that they were using. And this was for about 3 or 4 weeks out of a placement. It was every time I would go.

A preoccupation with test scores might be common in U.S. schools, but it had a special resonance and political meaning in Roanoke. As I'll explain further in the next chapter, Roanoke City had been in economic decline since the mid-1970s and grew progressively poorer than surrounding Roanoke County. Quality of life issues—education, for example—were important to city leaders' attempts to keep affluent residents from leaving and to make the city more attractive to county residents. Yet standardized test scores, one of the most obvious ways to compare schools and school districts, consistently favored the County over the City by a wide margin. Thus, in addition to its use as a control mechanism, the stress on raising scores stemmed in part from a need to improve the public image of the city's schools.

The result within the district, however, was a kind of punctuated curriculum in which elementary schools interrupted their teaching for weeks at a time to coach students for the tests. Outside of this test preparation, there was little consistency in curriculum from one elementary school to another. One of my colleagues at the university, who had worked with both Roanoke city and suburban Roanoke County schools, remarked on how different city schools were from one another, in part because of the relatively short tenures principals spent at particular schools:

> I've been struck by the differences among the buildings [in the city], and that would really hit somebody who's spent a lot of time in Roanoke County schools, because those [county] schools are more notable for their similarities than their differences. But the differences in the city schools—and I have a feeling that they're centered around the principal quite a bit—that they have a lot of authority. Which is interesting, because I know they [central administration] move people around; they're not there for a long long time. I think probably all the principals I work with, of the three that I work with, none of them have been in their jobs more than 3 or 4 years at the most. And there are very different styles, very different things going on in the schools.

This variability across schools was largely a result of a feudal dynamic running through Tota's administration. By *feudal* I mean a system in which administrators survived or perished not on the basis of their adherence to official procedure but by virtue of their loyalty to the top official (cf. Ball, 1987, p. 89). One of Tota's first moves as superintendent had been to centralize authority over principals. Previously such authority had been delegated to mid-level administrators (directors of elementary and secondary education), but Tota abolished these positions and placed himself at the top of a chain of command that included his assistant superintendents and instructional supervisors. The feudal flavor of this arrangement arose from the way Tota would detach himself from the actions of his mid-level administrators. Principals could get the superintendent's support for actions the other administrators might disagree with or take refuge under the superintendent's wing if these administrators attempted to intervene in the schools. The line of authority, in such situations, became a direct one between Tota and the principal. At the elementary level at least, this feudal dynamic meant that individual principals could acquire considerable autonomy in shaping teaching and curriculum—so long as they remained in Tota's favor and their test scores didn't decline.

In this highly differentiated, bureaucratic–feudal situation, in which parents had been effectively excluded as political actors, Mr. Watts, in his first principalship, was able to introduce striking changes at Thurber. The power structure did not *cause* these changes but simply created a space for reform, albeit a risky and difficult space. Innovations were possible, but only at the level of the individual school, without systemic support.[1] What drove changes were the principals, such as Mr. Watts.

---

[1]The exception to this statement might be the school division's magnet schools effort, initiated by Superintendent Tota to transform a number of schools within the city. As each magnet school had a different curricular focus, however, the effect was to reinforce the curricular fragmentation of the city school system.

MR. WATTS'S TRANSFORMATION
OF THE CURRICULUM

Mr. Watts had come to Roanoke after teaching middle school in Georgia for 6 years and getting a master's degree in administration. Within a year, he'd landed an elementary school vice principalship and had begun looking for ways to change the schools:

> When I [became an assistant principal in Roanoke] I had not read or heard the words "whole language," but I knew that the way we were doing things wasn't working. And I knew, I knew [*Pause*] in my mind that the Madeline Hunter model[2] was not working. And I was seeing a tremendous amount of teaching, teaching, teaching, teaching, teaching—but it wasn't getting us very far.

When I asked him how he knew that what he saw going on in classrooms "wasn't working," he referred to his own teaching experiences:

> Well, I taught in Georgia, and I had a large number of indigent children. And sitting and trying to teach—to get seventh or fifth graders, who've repeated once or twice if not three times by the time they get to that level—trying to teach them to add or subtract—and that's just an example—trying to teach them to do something that absolutely does not relate to their world and makes no sense to them—I might as well talk to the wall. And trying to go through a textbook with children who are absolutely not interested, because they have no need, to me is failure. It's just not doing what they need. And what I felt as an adult was that I had to create within these children a need to know. They didn't even have a need to know! I mean, they had kind of zeroed out on life, already. And...[it] was interesting, because there, we always had to write our objectives, and then we had to go through and show what we were going to do, and it was like—as long as it looked good on the paper, and the person who checked my plans read it and it looked good to them, then they assumed that what I was doing in the classroom must be okay. And it wasn't....Kids could go to sixth grade and, to me, not know a lot more than what they did when they were in fifth. That says to me the system isn't working.

---

[2]Madeline Hunter was a lecturer in education at the University of California who marketed an algorithmic teaching model (Hunter, 1984) based on the effective teaching research of the 1970s. Her model defined a series of teaching behaviors held to correlate with student test score gains. Teaching guidelines and teacher evaluation systems based on this model have been used throughout the United States (see Gibbony, 1994, for a critical discussion). For Mr. Watts and others, the problem with the model was that it focused on teaching behaviors stripped from their contexts in the flow of real classroom practice: It encouraged a mechanistic, teacher-centered pedagogy that precluded whole language approaches, cooperative learning, and most other strategies Mr. Watts wanted his teachers to embrace.

In the next chapter I discuss how this idea that teachers should be creating internal *needs* in kids (and its corollary that kids had "zeroed out on life") led Mr. Watts to experiment with the idea of reshaping classrooms to resemble businesses. Here, I merely note that this perspective intensified his feeling that the schools weren't working. He became determined to try something new once he became a principal:

> When I was able to make the transition from a vice principal where I took orders to a principal where I hoped to form a consensus, I was able to say, "Let's rethink this; let's relook at how children learn." And I don't think I even said it that way. I think what I did was, just very slowly began to introduce other options....Here in the division [teachers are expected to follow] the "elements of an effective lesson," and they are truly the sacraments—they are! And if you don't dispense the sacraments daily, you have done something irreligious. And I knew what kind of pressure that would put on people; that the whole division is performing the sacraments every day, and we aren't. And so the first year, I just didn't discuss it. I just—didn't talk it; just let it go. I didn't necessarily require it, but I didn't pooh-pooh it either. And so we went a year, year and a half, and it was just became kind of nebulous. And I think what people began to do was to begin to feel free from it.

At this point, *whole language* entered the picture. Mr. Watts seized on a remark by the superintendent and used it as a warrant for the innovations he wanted to introduce:

> I do remember that along the way, [Superintendent] Tota expressed interest in whole language and he liked the concept. And quite honestly I played that one as hard as I could play it, anytime I needed to. Because there are those betwixt us that are not predisposed to whole language....I've had many a lecture. I've had lectures one on one, two on one, and I've had lectures at meetings, when no one knew who was being barked at, but I knew who was being barked at. I've had a lot of those....[One administrator], for example, made it very clear that she thought whole language was "whole stupidity." And again, I just look at it as she doesn't understand what's going on. She does not understand what whole language is about.

During his second year as principal, most teachers at Thurber switched to a curriculum organized around novels, which was the operational definition of whole language at the school. Mr. Watts supplied this rough summary:

> What we started talking about was using literature....At the same time we were trying to obey the state guidelines in terms of curriculum. For example, third grade—*communities* is a social studies concept, so...they start out in third grade studying their own community, and then instead of just studying their own community the whole year, they do a unit on it, and then they go off to China, then to Africa, then to Israel, and study

communities there, and try to do some sort of comparing....Fourth grade, we want to continue somehow dealing with Virginia history and the beginnings of this country....And they also do a novel called *Phoebe the Spy*, which works around—Phoebe was a free Black that lived in the [George] Washington household....Then in fifth grade we pick up with the Civil War, with literature, and they do *Harriet Tubman*. And they will do an Indian story, *Sing Down the Moon*, that takes place about 20 years after the Civil War. Then they'll do an immigrant story from around the turn of the century, when many of the immigrants were coming. And they'll do a depression story, and then a World War II or after story. So we're using the novels to get to the global issues as well as our own history, as well as trying to create a meaningful situation for the children where they're making connections, so that things are studied out of a need to know rather than just out of textbooks, and "Today we're going to add, and tomorrow we're going to subtract, or tomorrow we're going to learn about World War II." [This is obviously only a partial account. Other novels were used, and math and science were taught as well.]

Although this approach to curriculum differed from that of other principals in the school system, the formal features of the innovation paralleled the change dynamics Superintendent Tota had introduced: They flowed top–down from a central administrative position (the principal, in this case); the process excluded parents or community groups from planning and participation; and the innovations rested on a concept of the teacher as a lone expert dispensing pedagogy.

With reference to this last point, Mr. Watts introduced the literature-based curriculum in the face of opposition from central administrators who favored a more traditional, workbook-based, test-oriented approach. Because the district power structure prevented those administrators from simply imposing their will on Mr. Watts, many of his battles with them were fought indirectly, on the terrain of staffing. On some level, as I show in the next section, the assumption seemed to be that teaching skills inhered in the bodies of particular teachers, that teaching itself was a form of "embodied cultural capital" (Bourdieu, 1986). Battles over a school's curriculum or teaching approach could thus turn into battles over which teachers were to work at the school.

STAFFING

When Mr. Watts was named principal of Thurber, he came to the school with a new faculty that included both veterans and teachers in only their second or third years in the field. Most of the newer teachers were willing to embrace Mr. Watts's innovations, in word if not in deed, but some of the more experienced teachers were unwilling to abandon textbook-based teaching styles that, after all, had been pushed on them for a decade by powerful administrators. Part of Mr. Watts's response was to look for new teachers, a task that required perseverance and political will. When I asked him how much control he had over selecting teachers, he explained:

> Let me give you an example. Mrs. Peel, for example, there was an interesting history with that one. I knew she was interested in whole language. The school where she was, the principal was very supportive of *her*, but there was no one else there interested in whole language. And I thought she'd be a great support for us, because the teachers had all been up to observe in her room; they respected her, they would be very willing to go into her room and observe, and learn from her. And I thought, "What a great person to have right here in the building; that's like having in-house staff development."…So I thought, now, how do I do this? How do I ethically, morally, how do I do this? So I trotted…down to Superintendent Tota and I asked him. I said "I'd like to know, what is the procedure for requesting a person, who is within the division, who you think would be good for your school, what's the procedure?" And he…said, you go to the principal, tell him that you would like to have that person, and tell that person if they're interested to put it in writing to personnel. And it shouldn't be a problem. And so I did.

> Well, there were all kinds of problems. All kinds of problems. In fact, the director of personnel told that principal that there would *not* be a transfer, that it was not going to happen. And so I just sat and waited until I got that piece of information, and when I got that piece of information, I went to Tota…and I said, "I want Mrs. Peel. I did what you told me to do, and I want her at Thurber next year." And he said, "She will be there next year." And the transfer happened.

This story shows Mr. Watts's adroitness at working the system and his willingness to take political risks. It also illustrates how the superintendent could disrupt the bureaucratic chain of command to forge a direct, quasi-feudal bond between himself and a principal. Still, in most cases the central office decided where teachers were assigned, and there was no guarantee they would end up with principals who shared their educational philosophies. Several Thurber teachers didn't embrace the literature-based curriculum and weren't particularly loyal to Mr. Watts. This lack of fealty created problems, since Mr. Watts's management style depended on interpersonal ties rather than on bureaucratic procedures or administrative directives (Ball, 1987). The reader might wonder, for example, why teachers stuck with him through the whirl of demanding innovations. The answer is that, despite all the frustrations, Mr. Watts was not harsh, intrusive, or threatening in his relations with teachers. He refused to impose his ideas on teachers or even to require them to reach a consensus among themselves. So long as recalcitrant teachers didn't publicly dispute his authority or broadcast their differences, Mr. Watts didn't directly confront them. Instead, he waited for them to come around or to leave the school. The result, at least in the short run, was that there was little continuity in teaching from classroom to classroom. Going from one room to another, even at the same grade level, could mean moving from one philosophy of teaching to another, one curriculum to another. At Thurber, these discontinuities confused parents and left some teachers feeling isolated.

TEACHING DEFINED AT THE INTERSECTION
OF THEORY AND ORGANIZATION

McLaughlin and Talbert (1993) noted in their study of secondary education that classrooms in the same school (or even within the same department in a school) often differ because teachers hold different interpretations of student capabilities. But classrooms also vary, at least in part, because pedagogy has been institutionally defined as residing in the person of the teacher. Teaching—not just at Thurber but at all the schools I'm familiar with in this region—is treated as a quality of *individual* teachers rather than of the faculty as a whole or of the relationships between teachers and the community. Although this definition might have suited teachers set in their habits, it created enormous problems for Thurber teachers who wanted to change how they taught but who had trouble finding opportunities for the conversation and learning they wanted and needed.

On the rare occasions when the faculty as a whole could talk about these issues, the format for discussion was to present an idealized picture of how whole language *should* work, without articulating a concrete pathway leading teachers to that promised land. During an in-service day before the beginning of my second year of fieldwork, Mrs. Peel, the whole language practitioner Mr. Watts had struggled to get transferred to the school, was "interviewed" by the rest of the faculty about her teaching. At one point, Mrs. Court, a fourth-grade teacher, explained that, after switching from textbooks and workbooks to novels, she was now having trouble turning the literature-based curriculum into a whole language approach. She felt that she was teaching the novels rather than integrating them into longer strands of thematically linked instruction:

> My problem is I have the novels and I'm making the transition and making really lots of really kind of strict plans for myself using those novels. So I'm using the novels and doing some neat lessons around that novel. I'm still keeping things so much more structured than the way I want for them to be. And it's hard to…to ask the right questions and, you know, how to, how to plan, even. How to really plan.

Mrs. Peel responded that the use of novels was not necessarily the same as the whole language approach: "I think one of the problems is...we kind of basalize the novel. We're afraid that they'll miss something out of that novel." Before her transfer to Thurber, Mrs. Peel had led whole language in-service workshops for Thurber teachers in which she'd apparently emphasized novel-focused teaching. Thus some of the teachers were confused to hear her now emphasizing thematic units. Mrs. Tanner asked her:

> Have your thoughts on whole language changed since you instructed us as a faculty in the beginning? A lot of us, I think, got from your information then, you know: We start with a novel and that is part of our springboard to do things and now...well, now it's changing. Now, it's do your theme and just let the novels just appear, you know. We always went, at least in our grade level we've gone with, you know, a time line idea theme. And we chose, and well, I mean, I guess they have kind of evolved, but how has your idea of whole language changed?

Mrs. Peel responded by explaining the evolution of her ideas in terms of her individual growth as a teacher:

> Well, the...more I have done this and the longer that I've done it, I have found that allowing kids to choose their novels, based on a particular theme, is probably the most satisfying thing I have ever done. And so that has helped me to get away from everybody doing one novel even though we have done [that]....Gradually move into that. I don't think next week you would want to give the whole class one novel and say, "Go off, kids, and read your novel."

Mrs. Peel then referred to a week-long summer workshop she'd attended a month earlier on outcomes-based education. The workshop had emphasized focusing on desired outcomes and then planning backward to thematic units and performance assessments based on teacher-defined rubrics:

> But I, what really has turned me on is what we did this summer, with, the going from the outcomes to the essential questions. And, and it really has, has made the picture so much broader for me too, and so now, a novel will be incorporated into what I'm doing, and will certainly have to be congruent with what I'm doing. But it won't have to be be just one novel.

Translating this broad picture into concrete practice was no simple matter, though. For Mrs. Tanner and for other teachers, the problem wasn't in the theory, but in their feeling of lacking the individual expertise to pull it off. Thus Mrs. Tanner responded to Mrs. Peel:

> Well, I was just thinking....I've tried to [refine things], at least the past two years, I've tried to, of course every year things have changed and it's

grown. But I've been allowed to refine what I've done rather than just—I don't know—I'm just not as good as you. I just can't cast everything into the wind and . . .

Mrs. Peel interrupted to reassure her that she wasn't suggesting that her way was the only way: "As long as you adopt the whole language principles, there's so many ways, I think, to implement the principles. And just, you know, you're not expected to do the way that everybody else [does]. . . ."

The other teachers, however, especially the ones who genuinely wanted to adopt whole language principles, felt they were navigating without a map. Mrs. Court asked: "Do you think it was easier to make the transition from where we were as a traditional teacher to where we might be now using our novels the way we do, than it is to go from where we are now. . . ."

"On to something new?" Mrs. Tanner completed the question.

"I had a huge, I mean it's such a big step," Mrs. Court began, and then as other teachers began to jump into the converstion, talking over each other, Mrs. Peel responded:

No it's not [a big step]. It's not. It's a progression. And you can do it. You can do it. Because you came from a traditional classroom to using, you know, having your things centered around your novel and, and you may not want to go this other way, but that doesn't make you any less a Whole Language teacher....Well then, if you are in your one novel, then divide your kids into literature study groups....You can grow into that. And, you know, it's a slow process....And I've been doing it all these years and this is where I am now. But it's been a steady and a slow progression because I've wanted it. I've learned so much over the years and nobody has made me do any of it. I've wanted to do it on my own. And I find something else and, man, I really like this. It excites me so much that I can see how that. I have this other to build on. But nobody is expecting you to go from one novel to, you know, this broad theme, where everybody does their own thing.

Mrs. Peel obviously meant to reassure the others, but by denying the difficulty they were encountering, denying the sense in which, for many, it *was* a huge step and not a "progression," she may have only confused the pedagogical issue. Mrs. Tanner and Mrs. Court knew they weren't doing what Mrs. Peel did, but they couldn't see how to make the transition. Teaching was so identified as an internal, individual attribute that Mrs. Tanner could only throw up her hands and tell Mrs. Peel, "I'm just not as good as you," while Mrs. Court suffered through the year trying to find her bearings and attributing her difficulties to some sort of personal failing. On the last day before Christmas break during the school year that began with the interview I've just summarized, I reminded Mrs. Court that at the beginning of the semester she'd been determined to do things differently but had been unsure about how to proceed. I asked whether she felt on firmer ground now. She replied:

> Only because I think I've backed off from my conviction—I mean, I'm not—I know I'm going to make some changes but I'm not expecting to do everything right now. I'm allowing myself to use the English book, and I'm allowing myself to use the spelling book. [*Long pause*] I feel more uncomfortable this year than I've ever felt. But I don't know how much of that is—I just don't spend that much time on school now. I think it really takes a lot of time. For me. I have to work at it. I have to plan, and I haven't been planning like I would in the past. Of course that was more direct teaching....And [now] I don't know what we're going to do from one minute to the next. It's a lot harder! It's much easier to teach directly, I think—well, no, that's not true. When I get to the point where I hope I am in five years, I'll feel more comfortable and it'll be easier. But right now it would be much easier if I could just go back to the way I taught. I knew I was *teaching* then. Now I don't know if I'm teaching....I was feeling pretty much on solid ground when I left. Although I've always been unsure of myself in a lot of ways. But I was feeling confident in my teaching. And I'm just not this year. But I feel better now than I did at the beginning of the year. I've just given myself permission to not take on too much. And I also am reminding myself that the kids are learning, even though it's in a different way.

Nias (1989), in her study of English primary school teachers reported that "virtually every teacher responded to my request to explain what it was to 'feel like a teacher' by saying that it was to be in control" (p. 187). Mrs. Court, in trying to change the system of control that organized her classroom by giving kids greater control over their work, experienced a kind of pedagogical vertigo. She no longer felt as though she were teaching and could only attribute this to a personal shortcoming.

Teaching, then, was defined as something found in the bounded bodies of teachers. The idea that teaching might be a function of biography and long-developing relations to materials and communities—or even more radically that teaching could be thought of as a collective accomplishment of groups of teachers working together—had no place in the dominant educational discourse that located the meaning of teaching in individual pedagogical expertise. That Mrs. Peel had taught for close to 20 years and both Mrs. Tanner and Mrs. Court had taught for less than 5 was irrelevant in the terms of the discourse.

Where did this "dominant educational discourse" come from? It followed partly from the spatial and temporal organization of schools: the physical separation of teachers and their lack of time to associate. Partly it was a function of school system policy, in which administrators evaluated and scrutinized individual teachers rather than collectives of collaborating teachers. And partly, as I suggest later in this chapter, the discourse of the lone teacher came from colleges of education, from people like me.

THE SHIFTING MEANINGS OF THE TERM
WHOLE LANGUAGE

The Thurber teachers were thus uncertain about the meaning of whole language: Did it refer to a novel-based curriculum, a theme-based curriculum, or what? In fact, the concept had been given myriad definitions throughout the school system. Mrs. Peel once told me she'd met teachers at other schools in the city who claimed to teach whole language with basal textbooks or to use a basal approach in the morning and a whole language approach in the afternoon. She remembered one teacher observing her classroom as kids worked collaboratively in groups and asking "When do you *teach* whole language?" Yet even Mrs. Peel, confident in presenting her work as whole language to other teachers, could be uncertain about the meaning of the term in her interactions with outsiders. The first time I visited her classroom, before she realized how ignorant I was, she approached me at the end of the day and asked whether what she was doing was whole language. Organizing instruction around novels, she explained, was more or less the way she'd always taught, and she'd picked up this whole language terminology only when she'd taken a couple of years off from teaching to work for a textbook publisher.

The term *whole language,* then, worked within the settings examined here like a *shifter* (Jakobson, 1971; Silverstein, 1976; see also Hanks, 1990), a part of speech whose meaning or "referent" "'shifts' regularly, depending on the factors of the speech situation" (Silverstein, 1976, p. 24).[3] The sense or referent of "whole language" varied with the speaker and the power dynamics of the speech situation. Teachers whose classroom practices might appear to me polar opposites could both claim to be doing whole language in explaining themselves to parents. To me, though, they might express uncertainty about the term and its relevance to what they were doing. In fact, in the instances I can find in my data where the term was used (and they are surprisingly infrequent), it seems to have been part of a boundary-generating discourse. Higher-status participants in unequal encounters (e.g., teachers talking to parents) introduced or used the term to define their domain of practice

---

[3]*Whole language* is not really a shifter in a technical linguistic sense, but, as used at Thurber, it had many of the qualities of a shifter. My apologies to purists.

and essentially to exclude others from the discussion by reducing them to asking for definitions of the term. When participants in a conversation were roughly equals in status, as in the discussion among teachers just reported, the meaning of the term slid about maddeningly. The teachers were simultaneously being told that there was an ideal model of whole language (exemplified by Mrs. Peel) *and* that all teachers could follow the model differently, at their own pace, by themselves. Each teacher, it seemed, was expected to define the term and reinvent the approach.

Because whole language functioned as a shifter, the term could flow freely across settings, as it was unattached to a stable collection of practices. At the same time, the meanings of the term were spatialized as purely local phenomena circumscribed by a particular teacher's practice, the space of the classroom, a space usually opaque to outsiders. "Whole language" could become a key element of a dominant educational discourse and more concretely the accepted approach of a school like Thurber. But it did so in such a way that made productive conversation with and about the term almost impossible, since different teachers used the term to mean quite different things.

Later in this chapter, I discuss the problem of defining whole language teaching in this individualized, localized way. My point here is that the situation among faculty at Thurber was a tenuous balance of stresses within a highly unstable political and community context; the innovations at the school were grounded in a fundamentally weak organizational base. As a result, some teachers were unsure of themselves, and most of the parents I met, saw, and heard at Thurber, did not support the school's approach to teaching and assessment.

PARENT RESISTANCE

I've described how it was possible for Mr. Watts to introduce his innovations at Thurber and I've suggested that the historical shaping of the school division pushed these innovations along certain paths so that they were theory driven, administratively centralized, decoupled from communities, and focused on the capacities of individual teachers. But the mix that came together at Thurber also included parents.

Waller (1961) once suggested that parents are inevitably at odds with teachers because they remember their own unpleasant experiences as students: "Each generation of teachers pays in turn for the sins of the generation that has gone before" (p. 59). But parents can also disagree with teachers when things *aren't* the same as when they'd been kids. The literature-based curriculum introduced at Thurber was a big change for parents and kids. Most had been satisfied with textbook-based teaching. For example, one afternoon I was talking to Mrs.

Longman and her son Neal and going through their collections of Neal's work from first grade through fifth. When Mrs. Longman couldn't find anything from Neal's second-grade year, she realized it was because he'd done nothing but worksheets and textbook-based activities:

> I don't know if I've got anything in here for second [grade]. He was in Mrs. Quirty's room. You know her? Wonderful lady. I love her to death. I think she was one of Neal's best teachers....I don't think I have anything for second grade. . . I don't know; it was just so different, second grade.

Mrs. Quirty had been teaching for 30-odd years and lived in the neighborhood. "You didn't do a lot of writing?" I asked Neal.

"Mrs. Quirty taught from the books, didn't she?" his mother asked him.

"She taught straight from the book," Neal replied.

"I mean," Mrs. Longman explained to me, "he had his little spelling book he brought home. He had to learn so many words. Of course, like I said, Neal never had to study, because he knew them."

Neal himself seemed to remember those days fondly:

> When I came to third grade, they didn't have spelling books; they cut them off the list of books. I don't know why, but then they pushed to novels, which seemed to bore everybody. [Laughs]. People just don't like them.

It wasn't that Neal disliked reading. Mrs. Longman told me: "He says, 'Give me a subject I really like and let me read about that.'"

"Give me a shark book or something," Neal interjected.

"They don't let you choose, do they?" I asked.

Neal replied with vehemence:

> No they don't! I was saying...on this book [Onion John] here they're letting us do our own vocabulary and test each other. But, they don't let us choose our own books. Most people aren't being very serious on their vocabulary. Of course I don't look that much either. I just look at what happened in the story. I'm not looking for vocab.

What he'd like to see, Neal explained, would be for the teachers to say: "'You have to have a novel. It has to be so many pages, at least 100 pages long—at least that—and you can have it, and you can read it. But you have to have it done by this deadline.'"

This, of course, is the same issue Mrs. Peel and the other teachers were debating. For Mrs. Longman, though, the issue wasn't pedagogy but her son's manifest dislike for the novel-based approach and her own uncertainty about why the school had made the switch to it.

Several years into the switch to novels, she was far from alone in her uncertainty. In the "interview" of Mrs. Peel I quoted from earlier, Mrs. West told the other teachers:

[I have] already had a lot parents with questions....And there are a lot of apprehensions and so forth, especially about, as you say, whole language and also about evaluation. How do you help parents? I mean, I've had conferences already this way. And a lot of, lot of questions.

"Have we ever had a letter or any, a newsletter, a Whole Language Newsletter for parents?" Mrs. Peel asked.

Mrs. West replied: "No we haven't, and I think, I wish, I've had it written down in my journal. I think we need to address this. Parents are quite concerned."

These concerns often came to rest on the most visible manifestation of Thurber's changes. Along with the shift to a novel-based curriculum, Mr. Watts made Thurber one of a handful of schools in the district to adopt an alternative marking and report card system. At first, the school switched from a five-category (A–B–C–D–F) system to one with two basic categories: Developing Understanding (DU) and Developing Comprehension (DC). That first year, the school sent home explanations of the new grade scale and held meetings to introduce the new report cards to parents, but there was still loud opposition.

One parent, Mrs. Hunt, recalled that the number of categories, rather than the specific letters, created problems for parents trying to translate between old and new systems. She contrasted Thurber's grading system with that of another school in the neighborhood, Gold Hill:

> Now, when they threw out the A, B, C, D number system, Gold Hill threw it out too, but they [Gold Hill] made four out of five, and the parents didn't get too excited. They could understand O in their mind was pretty good A or B; they could understand satisfactory was about like a C—you know, they had something there. But here, with DU and DC, only two categories, they couldn't understand anything about this report card.

Mrs. Graham, one of the parents interviewed in early 1993, recalled that immediately following the introduction of the new grading scheme at Thurber, "When you went to PTA it was like a chaos. Parents didn't like it. They said their kids didn't like it."

A year later, in response to parents' complaints, the school switched to an M-T-N—Mastered, Trying, Needs help—grading scale. The switch from a two-level scale to a three-level scale, however, failed to mollify the parents, and by late 1993, my second year at the school, they'd begun to organize.

Public Protest

I first heard about plans for a protest just before Christmas 1993, when Mrs. Grigsby, who had two kids in the school, stopped me in the parking lot and told me about a "rambunctuous meeting" of parents at which people were almost "out of control" in their criticisms of the school. The meeting had been set up through the PTA at Mr. Watts's instigation in response to a growing chorus of parent complaints. Later that day, after school, I told Mrs. Court of my conversation: "Mrs. Grigsby caught me out in the parking lot this morning, talking about the—they did have a meeting, right?—and she said it was raucous."

"Yeah," Mrs. Court replied, "I didn't know if I was supposed to say anything about it."

"Apparently Mr. Watts told them to do it?" I asked.

Mrs. Court explained:

> Well, he told them to, but—he told them to. But he never—I think they were planning on getting together in January, but they were so, there was so much, you know, concern was so heightened that they just went ahead and met now. And there was a lot of—I think there was a lot of angry feeling. Mrs. Moon said, "Yeah, we wrote everything down and typed it." And I think they're handling this so that if they have to present this to somebody who can make a difference, who can change things, they will. I don't know, I don't know what their plan is. But I think they really feel like Mr. Watts won't listen, and so if they're going to do something with it, I don't think they're going to go to him.

As Mrs. Court predicted, the parents sent Mr. Watts a letter instead of meeting with him. The date on the letter was January 24, 1994. The authors signed themselves "Concerned Parents." "In an effort to expand communications between the staff at Thurber School and the parents," the letter began, "we present to you an outline of concerns." Stressing their support for teachers, the parents nonetheless complained about what was taught, how it was taught, and how students' performances were recorded and communicated. They wrote:

> While we are receptive to the philosophy that it promotes a positive self-esteem, we are concerned that the current grading scale is not widespread enough to closely evaluate a student's progress.

> If the level of learning was more evident and the parents were assured of acceptable placement at middle school and beyond, the current grading scale could be tolerated.

> While using the current M-N-T system, some teachers "save" the Ms for the fourth grading period [at year end]. Hasn't the child "mastered" anything along the way? The lack of consistency among teachers is discouraging.

> With our feelings of a lack of basic structural learning, how can parents ignore rumors regarding the progress of Thurber students in the middle schools? . . .

Parents have little evidence of basic learning. The higher technology should be addressed by the middle and high schools.

. . . The students have come from and will return to, schools with more basic-learning structures and more traditional grading scales. We feel that [the] non-ranking...will only confuse and frustrate students further when they move on to middle school, where they will suddenly be ranked once again. We understand the reasoning for not ranking, however, we stress the need for a "reality check." Children cannot totally elude being ranked.

If we must divide the responsibilities of learning among schools and parents, we feel the most important lessons, basic instruction, must come from the school. Teachers cannot be responsible for teaching everything. Basic lessons must come first and foremost. Time constraints dictate what must be learned outside the classroom.

..... .

We welcome a system where parents are informed at least weekly as to the students' progress. Under the current system, parents feel left in the dark as to lesson plans. Some teachers are willing to go the extra mile to communicate with parents. Unfortunately, others aren't willing to meet with parents at acceptable times....We feel that Thurber caters to the low achievers. The average student and the high achiever are not challenged but relied on to "pull" the lower students. This "pairing" may be intimidating to the lower achiever and may also impede the progress of the others. We feel it is not in the best interest of all students to pair more aggressive learners with those who need more attention.

Fear and Protest

Parental displeasure doesn't routinely produce organized opposition and letters of this sort, and the authors of the Thurber letter would seem unlikely candidates to lead such protests. Most of them were working-class European American parents from the neighborhood around the school. Yet unlike the working-class parents Lareau (1989) interviewed, who "did not supervise, compensate for, or attempt to intervene in their children's program," who instead "'trusted' the school to educate their children" (p. 169), these parents were confrontational and organized themselves to openly challenge school officials. Many of the teachers, good middle-class parents themselves, wouldn't have dreamed of confronting their kids' teachers as they were being confronted. Even Mr. Watts, a highly articulate middle-class professional, hestitated to complain to the teachers or the principal at the public school *his* child attended in another part of the city for fear he'd "be viewed as pushy, a troublemaker, and it would come back on my kid."

Whether the parents in question are middle class or working class, such fear is predictable in a school system where ties between schools and communities have been ruptured. And some Thurber parents *were* hesitant to complain. Mrs. Graham, who was active and vocal in the PTA, acknowledged that some parents wouldn't talk to teachers about problems: "Some feel like it's going to hurt their child. Maybe some concern, they might think 'Well, that's going to hinder my child, the teacher's going to frown upon them.'"

Mrs. Kaiser provided an example from her son's fourth-grade year:

> [He and his teacher] just didn't hit it off at all. I kept hopin' all through the year that things would change and they would start to get along, but it never worked out that way....I talked to her a couple of times. But, uh, I talked to Mr. Watts—she, she has a way of hollering at kids. She did a lot of hollering. And I said something to Mr. Watts about that. And he advised me to—they have a journal that they wrote in, and he advised me to have Earl write in the journal, and then for both of us to sign it, and then that way she would get the message that she shouldn't holler. And I, I was kind of against that, because I figured it might cause him more problems than he was already having. So I didn't say anything.

This failure to "say anything" on the part of working-class parents does not imply, as Lareau (1989) suggested, that:

> Working-class parents looked up to teachers. They saw, quite correctly, a gulf between themselves and "educated people." Working-class parents talked, sometimes with awe in their voices, of people they had known who were "brains" or "walking encyclopedias." As high school graduates (or drop outs) who had never been to a college, the working-class parents feel keenly their lack of social standing and educational training in their visits with teachers. (p. 171)

On the contrary, the working-class parents from Thurber judged teachers harshly. At the end of the spring 1993 term, for example, Mrs. Longman told me of all the problems Neal had had with his teacher that year. She and her husband had discovered—only when the first report card arrived—that Neal hadn't been turning in all his homework. Mrs. Longman and her husband met with Neal's teacher, who suggested a scheme to coerce compliance by increasing surveillance: Neal would have to write out his homework assignment each night, then Mrs. Longman would sign it and have his father sign it. Neal, his mother recalled, was "tore up. The first day he come home with it—'Dumb homework folder!'—I mean, he was just really upset."

Neal's dad also grew quickly disenchanted with the idea and was puzzled by the notes Neal's teacher was sending home ("Crazy," he called them); perhaps he realized that he too had become an object of surveillance under the system of sign-offs. The Longmans had also been highly offended to hear from their daughter, a high school student who'd been doing volunteer work in the school, that Neal's teacher called her students "brats" in the teachers' lounge. At the time of our interview, Mrs. Longman told me:

> I hate that he's had to continue on. I really wanted to pull him out of Thurber. I really did. And I don't think my husband fully understood until this came up. I mean, he's been involved with the kids, and he cares about them and their education, but it's always been up to me to take care of them. And I told him, "I've had enough of Neal being upset. I've had enough of trying to sit down and talk to the teacher: your turn." So he took over, and he did it. And now I'm telling Neal: "27 more days. Just hang in there 27 more days." I mean, we're counting down the days off the calendar! Just because I want him to get through fifth grade—basically away from that and up to middle school.

Mrs. Longman's depiction of Neal's teacher doesn't suggest that she accepted the teacher's views or that they were too complex for her to understand. Rather, her actions provided an example of what Scott (1985) called the resistances of the "weak," where, "allowing always for the exceptional moments of uncontrolled anger or desperation" (pp. 286–287), weaker parties act publicly in the ways powerholders expect, but privately, in the company of peers, nurse their discontents.

The question, then, is how disagreements and resistances become open rather than remaining hidden. To unpack a text like the parents' letter, we must examine the historical and spatial processes that shaped school–community relations in such ways that some parents challenged or acquiesced, took voice or remained silent, banded together or acted alone. These issues can't be addressed without looking further at the histories and networks of relations that structured parents' interactions with the school.

THURBER AT THE INTERSECTION OF CITY AND COMMUNITY POLITICS

Schools have social histories. In some communities they function as centers of activity—sites of critical local events and ceremonies—and symbolize the shared experiences of the people who attended them. We're most likely to think of high schools in these terms, but elementary schools have their places in community memory as well. Thurber was an important symbol in the working-class European American neighborhood that surrounded it. One of the oldest schools in the city, it was for years *the* school for the neighborhood.[4] The first civic league for the area mutated into a parent–teachers association (PTA) in 1921 and

---

[4]The remainder of this paragraph draws on a privately published community history of the neighborhood around Thurber. I omit an explicit citation in an attempt to preserve the anonymity of the area.

shortly afterward began working with the county to build the school. When the school board refused to put up all the money to buy land for the school and to put in a sewer, the PTA assumed part of the debt and paid it off with money raised through community suppers. Throughout the 1920s, community members, through the PTA, stocked the school with equipment and supplies. As the area grew, the school itself expanded from 4 to 14 rooms and became a source of stability for the community. Thurber had only three principals from 1928 to 1981, and the faculty was relatively stable. A community historian, writing in the early 1980s, could claim that two or three generations of neighborhood residents had moved through the same classrooms.

Over the years, however, other schools had opened near Thurber. As the city's population stagnated and shifted to the suburbs, the neighborhood aged, and enrollments at schools like Thurber dropped. Rumors of school closings began to circulate. Finally, in October 1986, the school district's long-range planning committee recommended closing five neighborhood schools with old facilities, relatively small enrollments, and costs disproportionately higher than other schools in the district (Jones, 1986a; 1986b).[5]

There was immediate resistance. The PTAs of the affected schools, along with neighborhood associations and the City Council itself, opposed the closings. According to a newspaper account, the president of one neighborhood council argued: "The schools 'play a key role in maintaining the fabric' of the city. 'The periodic suggestions of closing schools...injects a degree of instability' in Roanoke....This leads to families settling outside the city limits" (Jones, 1986c, p. B6).

A city council member suggested that Superintendent Tota knew full well it was politically impossible to close the schools and had simply maneuvered the planning committee into making such a recommendation to, in effect, blackmail City Council into increasing the school budget. Tota denied this suggestion (Jones, 1986d), but he did acknowledge that closing the schools was an economic decision: Declining enrollments in the city system had meant a loss in state funds, and the aging schools were simply too expensive to keep open. The closings were portrayed as unpleasant but necessary moves:

> The public should remember that "for five years, the School Board and I have devoted energy to keeping schools open," Tota said....As more low-income children have entered Roanoke's schools, Tota said, the schools

[5]The long-range planning committee was a group of roughly 40 members, with indefinite appointments, who helped formulate policy for the school division. In 1991 a newly appointed school board member, Wendy O'Neil, complained that the group was dominated by a "'very close circle' from the wealthy South and Southwest quadrant of the city" who accounted for more than half the board's membership (Thompson, 1991, p. B4). By contrast, only 2 of the 42 members came from Thurber's quadrant. O'Neil was not reappointed to the school board when her 3-year term expired, apparently a result of her "outspokeness" (Turner, 1994b, p. C1).

have to meet needs throughout the city. Some schools may need additional staff to help with the special problems posed by disadvantaged kids, he said. (Jones, 1986d, p. A8)

A month later, in the face of continuing opposition to the closings, Tota suggested that the only way to keep the schools open would be to remodel them completely, by passing a $10.7 million bond issue. Even as he made this proposal, Tota warned that in preserving neighborhood schools the district still needed to act to reduce social divisions in the city:

"Unless classism, social, economic and racial issues are addressed in a positive fashion, they may forecast the 'white' and 'bright' flight evident in many larger cities in Virginia and throughout the nation," Tota told the [school] board....Tota's comprehensive plan is a delicate balancing act with the city's past and future. He wants to deal with housing patterns that have thwarted efforts to bring black and white students together while simultaneously honoring Roanoke's tradition of neighborhood schools. (Jones, 1987, p. A1)

Ironically, as I suggest in the next chapter, Tota's rhetoric of "disadvantaged kids" and fiscal crisis may have actually helped fuel county residents' fears of the city's racial diversity and economic stresses. In the short run, however, it was politically effective. A bond issue, including money for school renovations, passed in the fall of 1987.

Presumably in an attempt to address some of the class and racial issues Tota had warned of, the openings and closings of schools for remodeling coincided with changes in the boundaries of school attendance zones. Thurber's zone was expanded. Instead of drawing all its students from the surrounding European American neighborhood, the school now also drew students from two other areas in the city, both populated by African American families. Parents from the three segments of the attendance zone had different patterns of school participation.

The African American parents were not active in the PTA and were not among the "concerned parents" who authored the letter of protest. In part, this fact might have been a consequence of geography. The African American parents of Thurber students lived miles from the school in a city that lacked adequate public transportation. Mr. Watts and the teachers had briefly tried holding meetings at one of the apartment complexes where many of the school's African American students lived, but the effort was short lived. As Mrs. West recalled, "One of the reasons that we didn't get much momentum to do it again was that we'd go and one or two parents would show up. Out of a whole housing project." During my two years in the school, no meetings like this took place.

Even more than geography, the social atmosphere at the school might have made African American parents feel less than welcome. Most parents were European Americans and had a proprietary attitude toward Thurber. There were two African American teachers at the school at the beginning of my fieldwork; but neither had sworn fealty to Mr. Watts or embraced the novel-based curriculum, and by the end of my fieldwork both had asked for transfers to other schools.

The situation for many of the European American parents living around the school was strikingly different. Thurber had been *their* school for decades. In a group interview, about a dozen now-retired community members—former Thurber teachers, former students, and parents of former students—recalled a different relationship between school and community. Children, one person said, "didn't [act up] back then like they do now. There was no comparison." Mrs. Soltan, whose children had attended Thurber, explained: "A lot of it was the attitude of the child and the parent. The parents because [agreement from others in group] if you don't behave you're going to get it at home. That had a lot to do with it."

"We'd call for conferences," recalled Mrs. Mendes, a former teacher.

"The type of child changed with busing," Mrs. Sansome added. "When your children went to Thurber they were all neighborhood children."

"They walked there," Mrs. Goodman, a former student at Thurber and a parent of students, pointed out.

"Yeah, they walked there," Mrs. Sansome agreed, and added, "With busing you got a different group of children. And you got children who didn't have two-parent families, and it was a whole different ballgame."

Mrs. Hayes, who'd been a student at Thurber, suggested:

A lot of this, talking about discipline, goes back to the parents and the family. I knew if I got in trouble at Thurber or any other school that what they meted out was nothing compared to what the discipline I was going to get when I got home. [*Laughter*] It's because my mother had also taught school.

This shift from a situation where the European American parents saw themselves as the sole clientele of the school, a unified group sharing social capital and child-rearing attitudes, to one where they shared the school with little-known African American *Others,* was coupled to a second change in school–community relations: a shift from a situation where teachers and parents lived close to and knew each other to one where they lived apart, didn't know one another, and seemingly had different concepts of schooling.

Until the 1980s, most Thurber teachers had been either neighborhood residents or were known to parents through long tenure at the school. Teachers and parents belonged to the same social networks—or at least had access to one another through these networks. Mrs. Sansome, one

of the community volunteers I interviewed, was a former Thurber
teacher (her children also attended there), who had lived five blocks from
the school. Similarly, Mrs. Mendes taught at Thurber while living "just
a block away." Mrs. Joyce, who'd been a student at Thurber and later a
parent whose kids attended the school, remembered that her sixth-
grade teacher had "lived over on Weston Street [about eight blocks from
the school] up through there....Ms. Riley lived on Trenton Street [a few
blocks from the school]. Ms. Webster lived out here. Ms. Hudson lived
out here." Mrs. Mendes added that "the principal lived right down the
street at Trenton Street."

By the time of my fieldwork, none of the teachers lived in the
neighborhoods served by the school, and the faculty had become much
less stable. Mrs. Sansome recalled: "During the 12 years that I taught
at Thurber, for about 10 of them we did not have a change in faculty
members. We were a very stable faculty. It was only in the last two years
[which would have been when Tota arrived as superintendent, that
things changed]." One teacher, the community members marveled,
taught at the school for 41 years, in the same classroom. By contrast,
during my 2 years at the school about one third of the faculty changed.

This affinity and continuity between the school and its working-class
constituency had been nourished by clear lines of participation open to
parents. All the retired community members I interviewed who'd been
parents of Thurber students had been in the PTA, and in Mrs. Sansome's
words, "I guess all of us were room mothers." Room mothers organized
parties for kids and brought refreshments for the class.

Mrs. Joyce pointed out the contrast: In the old days at Thurber
parents were constantly in the classroom, organizing parties for all sorts
of reasons. Now, "they can only have one party a year. It used to be they
had parties all year long. Every holiday just about" ["And children's
birthdays," another parent interpolated] "you did something for the
class."

Having birthday parties for all the kids meant that even if only a few
parents actually participated, the community and community functions
had been frequently acknowledged and literally celebrated at school.
Now, however, there were only two parties during the year—on Valen-
tine's Day and just before the Christmas break—and parents were
rarely in the classrooms. The commonalities that community members
and school staff had once shared had now evaporated. And all of this
took place in a school where a decade of school system politics had
increasingly marginalized parents and community members from a
close and active role. This withering of once close school–community ties
in a context where community members still felt some ownership of the
school was a major reason, I think, that the collective discontent of the
European American parents came into the open at Thurber.

But I do not want to give the impression that the protesting European American parents were a homogeneous group. The protest brought together both long-term residents of the area and more recent arrivals. The former helped articulate a logic of strong parent ties to the school, grounded in the school's historical embeddedness in the neighborhood, and enrolled the more recent arrivals, who were also dissatisfied with Thurber on the basis of comparisons to other schools, into an oppositional structure similar to what Fantasia (1988, 1995) called a "culture of solidarity":

> Expressed in emergent values, behaviors, and organizational forms, these "cultures of solidarity" indicated that collective "consciousness" may be bound fairly tightly to the strategic encounter that has given rise to it, and thus such cultural processes can be seen as relatively independent of the previously existing ideas and beliefs of individual participants. (Fantasia, 1995, p. 280)

In other words, instead of looking at the parent protest as something flowing from the well-formed, pre-existing outlook of a stable group, we should look at the group itself, as well as its outlooks on the core issues, as emerging in the course of the dispute (and then likely evaporating in its aftermath). The weakening of parent–school ties in the school system, the history of Thurber in the surrounding neighborhood, the feelings of ownership on the part of some parents, and the visible contrast between Thurber's practices and those of surrounding schools all intersected with a tenuously implemented curriculum and an uncertain and divided staff.

The protest, then, was not a simple reflex of "traditional" parents resisting "progressive" innovations; it was a historically conditioned protest by a heterogeneous group that, as I show later, had a distinctive spatiotemporal orientation to the school.

MR. WATTS'S RESPONSE TO THE LETTER

I saw the parents' protest letter only on the first Friday in March, 5 weeks after it was sent. When Watts pulled me into his office that morning to show it to me, he seemed mainly puzzled:

> I think in several of these, one of the things that I would like to do is say, "What did you mean?" "What were you thinking?" For example, the one about the weekly student progress and the lesson plans? What did they really mean by that? What they've stated here I don't think they really mean. And I think rather than pouncing on this particular statement, I

first need to say, "Now, go back and tell me what you really mean about this."...They [the teachers] are not going to send lesson plans home. I'll say that right up front. And you are not going to see a progress report every week. Those things I don't mind just saying....But, I want to deal with these honestly. And honestly may mean me saying. "You're right; we need to change this," or "You're wrong; we're not going to change it," or "You are partially right, and we need to come to an agreement."

Mr. Watts's plan was to present the letter to the teachers at the next week's regularly scheduled Wednesday afternoon staff meeting and then to hold a public meeting the following night to respond to the parents. He asked me to come to the meetings and audiorecord them—in part so that, if necessary, he could "go back and listen to their comments and have something to fall back on to help us understand what they're saying."

Thus the next Thursday I set up my recorder in the school gymnasium where Mr. Watts, the fifth grade teachers,[6] and a group of 35 or 40 parents, many of whom came and went as the meeting dragged on, talked for about 3½ hours. Mr. Watts began the meeting with a 35-minute lecture on his philosophy of learning and then opened the discussion to parents. Although several spoke strongly in support of what the school was doing, the majority voiced concerns. Rather than giving a blow-by-blow description of the meeting, I synthesize the perspective the protesting parents articulated and compare it with the perspective from which the teachers and Mr. Watts seemed to operate.

Studies on parent involvement have suggested that a core difference between parents and teachers is that the former have a "particularistic" standpoint and think principally about their own kids in all their complexity whereas teachers have a "universalistic" standpoint and look at groups of students and at only some of their characteristics (e.g., Lareau, 1989; Lightfoot, 1978). At Thurber, however, both teachers and parents switched back and forth between particularistic and universalistic discourses, and other fundamental differences in parent and teacher perspectives surfaced. In particular, parents and teachers at Thurber mapped education differently in

---

[6]The fifth-grade teachers were the only teachers at this meeting, in part because much of the tension was over whether students going from fifth to sixth grade were adequately prepared. Mr. Watts asked the fifth-grade teachers to survey middle school faculty on how well prepared Thurber students were compared to students from other elementaries. The teachers apparently checked on a number of recent graduates who were now at the middle school in the European American neighborhood (they didn't survey the two other middle schools that African American students leaving the school attended) and reported that Thurber students were doing well indeed—in direct contradiction to parents' reports based on their knowledge about their own children. Another reason that only fifth-grade teachers were asked to attend the meeting may have been that it made it easier for the school to avoid showing teachers' differences of opinion.

space and time; the two groups fit kids' performances into different networks or circuits.

CIRCUITS AND FIELDS

By *circuits* I mean the networks of practices that orient people within arenas of institutional life. *Institutions,* in this sense:

> can be described as *cultural accounts* under whose authority action occurs and social units claim their standing. The term *account* here takes on a double meaning. Institutions are descriptions of reality, explanations of what is and what is not, what can be and what cannot. They are accounts of how the world works, and they make it possible to find order in a world that is disorderly. At the same time, in the Western rationalizing process, institutions are structured accounting systems that show how social units and their actions accumulate value...and generate progress and justice on an ongoing basis. (Meyer, Boli, & Thomas, 1994, p. 25 [italics original])

Institutions are mapped across networks of organizations. One way to talk about these networks is to say that they constitute *organizational fields* consisting of "those organizations that, in the aggregate, constitute a recognized area of institutional life: key suppliers, resource and product consumers, regulatory agencies, and other organizations that produce similar services or products" (Dimaggio & Powell, 1983, p. 148).

But what gets "recognized" as an "area of institutional life" depends on the observer's standpoint as well as on the interactions of organizational participants. The location of an organization in an organizational field is a social construction. That is, people from different standpoints looking at or participating in a setting such as Thurber Elementary—parents and teachers, for example—can see it as connected to different networks, can fit it into different cultural accounts, can understand its accounting practices in different ways. The sociologists just quoted, for example, produced work on the administrative and fiscal structures of schools and school districts (e.g., Scott & Meyer, 1994), but their maps of the organizational fields of public education bear little resemblance to those of parents, teachers, or kids. Indeed, these groups do not even appear on the sociologists' maps. The "organizational fields" the researchers described are only a few among many that could be defined by differently positioned participants. I'm not suggesting that circuits can be defined willy-nilly, or that participants necessarily disagree about the existence of organizational linkages. Rather, what varies is the importance participants attach to links and their explanations of the meanings of the linkages.

For Thurber parents, the school was a point on their kids' pathways to graduation and adulthood, one that played a key role in comparing and ranking kids to prepare them for different futures. Grades were mobile ways of representing kids that could move from one level of school to another and could be combined, averaged, and used for comparison and ranking. For some Thurber teachers, on the other hand, school was a workplace where they tried to perform as experts before an audience of students, peers, and possibly unfriendly district administrators. Grading practices were modes of communication directed toward students (as formative feedback on work), but they were also signs of a professional stance that linked the teachers using them to national movements of teacher professionalism and school reform.

Parents' Circuit: Comparison and Ranking

Case studies of parental opposition to school change have generally treated opposition as a technical problem, the product of political or organizational practices that fail to involve parents or community segments adequately in the change-planning process, or fail to monitor and address parental concerns emerging in the course of change (Gold & Miles, 1981; Smith & Keith, 1971). Other studies have focused on the ideological or cultural characteristics of parent groups which supposedly make them resistant to change (Moffett, 1988). By contrast, I suggest that something more than lack of involvement or ideological inertia produced the parents' resistance. Schools fit in different ways into the life trajectories of parents and teachers, and each group develops different vested interests in schooling and different ways of conceptualizing it. Instead of thinking only of their relations to a particular school (e.g., Epstein, 1995; Fine, 1993), Thurber parents oriented themselves to the *sequence* of their kids' schools. The parents' complaints about the system of representation embedded in the school's grading scale reflected their concern about how their kids' achievements would be mobilized and moved through that sequence. The judgments of curriculum and teaching that produced the letter of protest were grounded in comparative logics.

The parents' circuit, then, was the chain of school settings—elementary, middle, and high school—through which kids moved. Their movement was physical—kids traversed a sequence of spatial, temporal, and regulatory regimes that corresponded to a culturally constructed maturing of the body—and symbolic, in the sense that kids were translated into stable and mobile representations (grades, test scores), forms of institutionalized cultural capital (Bourdieu, 1986) that could be aggregated over time and used to rank kids, separate them, and connect them to the institutional identities that would shape the directions of their lives. The dual definition of institutions as cultural accounts and accounting systems meshed here: Parents saw schools as accounts of how kids matured and took their places in society (i.e., the school sorted them into appropriate paths and futures) and as accounting mechanisms (producing grades and test scores) to explain and legitimize this sorting.

This view may seem odd to those of us accustomed to looking at things from a teacher's standpoint. At a school like Thurber, a regular classroom teacher's acquaintance with kids generally begins and ends within a single school year. The histories of students in earlier grades and their fates in later grades are hidden. Only conversations with other teachers or their own experiences teaching in other situations give teachers a sense of how their classrooms relate to those of other grades or other schools. Mrs. Court, for example, recalled moving up a grade with the same group of students:

> in my experience, having taught third grade and then moved up to fourth grade, it's kind of humbling. You know what you taught them in third grade, you know what they've had, so you expect certain things. But, it's really eye-opening to see what they really remember, and how you really have to take so many steps back.

If teachers had visited other rooms in their building or at other schools, they would have been even more startled by the sharp contrasts in teaching and curriculum. Sociologists have talked of such discontinuities as aspects of the "loose coupling" of educational organizations—the way organizational units function independently of one another although they may be tightly linked in symbolic and ceremonial ways (Meyer & Rowan, 1977; Weick, 1976). But such discontinuities are not natural features of schools; they are the results of policies and practices limiting communications among teachers. And if schools are loosely coupled, they are so only from the perspectives of administrators and teachers. Parents do not see them the same way.

As I've said, at Thurber the parents I talked to saw schooling as a cross-grade, multischool process in which kids moved from kindergarten through twelfth-grade education along a single trajectory stretching toward adulthood. Many parents saved their kids' papers and tests and compared the work from different grades and teachers. Mrs. Longman, for example, told me that Neal wasn't keeping a journal in fifth grade:

> They used to have to keep a journal. In the third grade and fourth grade. And I've still got his journals. I hold on to that stuff. Because Neal wants me to keep every paper anyway. But when I feel like it's important, I stash them away. I like to get them out and take a look at them.

Other Thurber parents were already thinking about which middle schools and high schools they wanted their kids to attend. Mrs. Kaiser, for example, was planning to send Earl to a high school in the neighboring county system:

> Well, I don't have firsthand knowledge, but most of the people that I've talked to that have their kids in high school are in schools in the county. They seem like they've got a better—I don't know—they seem like they learn a lot more. And they're more advanced than the ones in the city.

Many of the parents' misgivings about the curriculum and the grading scale at Thurber were grounded in worries about the unorthodox marking system's affect on placements in middle school "tracking systems" (cf. Oakes, 1985). Mr. Dodd, the father of a fourth grader, was already aware (although he had no older kids) that the middle school used a traditional grading scale and tracking:

> The grading scale here [at Thurber] is quite wide, in my opinion. Now, when you go to middle school, not only is it lettered and not only is it numbered, but it seems to me that it's very much more pointed, and you're either in this group, or you're not. Now, there's got to be some adjustment, not only to the students, but to the parents as well, I mean, my gosh. . . .

Many of the parents had expressed similar concerns in interviews I'd conducted a year earlier. Mrs. Hunt, for example, had told me:

> We had parents last year that threatened to pull them [their kids] out of school, and a couple ladies did....And I tried to encourage them to stay, and what wonderful things we had, and they said, "I'm not gonna wait 9 weeks to know what's going on, and then find Ns when my child has done better work than this in another school." And so there, again, there needs to be more continuity between the feeder schools that send them down here, and here.

"The grading system they have here in the city," Mr. Hunt added, "they're not continuous [between schools] so you've got a problem for the child as well as the parent."

Mrs. Longman, talking about her son Neal, made a similar point in expressing her displeasure with Thurber's system:

> But what does it do to them when they go to sixth grade? That's my question. What happens to Neal when he goes from here to middle school, and nothing's changed in middle school? It's still the same grading system, still the same teaching. What happens then? "Oh, it's being changed, it's being changed"—yeah! There are three schools in the city of Roanoke that's doing different things, right? All the rest of them are still—oh well! Get me started! I have to cool off!!

At a meeting of the report card revision committee in the summer of 1994, Mrs. Fine, an African American parent, asked in wonder:

Is it just okay—doesn't the school system like work together, okay? So I notice that Thurber has changed, but a lot of the other schools haven't changed, going to the Ms, Ts, and Ns! So, can one school just actually up and change the grading system just like that?…So, do the different schools do whatever they want?

"They do different things," answered Mr. Watts.

This kind of answer frustrated parents enormously. At the meeting with Mr. Watts in March of 1994, Mrs. Massey had suggested that Thurber and the other schools get together and sort things out:

> I have one suggestion. Since we are in the city district, and there are a lot of parents that have concerns about their children's education. This system seems to have apparently worked really well. Maybe what we should do is possibly maybe get a lot of the teachers and parents from several different schools all together, to discuss what's going on, what's happened through the system, see how many parents really start thinking about it and really understand it and really agree with it, to see if we can just get it all across the board, every school. That way, we wouldn't have any problem with it.

But such collaboration across schools was inconsistent both with the political structure of the school system, with its independent principalships, and with the tightly bounded, inward focus of the faculty at Thurber. Mr. Watts and the teachers framed their activities within the boundaries of *their* school and resisted (and resented) comparisons with other schools. As Mr. Watts insisted during the meeting with parents (in a discussion of standardized test scores): "We cannot compare Thurber School to Pumpkin Hill [an elementary school in an affluent section of town]. Okay, they're not the same. If we compare apples to apples, we perform as well or, or better."

Although it might seem obvious to educators that school outcomes can't be compared because schools deal with different students, operate under different constraints, and draw on different resources—a perspective that focuses on differences in inputs—parents focused on outcomes and from that position countered that their kids should be doing as well as any others in the system. The Thurber parents could and did compare schools on the basis of their standardized test scores (which were published in the local newspaper), on the basis of their own experiences with different schools, and especially on the basis of anecdotes about other schools that friends from church or work told them.

It might be useful, in fact, to think of parents as participating in what Moll and some of his colleagues refer to as "funds of knowledge," household-centered social networks across which families share essential resources, skills, and information (Moll & Gonzalez, 1994; Moll, Tapia, & Whitmore, 1993; cf. Smith & Tardanico, 1987, pp. 100–101). Because Moll and his colleagues are mainly concerned with the experiences of working-class Mexican American families struggling to survive in unstable labor markets, they've tended to focus on funds centered on "sócial, economic, and productive activities" (Moll, Tapia, & Whitmore, 1993, p. 160) and they've generally viewed household funds of knowledge as ordinarily segregated from school-based activity.

The protesting Thurber parents, however, also working class but situated in a relatively stable labor market, were participants in funds or networks organized at least in part around reproductive activities such as schooling itself. The parents had social networks across which they shared information about school practices, networks composed, for example, of friends and neighbors whose kids had other teachers or went to other schools; of teachers from other schools who went to their churches; of knowledgeable casual acquaintences (e.g., Mrs. Longman had struck up an acquaintance with a central office administrator who attended her Weight Watchers class); and finally of the PTA itself. The networks were sources of information that helped parents make decisions about what middle and high schools their kids should attend and what preparation was needed for school at those levels, and also allowed them to situate Thurber within a larger organizational field.

An A–B–C–D–F marking system fit neatly into the parents' comparative logic by letting them compare their kids to others (or at least to a mythical average kid represented by a C grade—mythical because the assumption that grades are distributed on the same bases across schools is untenable; see Office of Educational Research and Improvement, 1994). These rankings could be taken as "objective" representations of students' abilities since they were based on a clear referent: the percentages of kids' correct answers on standardized, textbook-based tasks. Parents could thus assume that the rankings were reliable predictors of how the kids should do in later grades.

The alternative marking system introduced at Thurber disrupted these assumptions. Instead of marks based on percentages of right answers, the kids received codes based on the complex and unarticulated judgments of teachers. Grades were transformed from referential terms to shifters, indexical terms whose meanings depended on which teacher was using them in what context. Parents could no longer look over student work, check to see what scores their kids made, and then praise or cajole them as need be. The move to the literature-based curriculum turned schoolwork into a black box for parents and made them depend on teachers to tell them when things were going right or wrong.

As one result, marks ceased to appear *objective* and instead seemed more like choices made by teachers rather than mirrors of kids' abilities. Hence, when parents saw marks they thought unsatisfactory, their complaints went not to their kids, but to the teachers. By the same token, as the grades now appeared to be teacher rather than child produced, parents could no longer use them for comparison or for a gauge of future performance. The aura of objectivity once attached to grades had helped legitimize unequal outcomes, but many parents now saw the M–T–N system as an unnatural attempt to mask the "natural" inequalities among students. Thus Mr. Hereford could complain:

> I accept the, the…the equality of this process, but you have a class of fourth graders, and some, as you said, are working at a, a, higher level of accomplishment; they have developed further, maybe, in one area, maybe in all the areas, versus the others. Now, I understand you all have to test these kids at certain periods in their education now—but at what point do you come to a conclusion, a rational, logical maybe not altogether what seems like a fair conclusion, that basically if you put these children with these children—I think you hope that if these children who are not developing quite as fast stay with this group, it'll help them develop a little faster. I think many are sensing that the opposite is happening now. That to create this equality we are bringing about a learning-down.

At issue here was the question of whether the school was trying to promote a social agenda—creating "equality" among the students—that was overriding what some parents saw as its true educational function: creating differences. This is an issue that resonated with larger political debates going on in the state during this time.

Political Linkages

The literature-based curriculum, and the complex grading practices introduced with it, disrupted the assumption of a normal distribution of talent which schools should reinforce through their grades. As far as parents were concerned, teachers weren't there to make personal judgments about kids or to build their self-esteem; they were there to teach the "basics" and neutrally report on the kids' differential performances on straightforward tasks. Mr. Dodd, for example, complained that kids needed to be drilled more on their multiplication tables, and Mrs. Grigsby wondered why the teachers didn't just make the kids use correct spellings and punctuation the first time around rather than making them rewrite their work.

The old textbook–worksheet system had defined a small but clear role for parents in the basics-oriented curriculum. The steady stream of graded material going home from school allowed parents to monitor what their kids were doing, support the teachers' assignments, and reward or punish kids for their performances. There was a regular, albeit a very assymetrical, communication loop between school and home. In the new curriculum, by contrast, communication was more ambiguous

and much less regular, and parents' roles and opportunities for participation were much less clear.

The parents' emphases on teaching the basics and ranking students
and their demands for improved lines of information from school to home
thus might have grown partly from their traditional expectations based
on their own experiences as students. I want to suggest, however, that
the political climate of the time gave resonance and depth to their
expectations and encouraged parents to publicly articulate their differences with the educators at Thurber. The parents' letter of complaint
was drafted only weeks after George Allen, a conservative Republican
with ties to the Christian right, had been elected governor. Allen had
easily carried the European American neighborhoods around Thurber
(flyers supporting him were distributed outside PTA meetings during
the campaign), although he lost in the African American neighborhoods
by a 10 to 1 margin.[7]

Allen's campaign had emphasized "parental rights," charter schools,
and voucher programs. He had promised a return to the basics and a
new battery of standardized tests, to be administered every other year,
as a way of making schools more "accountable." And true to his word, a
year into his term, Allen began to push through revisions in state
curriculum guidelines which favored skill drills and rote memorization,
especially in the areas of Language Arts and Social Studies. This
conservative mindset on education is exemplified in a 1994 speech given
at a public meeting in Roanoke County to discuss the new curriculum
guidelines. The speaker was a retired university professor and local
Christian Coalition leader who supported the governor's standards:

> When I went to teach [college] in 1981, I expected my students to be as
> well prepared as I was when I went to University. And I was shocked, I
> was shocked to find out that their math was atrocious. They didn't know
> what the area of a circle was or how many feet in a yard—things like that.
> Now, that's memory, but believe me, it's useful, okay? [Applause]....There's
> nothing wrong with memorizing things! Anything you've ever learned is
> by repetition. Watch a little baby learn how to walk? How do they do it?

---

[7]One side issue worth noting is that the lieutenant governor candidate on Allen's
Republican ticket was Mike Farris, an ultraconservative with strong ties to the Christian
right. Farris had publicly called the public school system a "godless monstrosity" and after
losing the election, had become head of the Home School Legal Defense Fund. In this role,
in June of 1995, he led an attack on a Federal Trade Commission action against the makers
of the Hooked on Phonics program. Not all protesting Thurber parents agreed with
Farris—Allen carried the neighborhoods around the school, but Farris lost them. But
Farris's grounds for supporting phonics and for attacking whole language clearly showed
that parental control issues were at the heart of the debate. For Farris and others, phonics
was a technique that parents could use at home (either in conjunction with school
instruction or in home schooling). Whole language, by contrast, centered power in the
hands of teachers and excluded parents, unless roles for them were explicitly built into
the curriculum. The only roles educators at Thurber allocated to parents were listening
to their kids read and signing a homework folder each night.

They try and try again, right?...Repetition, repetition. If that's rote memory, tough! That's how you learn!! [*Applause*] Anyway, I found out that
these students of mine...they could not write. Their spelling was atrocious.
This so-called invented spelling is just for the birds [*Amens from the
audience*]. When you learn to read, you learn to spell. And that's with basic
systematic phonics! The look-say, whole language method has been a
disaster in this country [*Applause*].

How many of Thurber parents would have endorsed this view I can't
say, but there were many anticipations of it in their public objections to
the curriculum.

Having adopted a literature-based curriculum and a kind of portfolio
evaluation, the staff at Thurber thus found itself at odds with this
ascendant conservative movement. They had moved far from rote learning and memorization and had positioned themselves as the sole agents
of judgment in instructional matters. And although they probably did
not intend to, they had essentially excluded parents from the schooling
process. For if parents understood schooling within a circuit that traced
students' movements across grade levels, the circuit that Mr. Watts and
most of the teachers worked within, as I explain in the next section, was
one that supported the notion of teachers as autonomous experts whose
judgments on curriculum and assessment should simply be accepted.
From the school perspective, parental resistance seemed to stem mainly
from ignorance. At the meeting held to air parents' complaints, Mrs.
Moon, who had let it be known that she was praying for her child's
teacher, asked if parents could just vote on whether to go back to the old
grading system. Mr. Watts replied: "I would say, we would like to educate
first, and then we can have a vote. But we would like the opportunity to
educate everyone on why we do it the way we do it."

Mrs. Moon shot back:

Well, for three years, this has been educating, and parents still don't
understand it, and I'm one of them. Because my daughter went from here,
to middle school, and she was unprepared, and astounded as to what she
had to face when she got there. And I know Mrs. Hunt felt the same way.
I've had my child crying, upset. What I'm saying—just like this gentleman
was saying in the back—they are going to go on to 6th, 7th, 8th, on to 12th,
and they are going to face life. They're not going to have fantasyland where
somebody's going to say, "I'd like to see how your tone of voice is." They're
going to say, "I want to see what you can do."

The challenge here was directed beyond the grading system itself and
implied the parents' unwillingness to accept the notion, at the core of
the teachers' circuit, that teachers should determine what was to be
mastered and when it had been mastered.

The Teachers' Circuit

Whereas parents wanted their kids reduced to stable, combinable representations that could move through a local network of schools, the teachers at Thurber wanted to describe students with complex and unstable representations (portfolios, for example), whose networks of circulation were unclear. On the one hand, the portfolios were supposed to move in a very tight loop between teacher, student, and parent as formative assessments; on the other hand, assessments like portfolios linked the teachers and what they were doing to a disciplinary vision of teaching as an expert, professional practice.

The teachers' circuit was defined by their relation to an idea of pedagogy in which kids worked in groups, worked on integrated strands of curriculum, and were formatively assessed on complex products like stories or poems rather than on worksheets or simple tests. These ideas separated teachers from the community and connected them to national movements in educational reform and pedagogy. In the language of the French sociologist Pierre Bourdieu (1985), Mr. Watts and the teachers were redefining the *field* (a term analogous to my use of *circuit*) of educational practice. The traditional grading system was directed to a general audience of parents; the new curriculum and grading systems had a different ideal audience, one composed of other educators and educational researchers. I was more representative of the ideal audience for the new grading system than were the parents of kids in the school. I came from the university, was a vocal proponent of whole language and portfolio assessment, and had actively supported some of the school's innovations (by donating books like First, Kellog, Almeida, & Gray's *The Good Common School,* 1991, to the faculty, giving several teachers copies of books like Routman's *Invitations,* [1991], and later circulating articles about Kohn's [1993] work [Miller, 1994] on the problems of using grades as external incentives).

A circuit orienting teachers to an idealized, theory-based pedagogy helped create and sustain a definition of *teacher* as pedagogical expert. Teachers were supposedly self-sufficient constructors of instructional settings, the principal mediators of students' interactions with curricular materials (as opposed to the more traditional definition of teachers as transmitters of the knowledge encoded in textbooks). I do not suggest that all the teachers at Thurber thought they were experts in this sense; some were quite unsure of themselves. But this language and concept of expertise limited teachers' ways of talking about themselves and the public roles they could assume. As experts, for example, they should already know how to do wonderful, creative, inventive activities and use holistic assessment practices to make sense of students' performances on complex tasks. Most teachers, however, had neither the training nor the immediate support to develop such strategies and, like Mrs. Court, felt simultaneously frustrated and guilty.

At the same time, the definition of teaching as expertise suggested that teachers should be left alone, beyond the interference of parents or administrators. The teachers saw parents' attempts to participate as challenges to this pedagogical autonomy, and many of their responses to parent complaints seemed to be simple restatements of their expertise. At the meeting to address the letter of complaint, for example, Mr. Watts began his response this way:

> [*Reading the parents' first comment*] "While we are receptive to the philosophy that it promotes a positive self-esteem, we are concerned that the current grading scale is not wide enough to closely evaluate a student's progress." Any questions? I would be glad to tell you what we think and why we do what we do. And that's *very* simple. There's really nothing hard about it. Our thinking is, when a child has *mastered what we want him to master*, then let's say he has mastered it.

Such assertions of monopolies on relevant knowledge are a common feature of expert or professional claims to power (Freidson, 1970; Welker, 1991). But casting teachers as the sole arbiters of curriculum and evaluation raised tensions among the teachers as well as between them and the parents. Expertise and professionalism garner much of their legitimacy from the idea that professional judgments reflect collectively produced knowledge and not individual, idiosyncratic decisions. At Thurber, however, there were no opportunities for the discussion and debate that might have produced shared understandings. Instead, teachers worried in private about making assessment judgments and defending them to parents. "Math is easy," one teacher explained to me:

> 'Cause they either get a math problem right or they get it wrong. But in their writing I'm not keeping checklists. Like Mrs. Peel, she's very organized. She keeps points—like a point system—kids get certain points for doing certain things, and if they don't do it or didn't do a good job, they lose points. So she can back that up, so it's not a problem with the parents. I can't back up—a lot of what I'm saying about the kids and where they are, because I don't have any records. The only records I have is their work. So, I need to really—I have to have time. But I don't know how! I used to take a stack of papers home and I would grade them, and make marks on them. And now I don't want to make marks on the papers if I'm not going to grade them, give them M, T, or N, whatever, on their writing, really. You know, I need to conference with them, and I need to, when I talk to them, I need to take notes. So that makes me uncomfortable....I don't know what I'll show [parents]—if they want to see where I'm getting my Ms and Ts, I don't know.

At the March protest meeting, Mrs. Hereford raised this issue of inconsistency by pointing to situations where kids in the same class got the same grades for different levels of performance:

> If you have children, say I have a child that's in math, she's learning pretty good, and she gets on her grading a "masters." Okay, and my next door neighbor, her child is in the same classroom as my child, and gets the same grade as my child. And the two of them, one's learning more and does better, and the other one is slightly less. But they're both getting "masters." Then how—how do you compare that?

Mr. Watts could only respond by again insisting on the teacher's expertise and autonomy:

> The only way that you could try to explain that, what you're speaking of, is that the teacher who observes what went on in the classroom, based on what's in the child's portfolio, made that determination. That they both had mastered the material.

Mrs. Hereford responded:

> But at the same time, that's not letting the parents know exactly where their children are, like A, B, C—you know, when we were graded when we were young, our parents knew exactly where we were in our activities at school. We either got A, B, C, D, or F. Here, there's only three. So we don't really know exactly where our children stand as far as their education goes.

When parents questioned teachers' practices by constrasting them to practices at other schools or by contrasting the evaluations of their kids with performances of kids from other schools, their comments were not treated as reasonable questions or concerns but were seen as challenges to the teachers' claims of expertise. Yet the faculty as a whole was unable to agree on its response. For example, in one teachers' meeting to discuss the parents' letter, Mrs. Peel, who earlier in the year had reassured the faculty that getting to whole language was a slow progression traversed at different speeds, now complained about the inconsistency from one classroom to another: "We have a philosophy, and people who don't agree with it should move on."

Mrs. Marx responded immediately:

> I'm an individual; we're all individuals. We may have a philosophy, but within that philosophy we're all individuals, and I'm uncomfortable with any one person saying who should stay and who should go and what people should be doing in their own classrooms.

Mrs. Peel backed up a little and made it clear that she wasn't trying to force anyone to leave. Her point at the end was that "we can't keep showing the community different faces. If we all buy into the philosophy, we should be consistent in how we deal with parents and assessment."

"I agree with that," Mrs. Marx replied.

"We're supposed to be united," Mrs. Peel continued.

"But are we?" Mrs. Marx asked. Everyone, I think, knew the answer to Mrs. Marx's question: Teachers were widely divided about how they ran their classes. But just as they resisted parents' attempts to raise comparisons across schools, they judged attempts to compare classrooms inappropriate. The structure of the school system, which kept teachers separated from one another and masked one school's activities from other schools, made the comparative talk that parents insisted on impossible for teachers.

As one consequence of the lack of comparative discourse, arguments about teaching, among the educators at least, were reduced to arguments about decontextualized notions of pedagogy. Instead of critique and self-examination, teachers tried to make sense of their work by talking about the presumed connections between idealized ways of teaching and idealized student outcomes.

This view of teachers' activities as the deployment of discrete performance strategies is heavily promoted in many colleges of education. Professors discuss pedagogy as a *virtual system* in which certain pedagogical regimes—almost always conceived in terms of *classroom* practice—produce certain student outcomes, rather than as real practices slowly accomplished over time and space, continuously modified to deal with change and contingency.

The idea of pedagogy as flowing from an individual teacher and centered entirely on classroom processes closes off concepts of teaching as grounded in relationships with parents or communities, of teaching as a fundamentally communicative activity that stretches beyond the walls of the classroom. This idea also hides the fact that shifts in pedagogy and assessment require changes in how teachers interact with parents. The Thurber teachers tried to maintain a traditional teacher–parent relationship that would have been appropriate for a textbook- and worksheet-based pedagogy in which teachers and parents communicated infrequently and teachers were left alone to teach.[8]

To the parents, however, having kids working in groups on tasks spread out over several days or longer, with the work often going directly into a portfolio rather than coming home, implied a different parent–teacher tie. Because kids weren't bringing worksheets home every night, parents wanted more direct contact with teachers, like notes or phone calls, to monitor how their kids were doing. And because kids no longer performed the same tasks in groups separated by test-defined ability levels, parents thought they needed to give teachers more input

---

[8]The routinization of teacher–parent communications in traditional report card systems is attested to by books like McDonald's (1971) *Teachers' Messages for Report Cards*, a compendium of prefabricated paragraphs teachers can use to describe kids, along with an appendix of "appropriate adjectives" and "appropriate phrases."

about what their kids could do. How, they wondered, could teachers know what each kid was capable of if most work was group produced? But parents who tried to tell teachers about their kids' abilities were seen as intrusive and pushy by some teachers (e.g., Chavkin, 1989; Comer, 1984; First, Kellogg, Almeida, & Gray, 1991; Lightfoot, 1981). Although Mrs. Peel, the teacher everyone thought was most successful at the whole language approach, called parents at home to update them on how their kids were doing, other teachers balked at this idea when parents suggested it to them at a meeting.

Mrs. O'Brien explained:

> I don't want anybody to be offended by this—but when I leave school, when I go home, my time is mine. And I never, I never have enough time at school to make phone calls. So I have told my parents, if you need to get hold of me, these are the times that I'm in school—I'm at school before 8:30. Call me before then, and I'm usually here after 3:30, until 4:00, if you need me.

Mrs. O'Brien and most other teachers already felt overworked. To them, the idea of remapping the temporal borders of teaching by calling parents at night just didn't seem reasonable. Under stress and out of time themselves, the teachers seemed unwilling to acknowledge the constraints under which parents also operated. Most insisted that the parents really didn't *want* to meet with them, wouldn't come in to meet with them after school, and weren't there to take their phone calls at lunch. Mr. Watts thought the teachers should just post "office hours" (like university professors) and make parents responsible for meeting with them. The ideal of parental involvement that he and his staff embraced seemed to be the one articulated at a staff meeting by another teacher, Mrs. Engels: "Parental involvement, to me, means parents taking part in the child's activities at home....Someone to help them with their science project. Getting involved in activities."

These notions of parents staying home to take teachers' phone calls during the day or coming at lunchtime when teachers wanted to meet are what Epstein (1995) called the "learning at home" conception of parental involvement, in which parents are not considered as participants in school decision making or as collaborators in developing or strengthening programs. Indeed, some teachers felt the parents' complaints flowed not from a need for better communication or a desire for greater roles in defining curriculum but from simple ignorance and an outdated worldview.

LEGITIMIZATION THROUGH ECONOMIC DISCOURSE

The protesting parents were unsatisfied after their public meeting with Mr. Watts and the fifth-grade teachers. Several took their complaints to an assistant superintendent, who apparently telephoned Mr. Watts and told him to resolve the situation. A subsequent meeting of teachers was tempered by a realization that it would be politically necessary to appease parents. When Mrs. Tanner complained that "some parents just won't learn what it is that we're trying to do. And I mean, really, they need to be made aware of the fact that if they don't like it, they can move;" Mrs. O'Brien responded: "Their rationale is that this is *their* school and they shouldn't have to move, we should be the ones to change." Mrs. O'Brien continued,

> I think up till now we've had it easy in a way. We kind of hid in the school district. Nobody else was doing what we were doing; nobody wanted to talk to us or look at us. Now we're visible. Now people are looking at us a lot....What we have to do now is make what we do palatable.

Making it palatable meant more than just explaining novel-based curricula and portfolio assessment; it meant supplying parents with a frame of reference, a perspective that would justify these approaches, would show that they were necessary and desirable, not just fads. The resources for such a justification were limited, however. As it had set out on an independent path, Thurber couldn't legitimize itself by reference to school system practice. It had to justify itself *against* the weight of practices at other schools. Neither was it possible for Thurber to draw on support in the community. There were certainly parents who liked what the school was doing, but the traditional ties between school and community that had broken down after Tota's reassignments and the renovations had not been replaced. Whatever ties existed were between individual teachers and parents of kids in their classes. It was difficult even for teachers to call on each other for support because their isolation made sustained discussion difficult.

Instead, Mr. Watts offered as a legitimizing view the argument that new forms of pedagogy and assessment, such as those practiced at Thurber, simultaneously reflected "how students learned" *and* marked the cusp of new trends linking schools to changes in the economic system. He looked, in my terms, for a common point where teachers' and parents' circuits could connect. Preparation for work, a standard rationale for schooling, and a key component of the trajectories parents plotted for their kids, seemed to fit the bill. In the big March meeting with the protesting parents, Mr. Watts had tried to connect the form of teaching he favored to successful business practices:

> Children construct knowledge through their own actions and through interactions with adults, children, objects, and ideas. A perfect example of this is Japan. After the war, Japan moved to a totally different way of business and industry than the U.S. People worked in groups. What we've learned is that there's an explosion of information in a group setting that

there isn't on a one-to-one basis. That's why it's very important for children to have interactions with adults....You know what creates the highest percent of remembering something? When you teach it yourself. You will remember 90%, according to statistics, of what you teach yourself. That's why we like to have children teach other children. Not all day long...but to demonstrate their own knowledge....Children's thinking is not compartmentalized into subject areas. This is very important.

The parents' resistance, Mr. Watts thought, was tied to their working-class backgrounds and to the declining relevance of their experience for what he saw as the emerging postindustrial age. At the meeting to listen to their complaints, he had pleaded with parents that abandoning the new approaches of the school would be:

a tremendous step backward. And I think another very difficult thing for people to understand is that we are no longer in the industrial revolution; we are smack dab in the middle of the information age. Things were designed for the industrial revolution, and we—we're not moving out of it, we are *out* of it. We are *in* the information age, and it's hard for those of us who grew up in the industrial revolution, the industrial age, to understand the significance of that. They're going to be in a very different world.

Talking with the teachers in the aftermath of the meeting, Mr. Watts repeated these ideas and framed for the teachers the idea that new pedagogies and assessment systems were needed to prepare kids for the coming new economic order: "That's one of the other things that's registering with me more and more and more. These parents, like us, are on the end of the industrial revolution. They have not walked into the information age, and their children are in it."

As this reasoning depended on parents' acknowledging that their life experiences were no longer relevant, it shouldn't be a surprise that it wasn't entirely successful. Mr. Watts and the teachers finally had to revise the grading scale from 3 levels to 4 over the summer; a move explicitly intended to give parents something they could more easily translate into A–B–C–D–F terms. But the economic rationales Mr. Watts advanced raise some questions. In this chapter, I have discussed how school system politics, discursive constructions of teaching, and teacher–parent struggles shaped the curriculum and politics of representing students. The question of the school's place in the larger political and economic context of the city remains to be explored: Just how did Roanoke and its schools fit into the postindustrial economy, and how were ideas about the high-tech information age articulated in the school? In the next chapter I examine the intersections of these issues—intersections that involved not parents and teachers, but teachers, administrators, corporate consultants, and kids.

2 A Tangle of Cities, Corporations, and Kids

> Discourses that speak for and against the city, then, like all discourses, are strategic incursions into our imaginations.
>
> —*Beauregard, 1995, p. 77*

Several intertwined discourses were linked to the idea of information age pedagogy. One discourse portrayed cities as areas of decline, difference, and danger. Another portrayed the economy as shifting from a manufacturing base to one founded on knowledge- or communications-based services. Finally, a third cast education as the key to reinvigorating the city and to smoothing the transition in labor markets produced by the economic shifts. In this chapter I'll show how regional politics disseminated these discourses; then I'll look at how the discourses intersected (along with other flows of activity) at Thurber. I present a case study of a school–business collaboration, describe its ideological foundations and the stresses it created for teachers, and show how it ultimately floundered in the classroom. To begin, I sketch the urban context of Thurber's attempts to change.

INDUSTRIAL DECLINE AND ECONOMIC TRANSFORMATION

Imagine Roanoke as a circle divided into quadrants. The downtown sits at the center at the intersection of the railroad tracks and the interregional highways. The poorest neighborhoods cluster around this core. To the northeast and southeast several important commercial roads cut through European American working-class neighborhoods. The southwest contains the most affluent part of the city, with tree-lined streets, big yards, and large houses, both old and new. The northwest, on the other hand, is the poorest, the area where almost all the African

46

American population has been concentrated. Encircling the city like a doughnut is the more affluent, largely European American county.

To make sense of this spatial organization of wealth and ethnicity, we need to understand Virginia's unique system of separating cities and surrounding counties into independent political and fiscal entities. Until the 1970s, cities could grow by annexing surrounding county lands. As the demographic structure of the state changed, however, the legislature became increasingly dominated by suburban and rural lawmakers whose constituents resented these encroachments. Lawmakers passed a series of annexation moritoriums that culminated in a 1979 bill ending cities' rights to annex.

Frozen geographically, cities have since been unable to extend their tax bases in the face of increasing pressures from aging, declining populations and increasing concentrations of poverty at their cores. The annexation prohibition was especially painful for Roanoke, which, like other northern and eastern cities with industry-based economies, had undergone dramatic economic shifts in the 1970s.

Roanoke had grown up defined by its close ties with resource-based extraction industries: It was headquarters for the Norfolk and Western Railroad, in large part because of its geographic proximity to the West Virginia coalfields. Roanoke was also the site of the first artificial fiber plant in the South, the British-owned American Viscose Corporation's rayon plant.

For decades, the big industries provided stability to the working-class communities of the city, but in the 1950s the situation began to change. Demand for rayon slumped, and when the American Viscose plant closed in 1958, 1,750 people lost their jobs. At about the same time, 2,000 railroad workers in Roanoke's steam engine plants were put out of work by the switch to diesel engines (White, 1982, p. 118). The downtown began a long decline in the mid-1960s with the opening of several malls in outlying areas. The population of the county began to grow while the city's stagnated. In 1982, Norfolk and Western merged with Southern Railroad and moved its headquarters to Norfolk. A decade later, the only regional bank based in the city, Dominion Bankshares, was bought by the expanding First Union Bank of Charlotte, North Carolina.

Along with the rest of the country, Roanoke's employment base had shifted: In 1974, 8 of the 10 largest employers had been industrial or manufacturing firms; in 1994, 8 of 10 were service organizations or public bureaucracies (Employment since 74, 1994). Although unemployment was low, jobs were increasingly concentrated in low-paying sales and service areas (DeBell, 1993).

Combined with the prohibition on annexation, the economic transformation of the city generated a sharp asymmetry between the affluent and almost exclusively European American county and the declining city with its large minority population (Table 2.1). County policies

TABLE 2.1
Population Characteristics: Roanoke City and Roanoke County

	City	County
Population	96,754	79,332
Percent European American	74.3	96.0
Percent African American	24.2	2.5
Families Below Poverty Level	12.8	3.0
Median Household Income	$22,591	$36,886
Percent High School Graduates	68.0	79.4
Percent College Graduates	15.6	22.6

Data from U.S. Census Bureau, 1990 Census. At URL: http://venus.cen-sus.gov/cdrom/lookup/CMD=TABLES/DB=C90STF3A/F0=FIPS.STATE/F1=F IPS.COUNTY90/F2=STUB.GEO/LEV=COUNTY90/SEL=51,770,ROANOKE.

seemed geared to maintaining this asymmetry. For example, the city had 1,500 units of public housing and 1,333 units of subsidized housing, but the county had no public housing and only 64 subsidized units. This situation kept poorer city residents where they were and pushed low-income residents from the county into the city (Turner, 1993). State legislators, meanwhile, endorsed the growing disparities through inaction: State funding for cities did not increase relative to funding for suburbs, even as family incomes in cities fell beneath those in counties (Study finds Va. cities in decline, 1993).

Realizing the city was becoming a magnet for the poor and disadvantaged, political leaders began to advocate the creation of a regional government that could pool resources. In 1990 they tried to turn this idea into reality by proposing a referendum to merge Roanoke city with surrounding Roanoke County.

THE MERGER FIGHT

From its beginnings, the merger effort attracted strong opposition in the county. Some saw it as part of a scheme by the downtown business elite to expand its power. Just a year earlier this group, with little public input, had engineered major changes in the downtown landscape by tearing down structures and rerouting streets to build a skyscraper headquarters for Dominion Bank. "Isn't this really an attempt by big business to annex Roanoke County?" a county voter asked at a public meeting (Layman, 1990b, p. B2). It didn't help that the person leading the fundraising effort for consolidation forces was Warner Dalhouse, the high-profile head of Dominion Bank, who was able to raise an amount unprecedented for a local referendum in Virginia: over $220,000, most of it from city-based retail, industrial, real estate, and construction businesses (Layman, 1990a; Layman, 1990c; Yancy, 1990). Merger opponents, meanwhile, raised less than $10,000 to support their efforts.

But although distrust of the urban elite was an important factor, the main sources of county opposition seemed to be racial and class based, and their focus was public schooling. A prominant merger opponent, Harry Nickins, a county supervisor, argued repeatedly that city and county were incompatible because of their different concepts of a "neighborhood school": "The city's concept of neighborhood schools is diametrically opposite to the county's concept because children in the city do not necessarily attend the closest school" (Nickins, quoted in Turner, 1990b, p. B1).

Nickins claimed that at one intersection in the northwest quadrant of the city, kids waiting on the four corners could be going to four different schools:

> Not all children who live in the same neighborhood in the city go to the same school, he [Nickins] said. Within an area of less than one square mile in Northwest Roanoke, he said, there are attendance zones for nine different elementary schools. (Turner, 1990b, p. B1)

As northwest Roanoke was overwhelmingly African American, the unstated subtext of these arguments would have been clear to everyone. The kids being bused from their Northwest neighborhoods could only have been African American. The implicit threat was that county schools would have inner-city African Americans bused into them or that county students would be bused to schools in African American neighborhoods.

Consolidation advocates pointed out that the county would have a majority on the consolidated school board and that only 5% of city students attended "a school that is not the closest to their home" (Turner, 1990e, p. A12). But this argument was perhaps beside the point. Lee Garrett, a former county supervisor, pointed to the racial concerns underlying opposition to consolidation: "They say this is a philosophical issue—not a racial issue," the paper quoted him as saying, "but believe me, it is a racial issue" (Turner, 1990d, p. B4).

Beverly Fitzpatrick, an employee of Dalhouse's at Dominion Bank and a city council member, accused merger opponents of racial "hatemongering":

> Fitzpatrick claimed that "racists" have helped kill merger plans in recent years in several metropolitan areas across the country. Racial attitudes also have been a factor in opposition to consolidation in the Richmond area, he said.

If the city–county consolidation plan is rejected, Fitzpatrick suggested it might also be viewed by some as racism....Cooperation, touted by opponents as an alternative to consolidation, is a "code word" for those who "oppose Roanoke, are full of prejudice and don't want to have anything to do with the [city's] minority population," Fitzpatrick said. (Turner, 1990c, pp. B1, B3)

With race now an open issue, merger opponents accused supporters of deceiving the public on the issue of busing. One opponent, Charles Landis, a former city council member, charged that federal desegregation orders handed down in the early 1970s remained in force and would result in the busing of county kids into city schools. Merger proponents vehemently denied this, but Landis supported his claim with a letter (dated July 21, 1988) from city school superintendent Tota to the state department of education. Tota, apparently trying to get money for Roanoke city's magnet schools, had written: "'requesting assistance from the state to encourage nonminority students living outside the city to take advantage of city school programs and, thereby, assist in decreasing racial isolation'" (quoted in Turner, 1990a, p. B3).

According to Landis's interpretation, this meant:

"Roanoke city wants and needs county residents, their tax dollars, and their children to help the city solve its social, economic, and school problems....The city's crime rate is more than four times higher than the county's. The welfare budget is more than three times greater than the county's. City schools are more than 40 percent non-white compared to 3 percent in the county." (quoted in Turner, 1990a, p. B3)

Teachers, who might have played a key role in this debate, were divided by other concerns. A county high school teacher organized a group of "educators against merger" and submitted a petition with 654 signatures in opposition (Thompson, 1990). Perhaps remembering the house cleaning that Tota had initiated when he took control of the city system, county teachers feared his adminstration, which they saw as "more authoritarian" than the county's. According to one teacher quoted in the paper, "In the county 'they consult teachers before they make major changes.'...In the city, she believes, 'They don't have the same input'" (Thompson, 1990, p. B8). In the wake of Tota's attempts to close neighborhood schools, county teachers also feared the closure of smaller schools and transfers for themselves and their students.

In the end, the consolidation referendum failed; it lost in the county by a 72 to 28 margin (although it passed in the city by a 68 to 32 margin).

In the aftermath of the defeat, merger supporters blamed their failure on a perception among county voters that the city school system focused on the needs of the poor and of the African American minority. Ironically, as I showed in the previous chapter, these were precisely the issues

Superintendent Tota had focused attention on: threatening to close schools because of budget shortfalls caused by needy school populations; warning that the neighborhood schools threatened with closing could be saved only if steps were taken to end segregation; promoting magnet schools to draw European American students from affluent areas to schools in African American neighborhoods. As one consultant for the pro-merger side pointed out in a newspaper interview:

> "If everybody says 'We're poor, we're deprived,' what impression does that give the county?" Merger opponents didn't have to bring up the schools directly, he says. "It had already soaked into the consciousness of the people for five years." (Yancy, 1990, p. A2)

Reflecting on the defeat four years later, Roanoke city mayor David Bowers pointed to the need to improve the *image* of the city education system as a key to overcoming county resistance to ties with the city:

> I'm not sure that we really spent the time four years ago to talk about the schools. We have excellent schools in the City of Roanoke....I'm not sure that we ever really spent the time discussing that issue and allaying some of the multi-faceted fears that people had regarding good education for their children in this area. We should've done that better. (Echols, 1994)

Not surprisingly, education was to play a big role in the next push for regionalism.

THE NEW CENTURY COUNCIL AND CORPORATE-SCHOOL RHETORICS

The problems that had prompted the merger effort didn't go away with its failure. In spring 1993, the Roanoke Valley Business Council began a new planning effort to try again to promote a vision of regionalism. The group linked with the major university in the region, Virginia Tech, to create the New Century Council, a group jointly chaired by the president of Virginia Tech and the CEO of the largest employer in Roanoke. The 91 people initially invited to participate were mostly European American male business leaders: Only 11% of the participants were women, and fewer than 4% were African Americans; 7% were elected officials, only 1 was a neighborhood leader, and there were no representatives from labor unions or grassroots political organizations (Yancy, 1993).

The strategy of the New Century Council was to improve public perceptions of the city and to demonstrate the importance of its relations to the surrounding region by developing a "vision," a "mindset," which would make regional cooperation (the group steered clear of the word *merger* or any other concrete description of city–region coupling) not only palatable but desirable to the counties. The council would address the education issue head-on, not by talking about neighborhood schools or busing but by arguing that the whole regional educational system needed to be transformed. The group adopted the rhetoric then being popularized by corporate executives and by Clinton Administration officials, of a new economic order centered on technology-based knowledge industries that required highly skilled workers (e.g., Labor Secretary Robert Reich's vision of a "third industrial revolution" led by a rising "technicians' class"). The group drew attention to the decline of traditional high wage manufacturing and industrial jobs in the region and to the problems of "inelastic cities" (Rusk, 1993) that couldn't grow geographically and lacked cooperative ties with surrounding municipalities. References were made, full of longing, to the expanding cities of North Carolina—Charlotte, now a banking center, and the "research triangle" around Raleigh and Durham which a generation earlier had been smaller and less prosperous than Roanoke.

By January of 1994, With the help of a high-profile Total Quality Management facilitator and after some 4 months of work and retreats at a local resort, a group of about 90 corporate and political leaders revealed seven vision statements. The area, the council declared, should become

- A world leader in public and private education

- Among the most desirable places in the world to live and work

- Renowned as the safest and healthiest place to live and work

- A region in which the infrastructure links the region and the world

- A diverse and globally competitive economy

- A partnership of governments investing in tomorrow

- A model for America in leadership, regional identity and creation of 21st century opportunities (Wagner, 1994, p. B1).

A day earlier, another group, representing the regional Chamber of Commerce, presented its Roanoke Valley 2000 plan (obviously modeled on the federal Goals 2000 initiative). The plan's objectives included sending kids to school ready to learn; increasing the high school graduation rate to 90%; ensuring total adult literacy and a population of good citizens ready to "compete in the global economy"; and ridding schools of drugs and violence. As the president of the chamber explained, the goals were:

"a mindset, a way of thinking and doing, a way for business, educators and parents to pull together and achieve a consensus for the future....[The goals are] about increasing the potential value of our citizens through education." (Turner, 1994a, p. C4)

The key idea behind these efforts was that the region around Roanoke could survive in the present economic era only if its cities and counties collaborated to improve the region's quality of life, among other things by improving education to attract high-tech industries to the area. A representative of the Virginia Employment Commission (VEC), speaking on a New Century Council panel, was quoted in the newspaper as explaining:

> The problem is, employees more and more need higher thinking skills to use and understand technology at work. That's in contrast to 30 years ago, when many jobs involved performing repetitive tasks, Skidmore [the VEC representative] said. . . .
>
> The school curriculum of tomorrow, panelists agreed, should include more access to vocational training, studies that develop thinking skills and stimulations that prod students to consider a career path earlier.
>
> Without those steps, "What's at risk is to have an underclass of people that are not competitive," said panelist Carl McDaniels, who runs a career guidance program at Virginia Tech. (Sturgeon, 1995, p. B8)

This emphasis on promoting education for "higher thinking skills" belied a job market that was clearly shifting toward service sector jobs with low educational requirements. In fact, although unemployment, at 3.4% at the end of 1994, was very low in the Roanoke area, *underemployment* was already high (DeBell, 1993). Newspaper articles chronicled the exodus of educated young adults, driven from the area by a lack of desirable jobs (Williamson, 1993). Meanwhile, the Bureau of Labor Statistics projected that the top 10 "high-opening occupations" for the Roanoke area between 1988 and 2000 would be mostly low wage jobs with low educational requirements: retail salespeople, general office clerks, secretaries, janitors and cleaners, nursing aides and orderlies, waiters, cashiers, and heavy truck drivers. Only two of the projected job growth areas, general managers and registered nurses, required post-high school educational credentials or were likely to pay above $20,000 a year (DeBell, 1994).

It's not surprising, then, that the rhetoric of a high-tech, education-driven future resonated most powerfully not among the general public or county politicians but among business leaders (for whom the position served as a way to displace blame for economic ills from the business sector to the schools; see, e.g., Hull, 1993) and educators, college professors as well as public school teachers. The state had been tightening educational funding and cutting monies to universities since 1990, and by elevating the importance of education and linking it closely to the all-important and politically sacred idea of economic progress, educators could position themselves better to resist budget cuts. Indeed, the strongest opposition to Governor Allen's attempts to cut education funding further in 1995 came from traditionally Republican business leaders.

On the other hand, for educators such as Mr. Watts the idea of a new economic order demanding "higher," more sophisticated skills than in the past seemed to support innovators who positioned themselves as fighting against the pedagogies of an outmoded past. The New Century Council released its vision statements just days before the parents delivered their letter protesting Thurber's curriculum and grading system, so it's small wonder that Mr. Watts drew upon the council's rhetoric in defending his practices.

Mr. Watts's affinity for the corporate-educational rhetoric, however, was not merely a tactical appropriation of the New Century Council's agenda. In the remainder of this chapter, I track an episode that took place in early 1993, a full year before the parents' letter. Mr. Watts, working with Thurber's "business partner" (see, e.g., Brothers, 1992), a large, technology-based corporation I call Industrial-MagnaCorp, tried to concretize the new economic–educational order by transforming parts of Thurber into a space ordered by the logics of corporate economic practice. Unlike the controversy over curriculum and grades which spanned my 2 years in the field, this business–school partnership had a short, 4-month life span, which can be tracked from the complex, shifting influences that shaped it to those that nurtured and ultimately killed it. This story illustrates teachers' difficulties in implementing such schemes and the kids' reactions to them.

CORPORATE SPACES IN THE SCHOOL

After the 1992 Christmas break, Mr. Watts hooked up with Thurber's corporate partner, Industrial-MagnaCorp, and a teacher from another school, whom I'll call Mr. Tripp. Mr. Tripp had developed a scheme for transforming his elementary classroom—both its physical space and its activity structure—into a simulacrum of a shopping center. On a Saturday morning in January 1993, Mr. Tripp met with Mr. Watts, two Thurber teachers, and two representatives from Industrial-MagnaCorp to discuss implementing Tripp's approach. After introductions, Mr. Tripp briefly explained his method:[1]

---

[1]Pam Simpson attended and audiorecorded this meeting for me. I later transcribed the tape.

The first year I [taught elementary school], I kept thinking the children needed a place to practice what they were learning. And also there needed to be created a *need* for what they were doing. I wanted them to see the need. Even before I said anything or instructed or taught or whatever. And so I came up with this concept of having, bringing a shopping center in on a miniature level, and making it so [attractive] in terms of how it looked in the classroom that in effect I could seduce them into thinking, "Oh, this is fantastic." And I ended up coming with this transfer theory—what I call it— that they transfer this real love of this thing to me, that they believed in me, they thought that I, you know, [was] this incredible person, because I had set up this and made it; it was so different than what they were used to.

Physical versimilitude was critical for Tripp. The shopping center couldn't just be:

some wallpaper slapped together with pieces of cardboard and here's your book or some furniture contrived together and "This is our shopping center, this is our school." This had to be—once the material matched the physical structure, the children became so excited about it....For 13 years I did it. For 13 years. There were waiting lists to get into my classrooms because of this....The reading is there; the writing is there. Art is there, science is there, career education is there. Hands on is there. There isn't anything that the system really lacks.

In Tripp's eyes, his scheme was a *curriculum,* not just an activity, and it required a major physical transformation of classroom space. As he explained to the group:

I really feel that once the physical part is in place, and that in itself is a part of how you're going to do it, a controlling factor, because there's a disbursement of children. See what I'm saying: Their exhilaration when they come in—you need to have a camera person there that day to take pictures of the faces on these kids.

In some respects, this idea of turning the classroom into a simulation of a nonschool environment resembled ideas advanced by progressive educators early in the century. Rugg and Shumaker (1928), in their influential text *The Child-Centered School,* mentioned the construction of simulated cities by kids and emphasized the importance of "realness" and having school activity center on "real-life situations" such as a school store, bank, or newspaper. Robinson (1923) even provided a detailed description of a school laid out as a "shopping arcade" (p. 217). In the progressive agenda, however, the aims seemed to be encouraging kids to learn about the activity or settings simulated and to learn general skills through participation in such simulations. Whether these were Tripp's intentions too or whether he saw the simulations as simply a way to motivate kids, I can't say. Others at the meeting picked up his ideas and took them in directions he clearly never intended them to go.

The Industrial-MagnaCorp representatives at the meeting—Mr. Pither and Ms. Wooster, from the marketing and quality control departments, respectively—responded warmly to the general idea of "more relevant," function-oriented pedagogy. Mr. Pither, who was to be the corporate liason with the school for the project, explained:

> [When I] first heard about this I thought, gee, what a concept. I wish that somebody would have done something like this for me....[Kids] have to learn how to spell and how to write and how to do math and all that nasty stuff. If maybe somebody gets involved with them and shows them that this stuff is actually transferable and they're going to use it for the rest of their life whether they like it or not, it could become something very exciting. So I'm going to be here to learn, probably more from the kids than anything else.

Ms. Wooster, mixing the now-familiar themes of a coming demand for high-skill workers with a blunt statement of corporate self-interest, added:

> Adults think that when you get out of school you're done. And it just isn't so. And the amount of learning we have to do is, is—just to do our jobs day-to-day—is astronomical. In fact everybody, everybody is in the world spinning faster and faster with the computers and the communciations, that everybody you talk to is busier than a one-armed paperhanger. And we have got to get everybody, from the children through the adults, to learn to love to learn. Because it'll be a whole lifelong process for them. We also are selfish, to know that children are your end product: Whatever you deliver we're going to receive and we're going to use them. And so we need them ready for that.

Corporate and educational interests merged at the point where the supposed changes in the economy and the job market—the new high-skill, high-tech jobs—could be used to justify new forms of curricula and pedagogy, such as teams of students managing businesses in the school.

Economics and Education: A Pedagogy of Need

Everyone at this meeting agreed that the economic shifts described earlier in this chapter were creating new demands on the schools. Mr. Pither talked about how traditional manufacturing jobs were disappearing:

> When I went to high school, it was a decent-sized school; 425 graduated, a third of those got married within the next week—I think half of those had to—and I went back, and I was a kind of, I was a dork. A small, nerd—now being a nerd is fashionable [Laughter]. So these guys ended up getting out of school, the really cool guys, got jobs in the factories....And

now I go back, and now they're unemployed or about to be unemployed. And they don't know what to do.

Mr. Watts agreed and stated his view that a new age required new forms of education:

And what has happened with that, I think, is a shift from manufacturing in the old traditional sense into a manufacturing–technology age. And they're very different. And you have to be able to do different things. And I think oftentimes we in education are still in that old mode. [Noises of assent]. And the kids are not going to function in this new environment. If we don't get out of that old mode, it's going to be worse than it was. . . .

Mrs. O'Brien, one of the Thurber teachers present, situated the school in this perspective for the visitors:

Though...this is basically an inner-city school, you're looking at a very nice inner-city school. We're looking at a lot of children who have never had that opportunity of lemonade stands. I think we have more and more as the years go on of parents who are too involved in other places, because of whatever reason, that kids aren't getting those opportunities....And to me that just pushes them further and further away when they go to work. They've never had that kind of experience. They think job, they think work is, you go to work and they pay you. And that's what they think work is.

The business-oriented rhetoric distanced parents from schools, and this supposed gap in home life led Mrs. O'Brien to ask the group to "think about our community in this area....How are we going to convince the Mrs. Hunts of the world that her children are not going to lose" on basic skills if they participated in such a curriculum.

Ms. Wooster answered: "This is the danger I see. I look at the world today, and I see all the low-skilled jobs moving out, moving offshore, moving to the third world. The only jobs that are going to be left here are high-tech jobs."

This rhetoric, which seemed to suggest that blue-collar jobs migrate to the third world on their own rather than being exported there by corporate leaders, anticipates the broader argument, to be used a year later by the New Century Council, that because blue-collar jobs were disappearing, education must prepare kids for high-skill jobs. Mr. Watts, in words that fit neatly into this line of thinking, suggested that schools needed to be "preparing those kids to be good employees and thinkers and problem solvers, when they get to [employers such as] Industrial-MagnaCorp."

As I've already noted, these suggestions of high-skill futures and impending worker shortages were highly questionable (Noble, 1994). Industrial-MagnaCorp itself had laid off thousands of skilled workers and managers from its international operations during the 1980s and had transformed itself from a predominantly manufacturing enterprise to a predominantly service organization.

Mr. Pither, then, might have more accurately described the situation when he said that the key to the transformation of the schools was the creation of a pedagogy that mirrored the market-driven economy of the corporate world: "We'll come up with this program, so that the kids understand what they need to do. And we can teach them that *life is nothing more than need and satisfying need* [italics added]—recognizing needs and satisfying needs."

There are layers of meaning here, some of them probably not intended by Mr. Pither. A pedagogy of need defines a social ethic for crafting personal relationships based on exchange, a logic for accumulating social capital by means of people's shaping themselves to satisfy others' needs (for example, by bravely embracing the identity of "dork" at an early age). And, if we follow the logic of the Committee for Economic Development (CED), a group of executives from large U.S. corporations, the pedagogy of need locates the value of education in a congruence between the needs of the corporate world and those of the students: in gaining the reading, writing, and problem-solving skills required by employers. The CED argued that schools should abandon attempts to include students with disabilities in regular classrooms, should cease providing social services to pupils, and should instead return to teaching the basics (Manegold, 1994). This view raises an interesting question: Where did the basics fit in the idea of making and selling products in a simulated shopping center economy?

Skills and Simulacra

Mr. Pither's colleague from Industrial-MagnaCorp, Ms. Wooster, raised this issue of basics:

> Help me past something here, okay. This is a personal hangup. I tell you what my problem is—I hate to shop. I'm not a shopper. And everything you're doing here is shopping and malls and things like that. And I'm real science oriented, and I love science. And I'm having a little trouble finding it in there....Having my children to grow up to be real skillful at mall shopping is not what I want my children to be. Although I understand how you can pick up all the skills in there, computer skills and math skills.

Mr. Tripp quickly explained that he didn't see students as only selling goods:

> This isn't retail; these shops are, in effect, shops in two sense of the word: We're talking not only retail, but we're also talking about manufacturing. These things are being constructed here; you see what I'm saying. That's an interesting point: We could have three or four rooms manufacturing,

and then you have a mall where it's just sold. But space dictates that you
can't have workspaces, factories in effect, and malls.

Ms. Wooster wasn't entirely satisfied: She insisted that there must
be a bounded space for *teaching*: "But you still need a place, whereupon,
let's say you wanted to learn about the bank and they needed to go to a
quiet place to sit down and actually maybe team with other people. You
need some common conference areas."

Mr. Tripp tried to suggest that spaces could have multiple functions.
The simulated business spaces could be appropriated for instructional
purposes: "A teacher can go into these shops to teach. You can teach in
these shops while business is being transacted." Ms. Wooster on the
other hand, had a much more "disciplined" view of spaces as having
distinct functions (Foucault, 1979, p. 143).

It was up to Mr. Pither to supply a solution to the dilemma, and he
came up with one that would have pleased the French writer Baudrillard (1983). Baudrillard argued that representations have lost connection to underlying "realities," that instead they float free as
"simulations" linked only to other representations. Mr. Pither suggested
that Ms. Wooster was mistaken in objecting that Mr. Tripp's scheme
went too far in turning the classroom into a simulated economy: The
real trouble, he explained, was that the simulation didn't go far enough.
If manufacturing and retail establishments could be simulated in the
classroom, why not school as well:

> A thought that crossed my mind, and that was to include school in the
> model. It seems to me what we're developing here is a microcosm of society,
> a little economic system: You can call it a mall; you can call it anything
> you want. The concept, though, is to say, hey, let's demonstrate what you
> use education for. It's like applied education. Where do you use this? And
> it seems to me, to pick up on the point you were making, why not, in this
> model, also have a school? Tie that into the traditional role of the
> school...what its purpose is; to train you to do something like this, and you
> pull that whole thing in. And then they understand, well, why do I come
> to school anyway? That's part of what's the world about. The school is just
> as much an important part of society as the business, as the bank, as this
> and that.

Catching on to her colleague's line of argument, Ms. Wooster asked
why, if you could have a school-within-a-city-within-a-school, you
couldn't also have a church-along-with-a-school-within-a-city-within-a-
school:

> Let me take this reflection idea a little further. Here we're talking about
> this microcosm of area, and we're talking about the schools and bringing
> that in. And there is, in society, a reflection time. And here's another one
> you're going to have trouble with. It's called religion and church. Okay,

Sunday, a day of rest, reflection day, that we all need to survive. I know you'll have a real tough time with that....So you might not call that little area over there church, but you might need a little reflection area. You have to say that that's an integral part of your microcosm of society.

By now Mr. Tripp's scheme, complicated to begin with, had been transformed into a plan to produce a simulation of society within the classroom, wherein school, indeed almost all elements of everyday life, would become simulated within and subordinated to corporate space.

The Shift in Focus

Mr. Tripp seemed to sense that the discussion was moving outside his vision. He repeatedly cautioned Mr. Watts about how much was going to be expected from the teachers, how important it was to proceed slowly: "The thing you have to be careful of here is, you can't overwhelm. You have to start simple. You really do." Tripp also emphasized the importance of reorganizing classroom space:

It *has* to be real; something that they've seen in the community or on television. If they don't have that, and they're just working, that's okay. But you're not going to have that exhilaration, you're not going to have that starry-eyed fantasy. You're not going to get it. And I'm not going to sit here and tell you that in two or three months, it's just going to die. I don't know. It never died with me because of that. But it could die in your room if it's only paper and contrived furniture....I'd be interested in knowing what happens if you go that way.

His concerns grew in part from the drift away from the idea of physically reconstructing space toward simply instituting the formal mechanisms of economic activity. He was asked, for example, if the plan could start with setting up a bank as the first component of the economy. Mr. Tripp responded that they should "start with all of them, really," although the first practical step would be to collect the materials needed to remodel the classrooms. When Mrs. Wooster asked him, "But suppose that they're going to start just for a little while this year?" he replied, "But what's the bank? Then you're in your training mode then. You're not really an economy."

PUTTING IT INTO PRACTICE

Mr. Tripp's core idea of physically transforming the classroom was abandoned as being too elaborate and difficult. The idea of the economic classroom did not disappear without a legacy, however. Few educational processes are simple and linear. Although the school-as-economy scheme, as modified by the Industrial-MagnaCorp consultants, tied nicely into the Clinton Administration's information–economy rhetoric (which would later be echoed by the New Century Council), by itself the scheme did not produce action. The idea lay fallow for about 6 weeks after the meeting but re-emerged, transformed, when another element was added to the mix.

Dr. Tota announced that he would be leaving the superintendent's post at the end of June 1993. Mr. Watts, concerned that a new superintendent, possibly one unsympathetic to his innovative ideas, would be taking over, decided to try the waters of the doctoral program at Virginia Tech. He'd enrolled in a graduate course in educational psychology that spring and there he'd been entranced by the idea of *situated cognition* (as defined in a paper by Brown, Collins, & Deguid, 1989). We'd talked about it a few times, and I'd lent him a couple of related books (Lave & Wenger, 1991; Tharp & Gallimore, 1988). Now he wanted to tie the idea into a revised version of the business-in-the-school scheme to make the classroom more "realistic" and meaningful for students.

A school-based economy, he suggested to me, might be an example of situated cognition. The kids could form teams, do surveys, find a viable market, write a loan request, and apply to a bank (run by Mr. Watts) that would lend them money to produce their products. Once the loans had been made, the kids would market whatever they produced. In fact, Mr. Watts already seemed to have figured out what they'd make: "Cards," he told me—birthday cards, Easter cards, and so forth. He suggested the kids might even be able to sell shares in their companies and create a stock market.

I responded carefully. The idea of *situated cognition,* especially in the Brown, Collins, and Deguid (1989) version, *has* been invoked by proponents of school-based enterprises. Stern, Stone, Hopkins, McMillion, and Crain (1994), for example, cited the article to support the claim that "information and thought processes acquired in the context of problem solving that has a social purpose are more likely to be remembered and available for application to future problems" (p. 205). My own take on the idea was rather different. As I said to Mr. Watts, the question was not whether "something" was situated cognition but rather how a particular activity was connected to other activities. I suggested that he might want to talk to the kids about the kinds of buying, selling, and so forth they did in their everyday lives and then try to figure out how the activity that was being proposed—the simulated economy—resembled or could be connected to those activities. It was unlikely the kids had ever run businesses or applied for loans, but they probably got allowances or did chores for money and bought things with their money, and so on. I suggested he consider building on these practices.

As was often the case, my suggestions went nowhere. A week later, as I checked into the office in the morning, I saw Mr. Watts sitting at the computer working on an application form for the businesses kids were to set up. As I looked over his shoulder, Mr. Pither, the Industrial-MagnaCorp liaison, came in and began talking to Watts about the form. Mr. Watts asked what should be included and ran through some of the items he thought were needed: name, business, school phone number, personal assests; and some questions such as "Are you putting in your own money?" "Do you have investors?" He told Pither, "The product is where I'm having problems." He'd begun to think that having all the kids sell cards might be too restrictive: "I feel like we're limiting what they do." Pither agreed and suggested that the kids be allowed to come up with their own ideas about products. The two then decided to fuel the school economy with a paper currency, Thurber Dollars, made by reducing and photocopying one side of a dollar with Mr. Watts's face replacing George Washington's. Mr. Watts decided to begin the business scheme with one class participating at each grade level. Mr. Pither made presentations to the classes, getting the kids "all fired up," in one teacher's words, and distributed the application forms (Figure 2.1). After that, teachers were left alone with the project.

Up to then, I admit, I hadn't paid much attention to any of this: I hadn't yet listened to the tape of the January meeting, and the business simulation was something I heard about only in passing. This situation changed when I stumbled into a meeting of teachers frustrated in their efforts to implement the plan.

THE REBELLION OF THE TEACHERS

Mrs. Peel, Mrs. West, and Ms. Boggs, the teachers trying to supervise the classroom businesses, had been stymied in their efforts to help kids fill out the application forms. The kids were supposed to survey fellow students to determine demand; do cost analyses to know what to charge; and apply for loans (in Thurber dollars) from a bank run by Industrial-MagnaCorp volunteers. If they got a loan, the kids would produce and market their products, show a profit or loss, then liquidate whatever money they made in an end-of-the-year auction of goods provided by Industrial-MagnaCorp. Mrs. Peel told me she thought the goal was to give kids practical experience starting businesses. She described her students as "lower middle class or below that even" and said that many were just looking forward to futures of wage labor. But even though she supported the goals of the activity, she and the other teachers were uncertain about how to proceed. They wanted more support from Industrial-MagnaCorp and, in a teacher's words, "begged" Mr. Watts for a meeting with a representative from the corporation. Mr. Watts complied

The Name of Your Business _____

Address _____   Telephone _____

References: List at least two names and the addresses of each.

Assets: List any assets that you believe will help the bank make a decision in your favor.

What is your Business Plan? (It should include the following information) _____

Market Strategies _____

Please provide a description of your product and a sample

_____

Who will make your product?

_____

What kind of advertisements will you do?

_____

COST ANALYSIS

Material Cost per item   _____

Labor Cost per item   _____

Tax Cost per item   _____

Interest Cost per item   _____

Based on your market strategies what do you expect for a gross income per item?   _____

Based on cost and earnings what do you expect for a net income per item?

What will be your estimated profit?   _____

Based on the above estimates how much money do you need to borrow?

FIG. 2.1 Student business application form.

and arranged for them to meet with Mr. Pither. I happened to be sitting in the office on the day Pither arrived and was invited to the meeting.

Mrs. Peel did most of the talking. "The first problem is patience," she said. "They [the kids] want to go to the art room, get supplies, and do it today." The kids also wanted to bring money and supplies from home. They didn't understand why they should go through the process of applying for a loan: "If we have it at home," the kids told her, "we don't need to borrow as much." Mrs. Peel said they didn't understand about Thurber dollars, which the businesses and markets would use for an artificial currency. "And another thing," said Mrs. Peel, "how do they earn Thurber dollars? That needs to be clarified. And if the businesses don't make any money, do they have to pay it back to Industrial-MagnaCorp? That needs to be clarified." Mrs. Peel said that her kids weren't thinking beyond the classroom. They were thinking they would make a product and sell it to themselves. Mrs. West said her kids wanted to know whether the money they "made" would be theirs. "My kids say, 'Why do we have to do an application?'" said Mrs. Peel. "They say, 'Why can't we tell them what we need and they give it to us?'" The kids needed a consultant, Mrs. Peel explained, to help them fill out the application properly:

> They need day-to-day guidance, and so do I. I've never started a business. I know I wanted to do this, but now I don't have any idea where to go, and I have 28 kids depending on me for answers....Let Industrial-MagnaCorp people guide us; that's what we need. I can facilitate, but I just don't have a lot of the basic knowledge to do this.

"We need Industrial-MagnaCorp to guide us," echoed Mrs. West. "The kids are crazy about this," said Mrs. Peel, "and they were mad when we told them to put it on hold." All the same, she was beginning to wonder whether it was feasible to follow through with the plan this year:

> I'm worried about time. I've got a lot going, and I want to make sure I do credit to the literature that we're reading. Just doing what we've done so far took two or three days, and that's just scratching the surface. Could we limit this to Fridays?

Mrs. O'Brien added that the rest of the school (the classrooms not involved in the businesses) knew nothing about the scheme. "How are they going to get Thurber dollars so that they can buy things?" This question produced a string of suggestions for incorporating payment systems into the school routine. Kids could be paid for behavior (or rather, lack of bad behavior). They could also be paid for academic work. "How much is homework worth?" asked Mrs. O'Brien. Mrs. Peel suggested that if students did all the work for a week, they could get one Thurber dollar at the end of the week. She said she also required her students to read four novels a month, and if they did, they could gain four dollars at the end of the month.

I suggested that as it was just funny money, why not pay the kids a million dollars a week? It might sound like more of an incentive. Mrs. O'Brien ignored me and told Mrs. Peel that she didn't think the pay should be orchestrated on weekly or monthly bases. On a weekly scale, if kids didn't complete their work on, say, Monday, there would be no incentive for them to do the work the rest of the week as they would have already lost their chance for the dollar. Instead, she suggested, they should be paid daily, a dollar a day. This idea raised the practical issue of how the kids would handle the physical money. "They'll steal from each other," Mrs. O'Brien said. Someone suggested the kids sign on the backs of their dollars, in ink, to make stealing impossible. The irony of this conversation, in light of the debate about grades, should be obvious.

Mr. Watts finally interrupted and said we could make such decisions later: "What we should be talking about now is how to get you all going."

"Here's my concern," said Mrs. Peel, coming straight back to the point:

> We've got to construct a survey, administer it to the rest of the school, analyze its results—and if there's no market for the proposed product, go through that loop again—and then we've got to flesh out the plan, get the money, produce the good, and sell it. I just don't see where we've got the time.

"Let's look at it this way," said Mrs. O'Brien. "We have six Fridays left....You can't do all that in six Fridays." She suggested they omit the survey but do the application. The application form, however, asked for marketing strategies and earnings estimates, which seemed to presuppose a marketing survey. Mrs. Peel insisted that to do it right they would have to do the survey, compile the results, analyze them, and incorporate the activity into a math unit—which would take about "three weeks," she guessed. Mrs. West pointed out that in the coming weeks they also had Science Fair projects to set up and demonstrate, days of standardized testing to administer, not to mention the regular curriculum.

"The question is," Mrs. Peel said, "do we want to do this half-assed this year or do it right next year?" From her tone of voice she clearly wanted to do it the next year.

But Mrs. O'Brien responded: "I think we should do as much as we can, even if it's wrong, this year. That way we can learn from our mistakes and try again and do it right next year."

"But do we really even have time to do it wrong?" asked Mrs. West. "I want to do my novels right, and I really want to do the Science Fair right, and I'm worried that I'm not going to have the time."

"What's your recommendation?" Mr. Watts asked her.

Mrs. West replied: "That we do it in the fall. I will feel less pressured. I feel like 'When am I going to do this?'...We need more time. Back in the fall when I was developing my personal objective for the year[2] I had no idea something like this was in the offing."

"If we just drop it," Mrs. O'Brien replied, "we won't know what we'll do wrong or do right when we try it in the fall."

"My concern," said Mrs. Peel, "is that the kids will see an example of us starting and then stopping."

---

[2]Mr. Watts expected each teacher to develop a "personal objective" for the year—an issue or topic they would learn more about and incorporate into their teaching.

. "Let's limit it to Fridays," said Mrs. O'Brien. "We do as much as we can for the next 6 weeks and get Industrial-MagnaCorp to come and be consultants."

Mrs. Peel seemed to realize that Mrs. O'Brien and Mr. Watts weren't going to concede, so she turned on Mr. Pither. "All right," she said in a tight voice:

> You guys come and work with us. *You* look at the applications; tell us whether they're approved or not. We'll just do everything in an abbreviated form. But we need Industrial-MagnaCorp people here. We don't know how to do marketing, and we need that explained to us right now....Can you all come Monday and work with each small group on their application? I have six [groups] in my room. Help them finish their applications; then come back Thursday to let us know whose application you've approved or rejected?

Mr. Pither blanched and said, "Well, I was really just thinking of coming in and talking about the process generally, not working with each group."

"Mr. Pither should have the applications from Mrs. Peel's groups in hand before he leaves on Monday" said Mrs. O'Brien.

"Well, we could spend an hour or so explaining the forms," Mr. Pither suggested.

"No, I need you to help us *work* on them," said Mrs. Peel. She pointed to the questions on cost analysis. "I mean, this stuff is a real struggle; we don't know where to begin."

It was agreed, finally, that someone from Industrial-MagnaCorp would come Monday to help Mrs. Peel's class, and the plan would go ahead in an abbreviated form, without the marketing surveys.

By the end of the meeting, I'd become curious about the scheme and saw in it tensions between corporate and public aims, between the teachers and Mr. Watts, between the whole language ideology the school embraced and the commodification of school work explicit in some of the talk that day.

That night I called Mrs. Peel and asked what she thought of the idea of just leaving a tape recorder and a bunch of tapes and asking kids to record their deliberations. I would have preferred to observe myself, but I had unbreakable commitments at the university. Mrs. Peel liked the idea and told me that the kids had really had to think about a lot of issues. When they began, they had no concept of *consumers*. "We almost had to beat it into them," she told me, "that they had to have people interested in buying the products they were going to make."

SCHOOLWORK FOR EXCHANGE

The complex lesson that goods can be produced purely for their abstract exchange values actually emerged slowly over centuries in the Western world. Its end result is what Marx (1967) called *commodity fetishism*: the situation in which "a definite social relation between men...assumes, in their eyes, the fantastic form of a relation between things" (p. 72). In other words, the situation emerges when people spatially or socially distant from one another begin to interact by exchanging things they've produced. Marx was talking about economics, but the scenario is a familiar one in education. Kids write papers or fill in the blanks on tests. Teachers or grading machines give them scores. And instead of treating this process as a "definite social relation between" people, we say that the paper got a certain grade or that the test measured a certain quantifiable level of skill or achievement. The relations are between products and abstract attributes, not between teacher and student or student and test maker. Even as kids, then, we become familiar with commodity fetishism in the context of school. Kids see their work as being meaningful mainly in terms of its exchange value not only because of tests and grades but also because what they do outside school is often given no place in school activity. For example, Neal, a quiet, working-class boy who loved math but disliked writing at school, told me one day about riding in a pontoon boat on the lake. Neal usually didn't show much excitement; so when I heard him talking with animation about the experience, I asked him if he ever wrote about such things in class. He and Lucy, a fellow student, answered together:

Lucy:	Uh-uh. 'Cause you forget about them in the class.
Neal:	They don't give you that opportunity to write about your life.
Lucy:	You make up things. . . .
Neal:	We have to make up immigrant diaries [as part of their current curriculum unit]. . . .
Lucy:	I'm not doing it right....I don't like doing the immigrant diary.
Neal:	Me either. I don't really.
Lucy:	I think it's stupid.

The kids' understanding of the products of their work provided a lovely example of commodity fetishism:

Jan:	Let me ask you though, Lucy, do you think you all learn stuff about immigrants or slaves from writing about them?
Lucy:	No!

. . .

Neal: The only reason we write about stuff like that is just for samples. For the next grade.

Jan: Samples?

Lucy: I know. For the teachers.

Jan: Is that what she [their teacher] said?

Neal: Yeah. Well, they're mostly for samples, but there are a couple of them that are for grades. But all the others we just write for samples. So basically we're almost writing for nothing! But then everybody else can see how we used to write. So really we're writing kind of for a purpose; it serves a purpose.

Jan: Is that what [your teacher] told you?

Lucy: Yeah....[*Picking up her portfolio*] This is gonna go to sixth grade, all this stuff right here.

In this scenario, the portfolios functioned almost like grades by reducing students to two-dimensional, visual, disembodied forms that could be surveyed in their entirety by glancing at a file. And at least in some classes, the students understood the function of the portfolios to be exactly the same as that of traditional grades: to sort and rank students. Another fifth grader, Alf, explained in another interview that the sixth-grade teachers:

just look at it [the portfolio] and see how good we are, and see what kind of classes we have to go into. If we have to go in the high grade, low, or medium. And it goes, uh, till you go to college....Teacher....She told us we'd either be in a class that don't know very much or a class that sorta, sorta was on track, then, uh, if you're really smart.

In these kids' class, at least, commodities were familiar products of schoolwork and fit into a clearly articulated logic of exchange. Reality, in the sense of what they did in everyday community activities, had no place in this classroom system. The teacher defined the meaning of *activity*, just as the school-as-business scheme sought to insert reality into the classroom, not by drawing on what kids actually experienced outside school but by creating a simulation of a reality that adults experienced. Yet there were important differences between the portfolios and the products to be produced for the business game. For one thing, the kids didn't have to worry about the *market* for portfolios or about material costs, taxes, and the like. Neither did they have to consider what might be in it for them, what *uses* they might make of the activity of schooling or the objects that resulted from it. Would their familiarity with the logic of classroom commodities translate into an understanding of business practices?

COMMODITY FETISHISM
VERSUS THE FIFTH GRADE

On the day the Industrial-MagnaCorp employee was to help the kids with their applications, I approached Octavia, one of the kids I had permission to interview, and asked her whether she would take my tape recorder and record her group and herself as they worked on the business application. She readily agreed. I want to stress that the following portions of her recording are not representative of Mrs. Peel's teaching but demonstrate a corporate pedagogy into which Mrs. Peel occasionally intervened.

The recording began with the noises of kids milling around the room before class. Then Mrs. Peel got their attention and announced: "We have a busy morning so we have to get started. We have Mr. Pepper from Industrial-MagnaCorp, who's going to talk to us about our applications, very first thing this morning....Okay, is Richard here?"

"No," said some of the students, and a couple pointed out that Thurston wasn't either.

"They must have killed one another," Mrs. Peel joked. When she had finished with the roll, taken lunch orders, and let the kids sharpen their pencils, she asked me to explain about the taping. Although I'd been in the room several times earlier in the year, I reintroduced myself, explained why I wanted the recording, and told the kids that if they didn't want to be recorded, they could tell Octavia to turn the machine off. There were no questions, so after making sure Octavia knew how to operate the recorder, I left. Mrs. Peel then asked the kids to move into their already-formed business groups and turned the class over to the Industrial-MagnaCorp representative, a Mr. Pepper:

> Okay, you guys ready? We're going to try to go over probably the top half of this page. And I think most of you guys have already done this, and I just want to make sure that we all get to the same point before we go to the bottom half and continue on from there, okay? Has everybody chosen a name for their business? Everybody have a name?

There were cries of Yes and No from across the room, and Mr. Pepper, surprised that some groups lacked names, went around the room checking. While he looked, the kids in Octavia's group began talking among themselves. Someone suggested Daisy do all the writing on the application, as "she's got the best writing." The activity quickly became an occasion for talking about money and wealth. Rona complimented Octavia on her shirt: "I like your shirt, Otty."

"What?"

"I like your shirt."

"Thank you. It was worth it; I spent $45 dollars on it."

"I wouldn't buy that. $46? Say that again?"

"I wouldn't spend $46 on one shirt [*Laughing*]."

Mr. Pepper called for everyone's attention, and the class immediately became quiet. "Does everybody have an address for your business?" Several answered that they didn't, and one asked about using their own addresses. "Sure," Mr. Pepper replied. As they wrote in their addresses, he walked around the room and reminded them to put down the name of the city and the state they lived in as well. Finally, he stopped and spoke to the whole class:

> Okay, everybody understands why it's important to have an address and a phone number, right? How are you going to sell anything if people don't know how to locate you? You're not going to be very successful, are you? Now, does everybody know what we mean by references? Can somebody tell me what references are?

There was a quiet pause before a boy answered: "Like when you go for a job, and you've been transferred from another job, like someone before gives you a good reference."

"What's a good reference mean?" Mr. Pepper asked.

"Like something that you did, something about you," the boy responded.

"Tell the other person something about you," Mr. Pepper expanded, "some good things that you do, and maybe recommend you....Does everybody have a couple or three references written down on their page? Somebody that likes you; somebody that thinks you will do a good job."

"Your mother?" a boy suggested.

"That's good, your mother would be a good one."

Mrs. Peel told the class that she could be a reference too. Mr. Pepper tried to say something more about references, but the kids kept talking until Mrs. Peel intervened:

> Mr. Pepper, they're still not listening [*The class gets completely quiet*]. I want to say something about these references. You all know when you address a letter, that you've got to have the person's name, you've got to have the street address, you've got to have the city and the state? First name won't cut it. You've got to have it all. And in going around I think some of you have just put down first names. You've got to have the name, as well as the complete address. Industrial-MagnaCorp doesn't know that that person lives in Roanoke. And they don't know if it's a Mr. or a Mrs. until you write it down there. So please remember how we address letters. That's the way you've got to have it on there, that complete address.

Now Mr. Pepper explained the necessity of locating themselves in an abstract space of trustworthiness so that distant corporations could weigh their worthiness:

The reason that we have references is because most of the time you guys are gonna have to get a loan to get your business started...and that bank is going to want to know if you guys are good people. And so what you want to do when you write down your references is list people who like you, who think that you're, you're a good risk. Who think that you're going to pay the money back to the bank, and so the better person that you write down there—if you write down somebody that doesn't like you, they're going to tell the bank, "No, I wouldn't lend him or her the money, because they're not a good risk. They're not going to pay you back." So you want to make sure you write down somebody who's going to give you a good recommendation. Right? Okay?

Now, the next thing we need to fill out are assets. What kinds of things, what kinds of things do you own? What kinds of things—what kinds of things does your business have that are of value? Okay? The bank, the bank is going to lend you money, but they're not going to lend you money if you don't, if you don't have anything...[To Mrs. Peel] They don't know collateral, do they?

But they did, Mrs. Peel replied. She asked Elwood "What do you always give me before I give you a pencil?"

"A dollar," Elwood replied.

"He gives me a dollar," Mrs. Peel reminded the class, "and I hold on to the dollar until he gives me my pencil back. Okay? And if doesn't give me my pencil back, then I just keep the dollar."

Mr. Pepper followed this lead:

Okay, so you guys all understand that, right? So, another name for that dollar is an asset. Because you're borrowing a pencil, and in return you're saying, "I have a dollar, and if I don't give you your pencil back you can keep my dollar." Okay? So, an asset could be—for somebody like me it could be a car. An automobile. It could be, maybe it could be a bicycle for you guys. A Nintendo set. Yeah. Sure. A television set. A house. Things that you guys have that are of value to you, that you're willing to risk your business on. And this thing is a risk.

The kids began talking and trying to work their way from an understanding of use value to one of exchange value (which Mr. Pepper had unintentionally confused in telling them that collateral had to be something of value to them, rather than something of value in an exchange situation). One student apparently suggested putting down a sister for collateral, and Mr. Pepper patiently explained that they couldn't use brothers and sisters. Someone else suggested roller skates. In Octavia's group, Rona asked, "What about a hair bow?"

"That's not worth much."

"They're really pretty though."

"Oh, I know, I'll put a beret—it's a big, big, beautiful beret."

"What about a bracelet?"

"Uh, I can't think of nothing."

"What about your book?"

"You crazy! I'm not betting my book. Don't you dare write that!"

"You can have mine."

"No, no."

"Anything but my book, you can bet my little sister for all I care!...I don't even want to waste my book on it."

"I don't even want to risk my keyboard."

"I don't even want to risk my book."

"I care for my books more than my sister."

"I don't. Well, I value my sister."

Mr. Pepper, seemingly worried that some kids were talking as if they would inevitably have to give up their collateral, told the class:

> You're not going to have to ever give any of this stuff up; as long as your business is doing good, you're makin' the payments, then you don't have to ever get rid of this. But, if you don't make your payments, then I can take that, okay?...I really don't need Nintendos. I can sell them, but I'll never make my money back on those things. I'll end up losing money as the bank. So you guys have to come up with a good plan to convince the bank that you're a good risk, okay. So the first part of that is market strategies. Okay, what you need to think about, with the business that you're in, and the products that you have, you need to think about what your product is, you need to think about what kind of people you're going to sell it to. Are you going to sell it to old people? You going to sell it to young guys like yourself? Are you going to sell it to just girls? Are you going to sell it to only boys? Is it going to be for grandparents? Is it, is it for sports? Sure, you want to think about the kind of people who have money to spend on it, right? Okay? So think about those kind of things, and write down a little bit about your market strategies. What kind of people you want to sell it to, what kind of product it is. Okay? You're not with me, are you?

"No," Mrs. Peel agreed, they weren't.

Mr. Pepper tried again:

> Okay. When, when you think about your product, okay, there's got to be somebody out there who wants to buy it from you, right? You guys understand that, right? If nobody wants to buy it, you're not going to make any money. Do you understand that? I mean, what are you guys selling?

"Uh," replied a boy.

"You sellin' those?" Pepper asked.

"I don't know," the boy replied.

"What's going to be your product?," Mr. Pepper tried again.

"I don't know."

"Are you going to sell to boys and girls?" Pepper asked. "Are you going to sell to people like myself? Am I going to buy your product?"

"No," said the boy.
"Okay," Pepper replied:

So part of your marketing strategy is to, to make your product something that boys and girls want to buy, right? Okay. Now, I think part of what we've already done, I think, you're supposed to have a product in mind already.

"Right," said Mrs. Peel, "they all have a product in mind."
Mr. Pepper then continued:

Okay, you have to think about what kind of people are going to buy your product; okay, think about that. And you have to think about—are you going to be selling it to the people who are real, real rich; are you going to be selling it to the people who are somewhere in between? [As he talks on, the kids begin to talk louder and louder]. Are you going to be selling it to somebody that's on the other end? You know. Are you, are you going to do a lot of advertising? Are you going to put ads in the paper; are you going to put ads on the radio? [Quiet again]. Are you going to do those kinds of things?

"That costs money," said one of the kids.
"It does cost money to do that," Pepper agreed, "but you're going to be borrowing money from me to do that, right?"
There was laughter from around the room and a couple of kids called out, "Let me see your money!"
"Not unless I like your plan," Pepper replied.
"It's counterfeit money!" someone cried out, and the overlapping talk in the class became untranscribable. The conversation shifted to a discussion of advertising channels, but after a minute, Mrs. Peel intervened:

Stop! Mr. Pepper, we need to stop for just a minute, because we're not taking this project seriously right now. And I'm afraid that Industrial-MagnaCorp will decline us and we will have wasted our time. When it talks about describing your product, you don't say "all kinds of designs"—that doesn't tell them one thing. They have to know exactly what you are doing. So, Sondra, will you read yours please, so we can see what you've got down there about describe your product?

Sondra, who could be depended on to take things seriously, replied with what Mrs. Peel thought was an appropriate product description, "We are going to have to make hard candy, lollipops. We will give different kinds of flavorings. They will be covered with colored plastic wrap." With this model in mind, the kids resumed their work on product descriptions. In Octavia's group, however, the discussion turned back to the issue of collateral.

"Just put my walkman," Octavia said. "I don't want to give up my roller skates."

"Thanks," said Daisy.

"Put my watch down," Octavia added.

"Oh come on, keep your pretty watch; your momma gave it to you," Daisy chided her.

"Yeah, you better keep that watch." Rona pitched in, "Your momma will get really really mad."

"I don't want to give away my roller skates," Octavia explained. "I don't really care about my walkman 'cause I don't use either one of them."

The girls had obviously not caught up with the modern treatment of objects as affectless and autonomous items of exchange. The sociologist Norbert Elias (1983) claimed:

> From the end of the Middle Ages on we can observe a strong shift towards the idea that objects can possess an identity, an effective reality, independently of the affect-charged ideas associated with them here and now by the groups concerned through their traditions and situation. This shift towards...a greater autonomy of "objects" in the experience of "subjects," is closely related to the thickening armour that is being interposed between affective impulses and the objects at which they are directed, in the form of ingrained self-control. (p. 252)

For the kids, though, some objects remained affect laden and tightly connected to personal, in this case familial, meanings. Even for Octavia, one of the most affluent girls in the school, who'd boasted of her expensive blouse, the criterion for deciding which objects to "give up" as collateral was based not on their abstract worth in exchange but on their value in the context of her immediate, everyday, embodied activity. This difficulty in thinking of objects in terms of abstract value became even clearer as the kids tried to determine costs and prices for their products.

Shortly after the previous exchange, Octavia spoke, for my benefit, directly into the microphone:

> Hello, hello, hello. We're selling T-shirts called Butterfly Wear. Our market strategies are, we're going to sell our project to young adults, and, uh, I think children—is that right? And, um, we want to, our t-shirts will have animals painted on them. And the hats will have glittered diamonds and names with lines of paint on it. And we will make and manufacture our own project.

Mr. Pepper, walking around the room, moved along to the next topic, cost analysis:

> Now, for those of you who picked more than one product, this is going to be a little hard, so you better think about one product—think about your

number one product. And we're going to figure out how much you're going to charge for that and how you're going to make money off of this thing, okay?...The first thing you need to think about is your materials cost—and what that means is, how much money do you have to spend to get the things you need to make your product?

Octavia, talking into the microphone, explained: "We're makin' like material costs for items like—we're puttin' down T-shirts, glitter, and paint. Oh, we forgot hats."

"What do you think the T-shirts are going to cost?" Rona asked.

"T-shirts," Octavia replied, "they cost at least a dollar. Okay, you're talking about the paint? The paint would cost at least four dollars—I'd say about five dollars a shirt. With the glitter."

"Five dollars a shirt?" Daisy seemed outraged.

"Well, let's say three dollars a shirt," Octavia tried.

"Nobody'll buy!" Daisy insisted.

Octavia countered: "Well, it's expensive with all that stuff."

"I know," Daisy replied, "but nobody will buy it!"

"$1.65 a shirt?" Octavia suggested.

Rona, still thinking about collateral, said "I want to put up my hat."

"Your hat?" Octavia asked. "Daisy, Rona wants to put up her hat!"

"What?" asked Daisy.

"Her hat," Octavia repeated.

"Don't put up her keyboard; that's going to be expensive."

"A hat!" Daisy said scornfully. "Who wants a hat, Octavia?"

"Please, Daisy," Octavia pleaded.

"Oh my God," said Daisy. "Who wants to buy a hat; who'd want it when you put your head in it?"

"I haven't used it!" Rona insisted. "I just bought it!"

"Yeah," said Octavia, "We can use the hat and makeup."

"I haven't got any right now," said Rona.

"You ain't got no makeup?" Daisy asked.

"Yes I have," Rona clarified. "I don't want to use it."

The class became quiet again as Mr. Pepper addressed the next item on the application form which dealt with interest. This step was critical in the activity because it substituted for the standard pedagogical disinterest of teachers a clearly expressed corporate self-interest:

The interest cost per item is dependent upon the interest rate that you borrow the money from me at. Okay? And I'm gonna charge you 4%. Four percent interest from all you guys for all the money that you borrow from me. Now, that's probably—leaves most everybody in the dust.

Uh, I can't lend you this money for nothing. I have to make something off of this money, don't I? Otherwise what good is—am I just that nice of a person that I'd want to let you guys use all my money? No, I don't think so. I want to make some money off of this too, right? The way I'm going to make my money is to charge interest from you guys. So...every dollar that you borrow you have to pay me back a dollar and four cents....That's how I make my money....If you need a hundred dollars, then I'll make $104. So, don't worry about the interest costs right now; we can all calculate that together. It's a set thing; you don't have any control over it. Okay?

Judging from their later conversation, few followed this explanation. Mr. Pepper's attempts to explain something to the kids that they didn't know about and didn't care about remind me in some ways of my own efforts, described in chapter 7, to explain my research to kids. Both of us were trying to talk about complex practices for transforming experience into stable, written representations. In my case, the kids initially confused my research with the library research they'd been taught to do. In Mr. Pepper's case, the confusion went deeper. After all, I was still talking about the world kids inhabited bodily. Mr. Pepper, on the other hand, was trying to talk about a world they could inhabit only on paper, a world where they were reduced to purely financial terms.

In the last 25 years, corporate conceptions of control and strategy have been increasingly driven by the finance-centered logic Mr. Pepper was invoking (Fligstein, 1990). The assets, debts, cash flow, and stock profile now "together sum up all that is important to know about any given firm" (Fligstein & Freeland, 1995, pp. 34). Finance functions as a "formal and quantitative" abstract space, which "erases distinctions, as much those which derive from nature and (historical) time as those which originate in the body (age, sex, ethnicity)" (Lefebvre, 1991, p. 21). Filling out the application form was a mapping of the kids' lives onto this abstract space. And as Allen and Pryke (1994) have argued, "The abstract space of finance in particular" is "bound up with practices of power:" "The mode of power is not simply economic as expressed in the speed and magnitude of monetary flows, but also representational—through the abolition of meanings, the manipulation of codings, the translation of tradition and the seduction of built form" (p. 459).

The stakes of Mr. Pepper's effort were thus big: If he could begin the task of drawing students into the space of finance, he could simultaneously draw them into a mode of space dominated by corporations like Industrial-MagnaCorp, a space in which all activity, all entities, were reduced to quantities of a standardized unit of value. There were echoes here of the debate over the grading scale. With the grades, however, traditional A–F marking systems reduced schoolwork to a school-specific currency, coupons (Nespor, 1990), so to speak, which could be redeemed within the school itself. Teachers disregarded the external meanings of the grades and resisted the parents' emphasis on these meanings. With the classroom business scheme, by contrast, the kids' work would be categorized entirely in terms usually excluded from classrooms: in the vocabulary of cash, irrelevant to the teachers but critical to the concerns of the corporation.

But much of the lesson seemed to go right by the kids. Octavia and her group were arguing: "It does cost something, because we've got to get someone to make our shirts," Daisy insisted.

"No, we don't," Octavia responded.

"We can make them ourselves" Rona pointed out.

"We're gonna buy them!" Octavia explained.

"Miss? Mrs. Peel?" Daisy got her attention.

"What are your ingredients here?" Mrs. Peel asked.

"We gotta put our T-shirts," Daisy said.

"Okay," Mrs. Peel explained, reading what the girls had written. "So it'll cost approximately $20?"

"Miss," said Octavia, "if we got one of those big things of Hanes [a t-shirt and underwear manufacturer], it wouldn't."

"I don't know about the labor," Daisy complained.

"Right here it asks how much *materials* are gonna cost," Mrs. Peel pointed out.

Again, Mr. Pepper addressed the whole class:

Okay, let me explain something real quick. What we're trying to do is decide how much you're gonna charge for each, each item that you sell. Now, of that item, there are different things that go into making up what you're going to charge for it. You've got to buy materials; okay, that's one thing. You've got to maybe pay somebody some labor money to make it, okay; you've got a tax cost that you've got to pay the state, and you don't want to pay that out of your pocket....Those are things that you have to spend to get your product. The fourth thing is the interest that you're going to pay me, and you want your customers to pay that for you too, right? So if you add all those up, that's how much money you have invested in your product. Okay? You need to at least make that much to break even. But you don't want to break even, do you? What do you want to do?

"Make more, make more," cried students across the room.

"Make more money, all right? So you have to add a profit on to your, on to your, uh, the total of those four things. To make money."

Mr. Pepper began moving about the room talking to small groups. With Octavia's team he explained: "Now, what I want you to be thinking about is, how much profit do you guys want to make? Okay, you guys think about this too. 10% or 20%?"

"I want to make about a dollar," Rona replied, but this was not an acceptable answer. The idea of profit required that the activity be fragmented into abstract, homogeneous parts rather than treated as a whole. The kids needed to articulate a profit goal per item sold, per exchange.

Mr. Pepper asked his question another way: "You want to make about $6 on every one of these, or do you want to make $7 dollars. $10? You guys think about that and talk about that, because you're all partners here, okay? Think about how much profit you want to make."

"Six dollars," said Octavia.

"Six dollars?" Rona asked.

"That's good out of $20," Rona pointed out.

"What about $5?" Daisy said.

"Yeah," Octavia seemed ready to compromise.

"So what are we supposed to do?" Daisy asked, trying to fit the activity into a typical academic task format. "We gotta add it up?"

"What do you want to do for the income, for the net income? How much do you want to take home after we finish this whole thing?" Octavia asked, filling out the application.

"$5," said Daisy.

"$5," said Rona.

"$5," concluded Octavia.

"I expect maybe a million. Ha, ha," Daisy joked.

"Maybe $150," said Octavia. "I don't know."

"Maybe $150," Rona said.

"A million!" Daisy insisted.

"Do we earn any money?" Rona asked.

"Yeah," Octavia tried to explain, "we get to take some home. How much would you like to take home?"

"$150," Rona repeated.

Some boys nearby who were trying to fill out the same part of the form seemed to be listening. "How much money would you like to take home after you finish?" one asked.

"At least $10. No, at least $15," another answered.

"They said $150," another boy pointed out, speaking of the girls.

"They not gonna sell enough to get $150," said the first boy.

Mrs. Peel raised her hand to quiet the class:

You all need to have a seat. I expect you to be in your seat with your hand ready [*Class immediately quiets down*]. Okay, we're going to skip down to, what will be your estimated profit. And raise your hand if you know what the word *profit* means. Sondra?

Sondra replied, "Money that you're going to get after you give all of the money back to the bank."

"Right," Mrs. Peel said. "How much do you expect to take home with you? Your take home?"

"Out of the whole thing?" someone asked.

"After everything is paid out, what will you expect to be yours?" Mrs. Peel clarified and then let the kids begin to work it out among themselves.

"Well," said Daisy, "I expect to take, um, I expect to take a few things home that I bought."

"Not *things,*" Octavia said. "Money!"

"Oh, uh," Daisy began, "I expect to take—"

"I said $150," Octavia informed her.

"That's too much!" Daisy responded, "$50."

"Yeah," Rona went along, "that's what I was going to say. Maybe $50. To take home with me. Spend on whatever I want!"

Octavia's group wasn't alone in its uncertainty. At this point, Octavia took the recorder to another table to capture this set of exchanges: "What do you expect to take home with you for profits?" she asked a boy.

"Money," the boy responded, "I want to take at least 50, 60 bucks home with me."

"They won't give you no $50 for sellin' something when they gave you the money in the beginning!" a girl scolded him.

She tried to explain: "They gonna let us have money to buy supplies; we gotta pay them back. After we borrow money, you think they're going to give us money? Excuse me!"

"If we pay them back?" another girl suggested.

"Pay them back?" said the scolding girl. "We gave them the rest of the money; we gonna borrow money back from them to keep?"

"We're gonna *pay* them back!" said the second girl more forcefully now.

A third girl intervened: "You'all tryin' to share a brain—get one that works. 'Cause it's not workin' right now."

Back with her own group, Octavia responded to a boy's question about the cost per item for the T-shirts: "We're gonna make it like about—$3 to $4 for our T-shirts, right?"

"Yeah," the boy persisted, "but how much would it cost you to make one?"

"$20," Octavia responded.

"For one?" the boy asked. "Okay."

"Cause see," Octavia explained, "Like, it's $6 for this, $6 for that, and it's like a dollar or something for that; for everything else you're gonna get to sell it. You gotta buy it and stuff."

"So, yeah," the boy agreed, "you have to sell it for over $20 per T-shirt. In order to get a good profit."

"But then we won't sell" at that price, Octavia seemed to realize.

"I know," the boy agreed.

These exchanges show the kids' uncertainty and unfamiliarity with the notion of profit (not to mention the other categories on the application form). Mr. Pepper was trying to get them to see the outcomes of their activity in terms of standardized quantities of an abstract medium—cash. But Daisy, among others, seemed to miss the point altogether (she thought she'd be coming away with some of the products her group was going to make), and Octavia, although she was clearly comfortable with the idea of cash, seemed to have no real understanding of how it was generated through production and exchange. Her estimates of what she might make (like the kids' estimates of costs) were pulled out of the air.

These confusions had nothing to do with developmental levels. Given their lack of information, there's no way the kids could have made sensible projections of costs or prices. Mr. Pepper had introduced them to a *simulation* of finance in which the categories on the application form had no connections to "real" entities or referents. Mr. Pepper simply led them through the form like a priest leading initiates through some mystical ritual they couldn't be expected to comprehend.[3]

I'm not sure what happened in the immediate aftermath of this meeting, but the business game never took hold in the class (there were, after all, only about 6 weeks of school left). Less than a month later I ran into Mr. Pither at a volunteer recognition day at Thurber and asked him how the effort was going. The third graders, he told me, were really gung ho, but those fifth graders, they just didn't have any enthusiasm at all.

CROSSED CIRCUITS

Fifth graders, of course, have lots of enthusiasm. What they appeared not to have was a well-developed appreciation for the logic of finance. The goal of the activity seemed to be to introduce kids into the network of modern exchange relations, to give them a taste of real-world capitalism from the standpoint of the firm—although ironically they were shepherded toward forming manufacturing enterprises (Mrs. O'Brian's nostalgic idea of kid-run lemonade stands being the archetype), the very kinds of firms dying out in the region. More appropriate information age enterprises might have been ones where the kids supplied others with services or knowledge: a for-profit peer tutoring system, for example, or services selling answers to test questions, forging papers, or supplying information about how to deal with particular teachers.

The kids were supposed to learn how to make things that others would buy. What gave them trouble was that in the process they were supposed to learn to think of their own possessions—their collateral—as

---

[3]Had there been time, it probably would have been possible to move the kids into the kind of corporate space Mr. Pepper was mapping out for them. In 1995, a different Roanoke city elementary school was transformed into a "free-enterprise microvillage" magnet school run along lines strikingly similar to those Mr. Watts and Industrial-MagnaCorp were trying to implement at Thurber in 1993 (without magnet school funding). According to a newspaper account, kids at the school, "which is designed to help children understand the relationship of school to the business world and real life," were doing well (Turner, 1995, p. C1).

exchangable goods and their personal ties—their references—as exchangable for loans. They were supposed to reconceptualize social relationships and other things that had concrete meanings within the family sphere as abstract repositories of value. Outside school, however, the kids' interactions with retail markets were still largely mediated by their parents and hence were intractably social and personal.

Lila, a fourth grader working on a newsletter I was supervising, explored this issue during my second year of fieldwork. She'd rejected all my research suggestions, telling me, "You always think of grownup stuff, not kid stuff." Then she came up with her own topic: "How to get your parents to give you what you want." Here are some of the reponses she recorded:

> *Effie*: Um, the way I get my mother, well, really my grandfather and my grandmother, to give me whatever I want, is to beg all the time, get on their nerves about it. Most of all, be horrible until they give it to me.

> *Sheila*: When I want something, I beg my mom, "Please, please can I have this?" And then if she don't want to give it to us, then go back to the car....I get mad at her, and if then she'll give me the things I want, then I'm happy.

> *Carol*: I keep asking them until they say yes....I persuade them; I won't stop till I get an answer Yes. I don't care if they yell or scream; I won't budge.

> *Beavis*: Well, I have to beg in order to do that....Sometimes it's a little hard and they won't let you have it. That's tough. Sometimes you just can't get everything you want.

> *Tina*: I don't get everything I want. When I want to get something, I just pound my feet and yell and stuff.

> *Cicily*: Getting my mother to give me something I want, all I have to do is be good and obey her, and do good in school, and do everything she asks me to do [*Laughing*], and—sometimes cry to get it. Sometimes, pamper her to get it, and sometimes have a sad face.

> *Brenda*: I beg, pretty often. And if I don't get what I want, I say I hate them, but that isn't true.

> *Cindy*: I beg them, or I usually go and do chores, and they'll give me money, or I'll clean the house, and they'll give me like $2 for washing the dishes. Or if I want something, I save up my money, and my parents, I just beg them until they give it to me, or I work for it.

> *Lauren*: Well, I don't actually get everything. Well, to get what I want, like I'm in a store? I say "Mom, can I *please* have this?"
>
> She says "No."

> And I'll say, "If you pay for it, I'll pay you back." When we get home, I'll pay her back, out of my allowance. It's actually like me paying it. And that kind of works sometimes. And sometimes I'll just beg her.

Mel: I ask for my birthday or for Christmas.

Lila: Well, the first thing I do is beg, and beg, and beg, and beg. And if they don't still give it to me, I'll tell them that I'll do something that is embarassing when we're in the store, because usually I beg when we're in the store. And when we're at home and I'm begging for money, and my mother's on the phone, I will talk really loud, and make my mother embarrassed, and I'll put on my headphones and scream so loud that my mother's going to get mad at me, and yell at me. And when she yells at me, she owes me 25 cents.

These kids, even Cindy and Lauren who worked for allowances, relied on affect and emotion to manipulate their parents into getting them things (as Duxbury, 1987, has shown, even preschool children develop elaborate methods of manipulating parents, especially in public settings). Some of the objects of their desire, as we'll see in chapter 5, might have been commodity elements of transnational cultural flows, but the acts of acquiring them were deeply personal and localized in special forms of direct bodily labor: cries, facial expressions, pouts, the speech register of begging. Similarly, when I talked to kids about their grades, they thought of them mainly in terms of their immediate meanings: a pizza dinner or a sum of money in return for a good report card. The ideas that grades shaped long-term educational and economic opportunities, as their parents might say, or somehow certified their worth, as the Industrial-MagnaCorp people might say, were not shared by the kids.

I am not suggesting that the kids were in some sense insulated from corporate space: Advertisers target children, both for their own disposable income and for the income they can cajole their parents, as intermediaries, to spend for them on mass-marketed cultural products (Jacobson & Mazur, 1995). Indeed, one reason that the Industrial-MagnaCorp business classroom wasn't more successful in pulling students into the space of finance might have been that the kids were already there but positioned as *consumers* of cultural products rather than as entrepreneurs producing for exchange.

What would be the import of a successful business-in-the-school program? In Stephens's (1995) words:

> What are the implications for society as a whole, if there are no longer social spaces conceived as at least partially autonomous from the market and market-driven politics? Where are we to find the sites of difference, the terrain of social witness, critical leverage, and utopian vision, insofar

as the domain of childhood—or of everyday life or of a semiautonomous realm of culture—is increasingly shot through with the values of the marketplace and the discursive politics of postmodern global culture? And what happens to the bodies and minds of children in the process? (pp. 10–11)

In the last three chapters I begin an answer to some of these questions by looking at how kids moved from localized, embodied arenas of practice (the family, their immediate friends, the neighborhood) to networks of practice more extensive in space and time, articulated through representations (print, video, money). This shift from the locally defined, everyday spaces where kids are embedded in highly personalized relationships to the abstract spaces that span regional and national boundaries is a large part of what happens to children as they move through elementary school (although not necessarily a result of what happens in classrooms). In chapter 1, I discussed how city history, school system policies, and school politics shaped the curriculum and politics of representation at Thurber. In the beginning of this chapter, I showed how the image of the city was shaped in the intersections of multiple discourses and how those discourses partly manifested themselves in curriculum, and then crashed on the shoals of the fifth grade. What I haven't yet done is look at these kinds of intersections from the standpoint of the kids: how they experienced their neighborhoods and city spaces, how they made sense of embodied activity within the school, how they oriented themselves in the global economies of signs that dominate the "information age."

3 Neighborhood Intersections

> Places and neighborhoods, understood as social entities, are *produced institutionally* [italics original], within ecological and technical constraints, by social and political struggles over competing uses of space, resources, and people.
>
> —*Wacquant, 1995, p. 427*

To this point I've talked about community–school relations in terms of educators' interactions with parents and business sector influences on curriculum. This perspective is obviously too limited. The neighborhoods kids and parents reside in are positioned in larger cityscapes. Kids' relations with these neighborhoods and their schools are not static but are patterned in space and time. Of two kids sitting next to each other in a classroom, one can live in a house her family's owned and lived in since she was a child, and the other might have just moved into an apartment complex. The neighborhoods themselves can have different relations to the school the kids attend. One neighborhood might surround the school, and others might be miles away and have no historical ties to the school. In this chapter, I explore these kinds of positionings of kids in neighborhood spaces and begin by examining the histories of those neighborhoods.

THURBER AND ITS COMMUNITIES

When Thurber's attendance zone was restructured in the late 1980s, it expanded beyond the European American area around and contiguous with the school, and two African American neighborhoods, both far from the school, were added. One, Eaton, was an area of about 12 square blocks consisting mainly of single-family residences (with a few large houses transformed into apartments); the other, Farewell Estates, was made up of large apartment complexes on the edge of the city and a few streets of a small subdivision adjacent to the complexes.

Fragmentation of the African American Community

The connections between the Eaton and Farewell Estates neighborhoods are complexly tied to the last 40 years of Roanoke history. Although they are different neighborhoods, many of their residents share a past in the political–economic history of the city.[1] Once spatially compact and self-sufficient, the African American community in Roanoke had been fragmented and geographically dispersed. As in many urban African American communities across the country, the main source of fragmentation was urban renewal.

A large part of the geographic center of Roanoke developed historically as an African American community. It was one contiguous area, part of it in the northeast quadrant and part in the northwest, the latter section known as Gainsboro. A local historian noted that in the census of 1880, taken just before the coming of the railroad, African Americans accounted for over 43% of the population in Big Lick, the first incorporated town in the area that was to become Roanoke, and in "Gainsborough," "blacks outnumbered whites by 272 to 67" (White, 1982, p. 59).

Until the post-World War II period, African Americans, confined by real estate practices and restrictive deeds that prohibited them from buying houses in other parts of the city, developed a vital and largely self-sufficient economic and cultural community. A brief history written in the early 1980s described a setting in which, up to the early 1950s, there was a rich civic life and community identity punctuated by "parades...through the streets of Old Northwest, sponsored by local civic groups such as the Odd Fellows" (Booker, 1981, p. 3). As an oral history interviewee recalled:

> We had a regular Black community...and we had about all of the organizations you really needed, I mean, places of business you really needed. The library, Bean Electric, barber shops, the Claytor's Clinic building, the YMCA, the YWCA, Gainsboro public library, lawyers' offices on the corner of Wells Avenue and then on Fourth Avenue....And the dentist...and two undertakers....It was just wonderful at one time, and then, all at once, the Whites seemed to want that section, and that's when they began to move us out. (Eliza Louise Brown interview, June 12, 1992)

---

[1]The following passage draws heavily on two sources: a newspaper report by Mary Bishop (1995) tracing the course of urban renewal in Roanoke and its devastating effects on the city's African American community; and a collection of oral histories, *A Hidden History: The Black Experience in the Roanoke Valley,* conducted in the early 1990s and now housed in the Harrison Museum of African American History in Roanoke and in the Newman Library special collections at Virginia Tech.

Henry Street, in the Gainsboro area, had been the core civic, business, and entertainment district that drew African Americans from the surrounding counties and served as a node where the community came into contact with the national culture and saw performers such as Count Basie, Lionel Hampton, Duke Ellington, Chick Webb, and Ella Fitzgerald.

The Burrell Memorial Hospital, founded and staffed by members of the African American community, had provided medical service; a cluster of segregated public schools had educated the kids. Some houses, especially in the northeast section, had lacked indoor plumbing, but many of the residents had owned their homes, and almost everyone, at least in retrospect, described people as close and supportive, a real community.

The first stage of urban renewal aimed to "clean up" this northeast section of the African American cityspace. Residents were told that their houses would be razed and graded and that they would then be able to move back into new homes in the area. According to one official history of the city, however:

> Actual removal of the dilapidated houses was begun in 1956 when crews tore down about ninety houses along Orange Avenue. By the time the work was completed, 536 pieces of property, 452 of them dwellings, had been razed. The average price paid homeowners was approximately $4,300, not enough to purchase a house in another section. Many of the residents went to the low-rent public housing units at Lansdowne and Lincoln Terrace. The original idea was to remove the highest of the hills, rezone lots into a proper size and then sell them back to private enterprise for the erection of apartments and to individuals for home sites. Almost thirty years later, the clearing has been done, but few lots are occupied. The major tenant is the city itself with its Civic Center on twenty-two acres of the area. (White, 1982, pp. 115–117)

A European American city council member from that period explained to Bishop (1995) that "'it had to be done...for the good of the city, for the good of the future. Their kids were growing up in slum conditions....That was prime growth land....Some people had to suffer'" (p. 2).

The city took a clear-cut approach and destroyed new homes and churches along with older and less sound structures. According to all accounts, the displaced community members:

> were told very specifically that they were gonna come in, relocate them. They could move or rent for maybe one or two years until they graded out, divided, resubdivided the lot. Then they could move back and build homes. And this is when the antagonism began because of look at what you have on the blocks today: Holiday Inn, Magic City Ford, etc. etc. etc....Where the Civic Center is standing....Mount Zion had just built a brand new church. (George Heller interview, May 14, 1992)

The city delayed giving northeast residents any compensation, and what former residents did receive, even those who'd owned homes outright, wasn't enough to purchase new homes:

> Northeast was a strong focal point for Blacks in that area, and naturally, when they developed they didn't get the fair amount for their houses because the—you, you take, for instance, the houses in upper Northwest which were originally owned by Whites and they cost more [upper Northwest was the destination for most families pushed out of Northeast]. A lot of people lost out on it, you know....They owned their houses around Gainsboro and then also in Northeast but when they went to get another house, they couldn't pay cash for it. (Richard Chubb interview, June 17, 1992)

Residents were never given reasons for the clearance, especially for the destruction of structures in good condition. The city reneged on its promises to make the land from the northeast quandrant available for housing again because it wanted the land for a route to connect Interstate 81, running through the valley just north of the city, to the downtown. Federal policies, such as the 1956 Federal Highway Act, encouraged such practices by reimbursing cities 90% of what they spent on constructing interstates (M. Katz, 1993, p. 462). Throughout the country, cities commonly routed expressways through African American neighborhoods in this way:

> Freeways in every major city cut through the middle of Black settlements in order to connect the central business district to the outlying white suburbs or were deliberately planted as buffers to protect white neighborhoods from the "contamination" of the expanding ghetto. (Wacquant, 1995, p. 428)

The expressway created an barrier separating the African American community from European American communities to the east (the railroad provided the boundary to the south). The waves of urban renewal pushed African Americans west to the city limits and often out of single-family homes altogether. Even when homeowners forced out of the Northeast got money for relocation, it was insufficient to buy housing in the Northwest portion of the community. Bishop (1995) quoted Lawrence Paxton, a dentist who during the mid-1960s was the only Black school board member:

> Homeowners living debt-free in Northeast had little choice but to assume big debts to buy Northwest houses that cost twice what they got for their old ones. Either that, he said, or they "ended up drinking up the money" and living in Lincoln Terrace [a housing project]. (p. 4)

Bishop (1995) claimed: "The children and grandchildren of people driven out of Northeast are still in public housing" (p. 3). At first, Lincoln Terrace, the largest of the projects, seemed not to have been viewed negatively in the community:

> Lincoln Terrace was the first....At the time it was a blessing....By it being a government project, the rent was much better; the houses were neat; the plumbing, they had internal plumbing. See, believe it or not, as late as 1950 many of the houses in what we call northeast still had outdoor plumbing facilities. (George Heller interview)

Federal policy, however, soon began to undermine the viability of public housing. President Nixon placed a moratorium on public housing construction in the early 1970s, and Ronald Reagan radically cut federal aid to cities during his first term. In M. Katz's (1993) words: "The federal government virtually stopped building housing, shrank its aid to cities, reduced benefits to individuals, and raised the taxes of the poor at the same time it lowered them for the rich" (p. 463).

As funds dried up and it became clear that public housing would be less a temporary haven for families between homes, and more a permanent residence for the low-income families, the condition and reputation of the projects declined. The projects gathered together the poorest members of the old African American community (those who couldn't afford to buy or rent homes), spatially detached them from neighborhoods with businesses and churches, and confined them in isolated, inward-focused physical structures. Such shifts disrupted the ties of the project residents to the social networks that had originally sustained the community. At a reunion of former residents in 1993, many recalled the old northeast as a caring community:

> "Growing up in Old Northeast was a learning experience" [one former resident recalled] "I remember playing around the old gas house on Kimball. Everyone was neighborly and friendly and everyone did something."..."We were one big family," said Della Millener, coordinator of the reunion. "Now we don't see them unless it's because of death, and that hurts." (Brown, 1993, p. D4)

When urban renewal spread to the Gainsboro area, the last remaining section of what had been the original African American neighborhood, people were further scattered. Again, relatively affluent families were forced out of homes and went into debt to buy houses in neighborhoods abandoned by European Americans to the west and north (Bishop, 1995, p. 4). Paralleling what had happened when the northeast was razed, many of those who'd been renting were pushed into public housing. Bishop (1995) cited Walter Claytor, who'd been a resident and professional in the Gainsboro area, in a community analysis of the urban renewal effort:

First, Blacks were forced from their homes and into adjacent white neighborhoods. Whites then built houses in subdivisions farther from downtown. That fed the purses of developers, bankers, real estate agents, carpenters, roofers, surveyors, the lawyers who oversaw the property changes, and everyone else in the real estate and construction industries. (p. 9)

Zoning laws (especially a 1966 ordinance) encouraged more urban renewal and suburban development by requiring large minimum lot sizes, which made it impossible to develop small vacant lots for single-family residences and promoted clearance of existing structures to create lots of minimum size: "The main purpose of the 1966 zoning ordinance was to allow and foster growth in Roanoke's outer fringe belt or suburbs....[It] resulted in the destruction of old, inner-city neighborhoods" (Gallimore, 1992, p. 45).

This strategy obviously became untenable when the city ran into the annexation ban a decade later, and the ordinance was revised. But by then, most of the damage had been done. The multiple waves of urban renewal had resulted in the destruction of 1,600 homes in the Black community, 200 businesses, 24 churches, and several schools (Bishop, 1995, p. 1). In the mid-1990s, fewer than 200 homes were left (p. 12), and there were no African American business or cultural districts. The human costs matched the economic and housing disasters. As one of the oral history interviewees recalled:

> My sons have said that they lost a lot of their friends. It's amazing because during the time of segregation that we were all closer together, the Black families knew each other; and now when they scatter, you have more trouble finding where they live and so forth. (Howard B. Hopkins interview, June 1, 1992)

No one, I think, was nostalgic about de jure segregation, but most of the economic and cultural infrastructure of the African American community had been sacrificed with little return to the community. De facto segregation continued. Although the African American community had become more geographically dispersed, it was still largely confined to the Northwest quadrant. Now, however, the Northwest had no African American–owned commercial centers, no hospital, and no theaters.

Federally mandated busing had been imposed in the early 1970s to remedy the continuing racial segregation of schools in Roanoke, but one of the oral history interviewees who'd been a student during the move from segregated to integrated schools, Sandra Smith Jordan, recalled:

> During segregation time...I felt like Blacks had more money and better opportunity then....During forced integration time, it was several groups or several generations of kids that was just thrown away because I, myself, was put in a school that teachers point-blank told me, "Hey, we didn't ask

you niggers to come here; and I got mine, you get yours the best way you
can." My ninth-grade education was nada—nothing....That was a wasted
year for me. That was a year of pain, a year of anguish....I had never
known that kind of pain and hurt ever before in my life....I was always a
good student at Harrison and Booker T. [African American schools during
segregation]. I had teachers that made me feel like, "You are going to learn.
You can learn. And I'm here to teach you." And I never in my life dealt with
a situation where people are gettin' paid to teach me, but yet and still they
are tellin' me because I'm Black, because of the color of my skin, they were
not gonna teach me, and anything I did learn I'd have to do it on my own.
(May 30, 1992)

Many European American kids, by contrast, avoided busing when
their parents sent them to private schools. One European American
parent I interviewed recalled:

The year [my daughter] was going into sixth grade, schools had been
integrated but it was not—they didn't have enough Blacks. We were in a
forced pattern of integrating, and she was gonna be bused to Hurt Park
School [a school in a predominantly African American neighborhood].
They had a five-block area from right in here that they were going to bus
to Hurt Park. And my husband said, "She ain't goin' to Hurt Park. If she's
goin' to be bused, I'll bus her myself." So she went to [a private school].

The school system's response to this White flight under Superintendent Tota was an aggressive campaign to transform schools in
African American neighborhoods into magnet schools.[2] European
Americans were bused into these schools, and African American kids
from surrounding neighborhoods, who might have attended the magnet schools, were sent elsewhere (thus the situation described in
chapter 2—children at bus stops on four corners of an intersection
going to four different schools). The Eaton neighborhood and the
Farewell Estates area were both much closer to predominantly African American schools than to Thurber, but the schools had been
labeled magnets. As a result, the social lives and activities of the
bused kids were rigidly segregated from their school activities. For
example, Cicily, one of the fourth graders I interviewed, who was
bused several miles to Thurber although she lived only a few blocks
from one of the magnet schools, Wharton, told me:

---

[2]Varady and Raffel (1995) reviewed research about magnet schools as a means to
attract European American middle-class residents back to the cities and presented a case
study of the effects of such schools in Cincinnati, Ohio. They argued that magnet schools
can improve a city's attractiveness to some extent (although not sufficiently to solve the
problem of European American middle-class out-migration) but conceded that such schools
also raised serious equity issues, especially about which children are selected to attend
the magnets. I have discovered no research on the impact of the magnet school program
in Roanoke, although the school district continues to pursue such programs actively.

I can't go to Wharton because of the side of the street I live on....[My] cousin, he goes there....And other kids I know, they go there too. I went there before in kindergarten, but they had to send me back to Gold Hill. 'Cause see, in kindergarten, I learned about it too.

Although she didn't attend the school, her friendships and associations centered on the surrounding neighborhood. She was already cheerleading for a football team that held its practices at Wharton:

One day I rode by there and I saw people playing baseball and stuff. Then I saw *football* and stuff. One year, I really did want to cheerlead, but I was too late to sign up. Then the next year I was into cheerleading, and I got on the team....And at, uh, Tupler [the recreation center serving the Thurber area], I think they're [*Makes a face*] because we *beat* them all the time in football. And we're better than their cheerleaders anyway.

Cicily's identification with her local neighborhood was a small victory against the city planners' and school administrators' fragmentation and abstraction of space. Cicily, for them, was part of a quantity—the school-age African American population—to be divided and distributed according to a logic that paid no attention to the meanings of neighborhood and school created by kids and parents. As Lefebvre (1991) suggested, the abstract space of planners is space considered as a Euclidean geometric environment of equal, interchangable elements, emptied of any meanings except those supplied by administrative agendas. By contrast, the dense community textures of the old African American community were *lived spaces* that took their meanings from the ways people did things in them, from the smells and noises and routines of everyday life. For planners and administrators, these neighborhoods occupied a segmentable commodity—abstract space—that could be manipulated and exchanged. On paper, the exchange built into urban renewal was simply money for housing. But the residents' sense of place was filtered out in such an equation, along with the spatially grounded webs of social relationships and community support that allowed them to locate themselves in the social world (cf. Lefebvre, 1991, p. 314).

By the same token, the relations of the African American community to the public schools, once strong and grounded in a sense of ownership, had also been remapped onto an abstract space. What education meant now was not a substantive, long-term social relation; it meant serving a certain number of years in an institutional space designed for, mainly populated by, and controlled and staffed by others.

Now, perhaps, the reasons for the lack of African American parental involvement at Thurber become clear. Not only was the school geographically distant from their neighborhoods (a real constraint for many low-income parents working multiple jobs or dependent on public transportation) and socially coded as belonging to the surrounding European

American community, the school was also transformed into an abstract commodity with no clear meaning in the everday lives of the parents in the new, fragmented neighborhoods.

As for these new neighborhoods themselves, community-controlled legitimate commerce, adult cultural institutions, and neighborhood schools had disappeared. The housing projects and large apartment complexes were spatially isolated and inward facing, bordered by parks, expressways, golf courses, and busy streets that functioned as moats. In residential areas, where African Americans were pushed west into what had been European American working-class communities, people still sat on porches and gave some life to the street, but absentee landowners were slow to maintain their properties or built cheap, crude "in-fill" houses on vacant lots. Homeowners and neighborhood organizations fought a constant battle to preserve and improve the areas. In the 1990s, however, the city and its boosters were again razing houses in the Gainsboro area, grinding down the bones of the neighborhood to create a new conference center and improve traffic flow to a strip of downtown being "revitalized" as a tourist attraction of boutiques and restaurants.

Domesticating the Landscape in Tupler

The city leaders' devastation of the African American neighborhoods near downtown did not prevent the decline of the downtown itself. The clearance of the northeast opened routes linking the city to the northern county, and the interstate spur and its extension southward created new commercial concentrations south of downtown and outside the city itself. For the county, this brought a burst of growth. For the Tupler area, where Thurber School was located, it brought a not altogether welcome transformation.

Tupler was largely farmland until the 1920s.[3] In the boom following the First World war, the farms were parceled into housing tracts. Advertisements from this period described the attractions of the area:

> 2 Miles from City Limits; National Highway Leading to Valley of Virginia; High-Class Neighborhood; Ideal Location; No Negroes or Foreigners. . . .

> With electric lights, gravel streets and building restrictions with fine school facilities and wholesome, invigorating country-like atmosphere, possesses both a charm and a healthfulness that must appeal to every person seeking to escape the dirt of the congested sections.

---

[3]Information in this and the next paragraph is from a privately published neighborhood history. In an attempt to preserve the anonymity of the area, I did not include a citation of this work. I also omitted several details about the neighborhood to preserve the anonymity of the school.

The working-class residents, many employed in the factories just to the east, moved into the area where building restrictions included minimum costs for homes along the various streets, a 40-foot setback from the street for all houses with front porches, and a prohibition on purchases by "Negroes, Greeks, or Syrians."

Thurber, as I explained in chapter 1, was the neighborhood school from the time of its creation until the 1980s. Kids in the area walked to school, and when they grew up their children attended the school. The principal and many of the teachers lived in the neighborhood, were known to residents, and had meaningful social roles in the community. The school, however, was just one of several community organizations that catered to kids. The group of retired Thurber community members I interviewed recalled that one of the churches: "opened up the fellowship hall in the afternoon I think one day a week for us to come over there and play records and dance. They'd have refreshments. Seems like they had a shuffleboard in the floor there." At another time, the church operated a coffee house that would attract "a hundred kids or so. That was wild. That was in the evening."

By the 1980s, however, Jackson Road, the main thoroughfare through the community, had become a commercial strip lined with restaurants and small retail stores. Businesspeople in the area had begun to worry about the neighborhood's reputation; they started a campaign to "revitalize" the area. In part these moves reflected the desires of long-time residents upset by the commercialization that had opened the area to outsiders. Instead of a space controlled by residents, Tupler had become a public space dominated by transitory visitors. In part too, the revitalization campaign stemmed from the recognition by local business leaders that new malls were draining the desirable businesses away from the area even as the downtown was trying to salvage itself with new upscale facilities. Tupler leaders felt squeezed and were desperate to improve the area's image. Revitalization meant putting up welcoming signs, pushing out undesirable businesses, and reducing the traffic and commerce through the area. By the 1990s, neighborhood space had been brought under some semblance of control, and the neighborhood had been redomesticated.

KIDS' MOVEMENTS THROUGH
NEIGHBORHOOD SPACE

Here we have only a sampling of drawings that were made for us, to which must be added all the discussions with the children. The material has all kinds of policy implications; I can start by isolating three. One is the importance for children of living in a community that has a strong identity—social identity surely, but also physical identity. Another can be described as the importance of engagement: each child needs a role of his own in his community. A third is the importance of the city as an educational facility, a place to explore and learn about the world. (Lynch, 1979, p. 115)

The descriptions of neighborhoods in the first part of this chapter identified the spatial regimes, externally imposed in one instance, partially self-designed in the other, that defined the landscapes of kids' out-of-school activities. But as de Certeau (1984) and others pointed out, space can't be treated as a static totality. It is constantly lived, experienced, reordered by those who move through it. Kids differently positioned in their communities and in the larger economic system can interact with neighborhood spaces in different ways. To understand these ways of acting and the positionings that make them possible, we must look at kids both historically and spatially. I can only hint at this, drawing on interviews with fourth graders in which I asked them to draw and to talk about maps of their neighborhoods. My inspiration was Lynch (1977), but what the kids talked about was less the spatial environment (Lynch's focus) and more their spatial histories. These histories seemed to follow three broad patterns, which I call embeddedness, displacement, and mobility.

Many of the kids at Thurber had lived in the same houses for most of their lives, embedded in well-defined home- or neighborhood-based routines of movement and interaction. They lived in houses rather than apartments and were connected to spaces across the city through family relationships and parents' workplace connections. Their routines of activity kept them outside the house a good deal, moving through their neighborhoods with networks of friends.

By contrast, a second group of students had moved into Thurber's catchment zone in the last year or two from other cities where they'd spent most of their lives and with which they still retained a strong sense of identification. They lived for the most part in apartments, had no family connections in the region, and spent most of their time indoors or in the immediate vicinity of their apartment complexes.

Finally, there were students who'd moved many times in their lives and had changed schools frequently. Like the displaced kids they lived in apartments; unlike them, they lacked feelings of identity with or membership in the communities they'd once lived in.

The boundaries of these categories are obviously fluid: Displaced or mobile kids can become embedded over time; embedded kids can become displaced or mobile. My point is that kids' relations with a school and with the social and material spaces they move through, are products of their ongoing histories and geographies. These histories and geographies are in turn shaped by sociospatial processes that articulate certain intersections of community politics, economic development, and gender, ethnic, and class relationships. Focusing only on schools or on kids' lives seen from the perspective of schooling obscures many aspects of these processes. Here, instead, I try to situate school in the kids' lives. I look at how some of the fourth graders I worked with negotiated space and activity outside of school and at how some responded to my requests, borrowed from a UNESCO study of adolescents growing up in cities (Lynch, 1977), that they draw their neighborhoods.

Embeddedness in Familiar Spaces

Cicily.   Cicily, an African American girl a few months away from her 10th birthday, had lived at her grandmother's house near the Farewell Estates since she was 3 or 4 years old. She could remember, though, when she'd lived in one of the city's public housing projects, and she told a story that illustrated some of the contradictory transformations of community engendered by life in the projects:

> I was three or four. But one time, this lady, she *hated* my mother. I mean she hated her. 'Cause she didn't like how she would dress—like she was her mother or something. And one time she called the police and stuff? My mother had went to the store, a store right near the projects, and she went to the store and went and brought some stuff. And I was in there, and I was playing with my friends and stuff, outside. She said, "Where's your mother at?" And I said, "She's gone to the store." 'Cause I was young enough to remember that. But when I was 3 I couldn't remember anything, but when I was 4 I could? And I told her she was gone to the store. And then I saw her walking in the house, and she came back out, and she was smiling like she was happy or something. Then the cops pulled up, and these foster home people pulled up. And I had to go to a foster home for about a month or so. And they found out the old lady hated my mother, and she didn't like her, and they moved me back with my grandmother. And then my mother moved in. I don't see how they let her get away with that.

The lady's concern for Cicily suggests a kind of twisted community spirit. A young child playing outdoors for an extended period (and as there were no stores near the project and the city has only a minimal public transportation system, Cicily's mother might have been gone for a fairly long time) was assumed to be neglected. The first line of recourse was not to address the problem directly or through the community but to bring in outside agents of surveillance, who responded by removing Cicily from the community altogether.

Cicily's situation changed radically when she moved. Her grandparents had had steady working-class jobs during the city's industrial heyday and in the mid-1970s had been able to move out of the Eaton neighborhood and into a house near the Farewell Estates area. Cicily flourished there. When I asked her to draw the neighborhood, she began with a picture of her house, then detailed its windows and flower beds, and moved out from her yard to the area around her home (Fig. 3.1).

I'll show you the whole thing. It's small [*She draws*]. Here's my house: It's a *very* big house. Looks like it's small, but it's big....We have a huge backyard and a huge front yard. We have another back driveway with rocks. We're going to get it cemented. That's the front driveway. There's a golf course over here....This, right here, is Burton [Road]. Burton right there. And I think this one over here is Moore [Road]....And then here's our neighbor's house over here. The house is long. If our house was stretched, it would be that long. Here's their door. And the window [*Draws*]....We have another neighbor back here. We're *really* close to the one behind us; you just have to walk across our backyard, and you're there. This boy named Anthony has a basketball goal and a volleyball thing. *This* is what *I* would call playing. And my cousins go over there. They're boys. There're not very much girls in our neighborhood. There's just a 3-year-old

FIG. 3.1. Cicily's map.

girl who lives over here named Kristi. We play volleyball. And he has a
tent, but I don't stay over there in the tent. And we play basketball and
stuff. And I play baseball with my cousins sometimes. And over here, the
little girl I talked about, Kristi, she has a whole bunch of more brothers.
And they have a trampoline. And we, I play on that.

Cicily gave her house a distinctive character and an explicit geographic position at the intersection of two named roads. The neighborhood was defined by spaces of bodily activity and social interaction;
friends were named and located within family structures. Cicily explained that her favorite outdoor activity was riding her bike, a 10-speed
she'd got for her 9th birthday. The golf course near her house, a remnant
left after a speculator's attempt to create a luxury country club went
bust in the 1973–1974 recession, supplied her with a contested arena of
pleasure:

We have a golf course over here [*Pointing to an area off the map she has
drawn*]. Like, this is a road right here? And this road right here?...It's not
a pattern—you know how usually golf courses have patterns? This golf
course doesn't. It has one over here—it's like up, kind of, like a hill kind
of. And then it has sand shaped close to it. Here's the sand right here. Like
that. And then it has the golf course part right here. And people have to
walk up here, that way. And people walk up here that way. And they get
out of their carts; they leave their carts right here. So I have to be careful
where, where I ride my bike at. Because, because, uh, I ride down this
road—I may go halfway up in there, but I don't go all the way. Because
before we moved, my grandmother, she made a deal with the owner. She
said that we would be careful of where we go and things like that. And he
said it was okay for us to ride our bikes anywhere we wanted to as long
as we don't bother the people over there, don't holler and things like that.
And we'd go riding up there. But now they have a new manager, and our
grandmother, she didn't, she doesn't have time to go over there and talk
to him, because she's too busy. And it's this old man, and every time we go
over there and ride our bikes through the path the old manager said we
could, he comes out and yells, "You stole my golf balls! You stole my golf
balls!" And all of that? And we don't pay attention to him; we just go
somewhere else where he's not at. 'Cause my cousins ride with me
sometimes. And you go up through here, and this other road goes up like
that, and we'll zoooom down it and up again. And then you just go straight
till you turn up here, and you can see my house again....Like my house
would be right there, and then you turn over to this road right here, and
it's townhouses. My cousin used to have, his best friend lived over....And
if you turn this way, you would see another big giant part of the golf course.
If you go *this* way, you see Sybil's house. And this other boy named Kenny
in Mrs. Tanner's class.

The golf course manager's actions reflected a general European
American suspicion and hostility toward African American kids who
ventured outside their immediate neighborhoods. Older participants in
the oral history interviews spoke of being "stoned" or harrassed in

earlier decades when they ventured into European American districts
of the city. Cicily was unfazed, however, by the manager's verbal abuse.
For her, the golf course was like the "unprogrammed space" Lynch (1977,
p. 13) spoke of: the streets and courtyards kids appropriate for their own
uses. For Cicily, these uses were mainly the semisolitary pleasures of
bike riding and the bodily exuberance of rushing through the streets
and dodging cars. She was not so much "colonizing" the space (Ward,
1978) as consuming it bodily. A golf course, after all, is a space of elite
consumption, where men (and some women), usually European Americans, cement social networks and demonstrate their affluence through
the conspicuous consumption of time and space. Cicily simply claimed
the space, for a short time, for her own uses. When I asked her about
her favorite place to hang out in the neighborhood, she replied:

> [*Pause*] Well, *by myself*, to hang out, riding my bike on the golf course. I
> may stop on the hill, look around. And fall asleep on the grass or some-
> thing. But, with someone else, it'd be—[*Pause*] ummm, our neighbor
> across our grass, across our backyard grass.

This claiming of uses in spaces laid out and controlled by corporate
powers (i.e., the golf course) characterized Cicily's spatial practice. She
rode her bike, for example, not just around the golf course, but down a
busy street to a small strip mall where she'd buy candy at a drugstore:

> Well, that road is busy, but the way the road is, there're not sidewalks or
> anything. There's a big giant church—and in the summer time there are
> snakes over there, so we don't go on that side of the street. But there's
> grass over there, and we'll just ride in the grass and go down there. And
> then there's this big back parking lot for Safeway. And we go up in this—it's
> this big dirt part, and it's the back driveway or whatever you call it, to
> Safeway. And we ride up there and turn there and go to Safeway. But my
> cousin. He take big things. He's 14, but he's very short. And he goes all the
> way to McDonald's! I may *walk* to McDonald's, but I don't ride my bike,
> because there's this hill that goes down like that [a steep hill].

Her itineraries, her routes through space, were defined by reference
to fast food stores and corporate wastelands like parking lots and golf
courses. Like many of the other kids, she was fond of big shopping
centers. But unlike Doug, the boy we meet next, what drew her to the
mall were clothes, not toys:

> I *love* the mall! Especially shopping! Take me shopping, and I'd probably
> buy the whole section of girls that's my size. Especially at J. C. Penny's.
> The other clothes, that I don't like, I wouldn't wear them. I just wish I had
> some kind of machine that would send me…an outfit when I wanted one.
> Or anything I wanted, when I wanted it.

Her favorite place in the entire city was a commercial site for the expression of bodily pleasures: What Cicily loved above all, and I'll talk about this more in chapter 4, was to roller-skate all night at a local skating rink, from 7 P.M. Saturday to 7 A.M. Sunday, an activity that gave her an intense sense of "freedom."

All these activities locate Cicily bodily in the open spaces of consumer capitalism—the elite spaces of the golf course, the popular spaces of the malls—where she extracted pleasure from bodily activity or through the purchase of commodities. The scope of her movements, her comfort in these spaces, seemed distinctive to kids who've lived in the same place for a long time. Another trait distinctive to such kids was their engagement in activities associated with cultural self-improvement.

Cicily's grandmother, for example, was able to create an analogue of an elite space in the home by buying a piano for Cicily and paying for piano lessons. As Cicily explained, the lessons were "my idea—*and* my grandma's idea. It was her idea to *pay* for it! [*Laughs*]." The lessons expanded Cicily's spatial range—they were the only things that took her downtown—and brought her into contact with a certain kind of pedagogical tradition characteristic of the middle-class aesthetic of distancing oneself from art (Bourdieu, 1984). The lessons exposed her to the "petrifying effect" of European classical music instruction (Bailey, 1980):

I play—I like it. It's just *learning* it that's so hard. But when you get—like I just play—it's fun! But learning it? You'd like wish the teacher would shut up! You just want to tape her mouth! And it's a lot of years to learn how to play good. But if you want to play just "good"? A couple of years. But if you want to play really really good and get on *Star Search* or something like that, you have to take a lot of years of practice. Plus you have to practice *extra* time at home.

Cicily was conscious of the fact that her opportunity to practice at home was due to her grandmother's ability to work multiple domestic jobs: "Yeah, 'cause we have a piano. 'Cause my grandmother works for three people: Friday she works for two, and during the week she works for one."

Her grandmother's employers were wealthy European Americans who paid her to look after their kids. This activity also offered Cicily access to social spaces different from those she found in her neighborhood, although these spaces were more difficult to capture for her own uses than was the golf course:

[My grandmother] babysits these rich kids. Their parents are rich and everything....They live in Heston [an elite residential area]. And they, they have a lot of toys, I mean, a *lot*! They never tear up their stuff! And she goes out of town with them to Virginia Beach; she babysits kids while the grown folks are gone. Like they go to Vegas—she'd have her own room and stuff. She order anything she want to; they'll pay for it. They don't care what it is. The kids, they stay in the room where she is. The momma and daddy, they have another room. Maybe the kids will walk in there when they feel like it or anything. And they order pizza, cookies, soda. All of that. One of them, they really like yogurt. They eat it all the time. It's only one kid that acts normal; the rest of them are weird..... [The little 6-year-old girl], her friend comes over, you say hi to her friend and she sticks her nose up at you! You come in the room, you wanna like play with them or something, and they say, "We don't want you playin' with us. Go out! Go with your grandmother." Because the [rich kids' parents] will let us, let me spend the night or something over there, while they're out of town; I stay with my grandmother. They just say that stuff. The little boy, I'm older than him, I'm 1 year older than him because his birthday is in December—he's very weird. His friends, they play baseball and stuff—you want to play with them? They'll look at you like you're dumb. Very silly....Well, they don't get to go to the grocery store and stuff with their mom, because they ask for too much, but like, she'd take one of them with her, not all of them, never.

Cicily seemed less bothered by the racism and class bias than fascinated by the strange habits of the kids: their behavior, their treatment of toys, their affluence, their spoiled or immature behavior outside the home. She might have learned the same things by observing her classmate Doug, but Doug, even though she sat near him for 180 days, was in some ways socially more distant than the rich kids her grandmother looked after. Them she could meet through the mediation of her grandmother's work. *Within* the school, she had no opportunities to move across social spaces.

Doug. When I asked Doug, a European American boy who'd lived in the area around the school since he was an infant, if he remembered how long he'd lived in his house, he replied with a story that began before his birth:

I came there—In Christiansburg, my granny built this house over an Indian graveyard, and stuff. And after we left it's been *hauntin'* the house! They've been hauntin'. My aunt's been up there and seen things. They never bothered us. Because my great great great great great great—see, my uncle, and my mom, and me, are a little bit, have a little bit of Indian blood in us. And we had to move, and we went to our grandma's and stayed for a while. And then we got this other house and stayed for a while. And then we went—then we went to my house up the street. And—I made a friend there. Met some of my friends [*Pause*]. And then, I didn't want to deal with anything with that one friend and this other friend. So, my other friend, Jeremy, we played for a long time, and, till I got—we're still playin'. But, he's copying the things I do. He's about like 7 years old, and, I ride wheelies, popped my bike over in the middle of the road one time. Hit my head smack dab in the pavement! Uh, and, pop wheelies up in the air. And one time, in the second grade, after school, on this TV show? On news? Um, my mom watches it, and there's this guy with grey hair and a beard, was walking around our, in our area? And I got scared. And I wanted to go outside, and I ran on the porch. Of course, I had these old slippery shoes, and I slipped—it felt like somebody's hands were grabbin' my feet, and I went straight through the glass, feet first! Up, all the way to the top of our house, and fell back down and turn over smack dab on my stomach. 'Course, you can see the place where I cut my thumb. And I still have a little scar right there. I had scars all over me. And, that was it, until now.

For Doug, where he lived wasn't a physical structure on an abstract grid; it was a history, a set of friendships, a place located by coordinates of particular bodily activities and experiences. The map Doug drew for me, like Cicily's, showed a house, the houses of neighbors he knew, and the streets he traveled on (Fig. 3.2). But the differences in the maps are striking. The diversity of sites in Doug's neighborhood gave his map more differentiation, and he included valued sites that he couldn't reach by bike—the mall and its surrounding stores:

Okay, here's the back of Thurber, where me and my friends, we come over here a lot and play baseball. And I said if we ever came back here and played baseball again that I'd pick up some dirt, some grass, and if Mr. Watts is out there, I'll throw it at him. Here's the ballfield. And the road goes up from this church...this church right here. And there's a road that goes to right here....And this other road leads to the fire station, this ambulance thing [a rescue squad station] right there. And we run up there, for a few minutes, and there's my friend's house...and then we pass my friend's house, and there, down here on the far side, is my house....Right here....That's my house. And that road has an empty spot right there. And leads to this other road. And then, we go places a lot. We go to Wal-Mart....And the road goes up, and you take this way, round our house. Sometimes we go to Wal-Mart, which is on Jackson Road. That little mall. And then we go all the way down to Toys "R" Us, when I have money. I go to Toys "R" Us. And if I don't want to go to Toys "R" Us, I go in the mall....Oh, and there of course is the church parking lot, where I always ride my bike. This is the parking lot, and this could be the church. And we go, me and my friend go across there, and sometimes I take my bike out of my driveway, out of the porch right here, and I take it down and go all the way down here, to there, to there....Sometimes we go over and play baseball; sometimes we play baseball—they have a basketball goal right here [in the church parking lot], but it's always broke. . . .

The difference in the maps was partly gender driven. As C. Katz (1993) reported, girls are as mobile as boys in some societies, but in industrialized settings, "All studies of children's outdoor play...have found significant differences between girls' and boys' autonomy, the extent of their free range area, and the ways in which they use space" (p. 101). Lynch (1977) noted that "girls are more often kept at home or must travel in pairs, while the boys are, at least in theory, free to roam" (p. 23). Both C. Katz (1993) and Ward (1978) pointed to parents' fears of harm to girls, their supposedly greater vulnerability, as a major reason

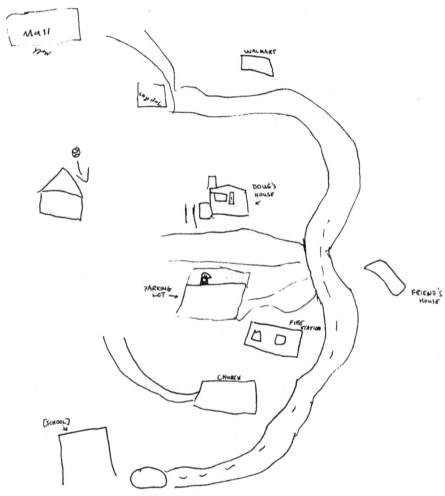

FIG. 3.2. Doug's map.

for restrictions of girls' autonomy and mobility (Katz likened it to purdah in some Muslim societies). Boys are seen as less vulnerable and are allowed to stay out later and travel farther from home. Ward (1978) also noted that girls are likely to have greater responsibilities around the home (household chores, caring for younger siblings) which may limit their mobility. In this light, Cicily, riding her bike down a busy street to a shopping center (although never after dark) or appropriating space around the golf course, was strikingly mobile. By contrast, Carol, a European American girl who lived near Doug, described a daily trajectory circumscribed by fear; she never left her fenced backyard without an adult escort. She told me of her friend:

Hetty, she's bossy, but she also asks if I can spend the night, and my mom says no, because one night, at 9:00, I was in bed, 'cause I have to go to bed at 9:00, sometimes 9:30, sometimes 10:00. And my dad, he was outside switching the cars around, for work. And Hetty, she was outside, and she's 7—but now she's 8—and she was walking her dog outside, outside in our street at 9:00. And someone could have grabbed her. And my mom and dad won't let me go over there because, because, you know, she might, you know, her parents don't even, her parents didn't even know she went out. And Dad goes, "Someone's going to pick her up, and that dog ain't gonna save her."

Doug, of course, expressed no such fears (in his story, reports of a suspicious man in the area made Doug want to go *outside,* he got so excited he ran through the door). His local play space was organized around familiar sites—school, church, fire station—community organizations (at least in principle) rather than the privately owned and potentially unfriendly spaces that dominated Cicily's landscape.

All the same, the comfort Doug felt on the streets of his neighborhood didn't translate into activity that could allow him to build or sustain meaningful identities in collectives centered outside the school. He didn't participate in self-improvement schemes as Cicily did in taking piano lessons or cheerleading, and his neighborhood demographics meant there weren't a lot of kids around for him to associate with informally. Moreover, the neighborhood's domestication, which probably made it safe, also made it dull. Bike riding provided a venue for bodily expression but not a basis for constructing a public identity outside school. For that, Doug's only options were organized recreational activities and the imaginative worlds articulated through popular culture. He wanted to play in the community baseball league, for example, but complained that his mom had forgotten to sign him up for it.

She was supposed to sign up for baseball. I'm a good hitter. I hit a baseball all the way into this girl's backyard. Over from like here—that girl's house was like there. And I hit the ball and the ball went [Gestures] and dropped. I can hit a baseball pretty far.

Doug also included on his map sites of consumption outside the neighborhood. His favorite place, he told me, was Toys "R" Us, followed by Wal-Mart, K Mart, the mall, and McDonalds. The school, by contrast, was useful only insofar as it could be appropriated for nonschool uses: "I hate the school!" Doug insisted. "I wish it'd blow up! I never like school." It was finally, as I'll show in a later chapter, popular culture that provided Doug with materials for constructing a public self. He was a fanatic television watcher: "I watch TV!" he told me. "That's all I do. I watch TV and I play."

Kids embedded in local neighborhoods, then, nevertheless experienced these spaces in different ways that depended on what the spaces afforded, the kids' means of mobility, and the race- and gender-based constraints they had to endure. Where Cicily and Doug were similar is in the relatively large landscape through which they moved; their sense of the histories of the places they lived in and moved through; their centers of activity away from home (i.e., the skating rink and church for Cicily, the mall for Doug); and their struggles to define identities grounded in community spaces outside the school (even if, in Doug's case, these efforts didn't get far). Although common sense might suggest that all kids experience neighborhoods in these ways, this is not the case.

Displacement From a Comfortable Space

Talking to kids who'd moved to Roanoke within the last year produced very different maps and narratives. These kids drew apartment buildings and immediate surroundings but did not label streets or friends' dwellings, and did not talk about friends by name in their narratives. They did not describe itineraries through neighborhoods so much as simply enumerate the items in the immediate areas of their apartments. They still thought of their former places of residence as home and hoped to return to them.

Lila.   Lila, an African American girl, had moved to Roanoke at the beginning of the year from an apartment complex in a more densely populated urban area in the state. She already knew that she would be moving back at the end of the school term and seemed happy at the prospect. She had more friends there, she explained. When I asked her to "draw me a picture or a map of the area" she lived in now, she asked, "A map? What do you mean?"

"Well," I tried to explain, "just a picture. And you don't have to be a great artist."

"Where I live in?" she tried again to get me to explain.

"Where you live in now," I said.

"Okay," Lila asked, "so I draw a picture of Roanoke?"

"Roanoke," I repeated, surprised by her question. "You could. I was thinking first of all of just your neighborhood, where you play after school, if there's anywhere around there. Wherever that may be."

"Okay." Lila asked again, "What do I draw, the playground or something?"

"Well," I asked her, "if I said, 'What's your neighborhood?' could you draw what you think of as your neighborhood?"

"But," she asked, "do I just draw the sign in front?"

"The sign in front of the playground?" I asked.

"No," she explained, "the sign in, in the uh, you know how, it's kind of like a welcoming sign. But instead of it being a welcoming sign it says 'Farewell Estates.' And that's where you just drive into."

"Okay," I tried to clarify again. "No, I guess I'm more interested in where you, as a person, go. So I'm interested in where *you* go in that neighborhood."

"To play?" she asked.

"To play or whatever else you do," I replied. "Or do you mostly stay in your building?"

"Well," Lila asked, "What if there was kind of like, kind of like, well, me and my friend walk down to the golf course store, and so, and the golf course store is just like on the golf course, not where I live. So do I just draw the golf course store?"

"That's a good question," I replied. "Do you go down there a lot?"

"Uh-huh," Lila replied. I explained:

Maybe you just need to draw that whole area. 'Cause what I'm trying to find out is what kinds of places, where you go—I was trying to figure out *what* your neighborhood was. So why don't you, yeah, why don't you draw, hmmm, show me where your house is and what kind of places around there you go....So it would be your house and maybe the store and maybe a playground. Wherever else you might go. Does that make sense?

Lila finally began drawing, working for several minutes in silence, not talking aloud and giving me the tour as Cicly and Doug had (Fig. 3.3). From time to time I had to ask her to identify what she was drawing. Her descriptions were brief. Instead of referring to spaces or to activities, she referred to objects in her environment:

This right here is the window....Okay, that's where I live....And this is the playground....This is a place where you, kind of like, when you have picnics and stuff....This is a playground, with a sandbox....This is a sliding board [*Silently drawing*]. And this is a merry-go-round. I don't know how to draw it [*Silently drawing*]. I don't have space for those others....I'll just draw it in the corner....It's kind of like a circle thing. And then it got bars on top and stuff [*Silently drawing*]....Okay, the golf course store is on the golf course.

"You go to any other stores except the golf course store?" I asked.

"Not with my friends," she explained. "I'm not allowed to walk to stores, 'cause the stores are all the way up in the front, near the road."

Cicily, by contrast, had told of riding her bike down a different section of the same busy road Lila referred to here. I don't think Lila's questions when I asked her to draw reflected an ignorance about the idea of maps; I'd seen her work with them in class often enough. Perhaps she had trouble with the idea that maps could describe patterns of lived experience and thought of them only as representations of abstract spaces: the

FIG. 3.3. Lila's map.

city itself or the sign representing her apartment complex. Lila *did,* after all, live in a setting organized by conceptions of abstract space, not in a *residence* but in *housing,* the latter defined functionally in terms of "minimal living-space," "modular units," "minimal facilities and a programmed environment" (Lefebvre, 1991, pp. 314, 316). Or perhaps Lila simply hadn't lived at Farewell Estates long enough to get a sense of its boundaries or distinctive regions. Perhaps it was hard to get a sense of the apartments as elements of a neighborhood. They were geographically isolated, near only to other apartments and the golf course complex that Cicily spoke of. It's even possible Lila was just having fun with me; she had a remarkably droll and deadpan sense of humor for a 9-year-old.

For whatever reasons, Lila defined the landscape by its few kid-focused elements—the slide and so forth—although she described her own activity as mainly walking. She sometimes went to the golf course store to buy candy but rarely went even into friends' houses: "I'm not allowed to go in other people's houses. Like my friend Destiny, I'm only allowed to go in her house. 'Cause my mother knows her mother."

Unlike Cicily, who had her cheerleading, bike trips to the store, and piano lessons downtown, or Doug, who had his adventures in consumption at the mall, Lila didn't get out of her apartment complex much, and then apparently not for purposes that centered around *her.* Rather, her mobility seemed limited to trips as a passenger on her mother's errands. The focus of her activity turned inward, but at home she lacked spaces of her own. When I asked her if there were a "good place" for her to be alone, she answered that she wanted to be alone sometimes:

> When my sister's messing with me. Like yesterday morning my sister was messing with me, and it was time for me to go to school, and we were yelling and fighting and stuff, and me and her share a room. And she locked me out of the room. And my homework was in my room.

Although I'm not sure I would have called Lila "poor," Ward's (1978) comments apply to many children from low-income families: "The poor child, who is usually the most isolated from the life of the city *as* city, is also, paradoxically, the child who is denied the solace of solitude. He [sic] is seldom alone" (p. 47). Like the children in Lynch's (1977) international study, meaningful activity had been emptied from Lila's spaces of activity: "The children seem to suffer from experiential starvation....In most of these settlements there is little for the children to be responsible for—no places they control and manage" (Lynch, 1977, pp 24–25).

Unlike Doug, and Tina whom I discuss next, Lila didn't even have access to popular culture as an alternative. Her family didn't have cable television and thus couldn't get some of the key channels carrying kids' programming. With nothing else to draw on, she was, of all the kids discussed in this chapter, the most outwardly committed to school (and of this group, was the student most liked by her teachers).

Tina.   Tina's displacement was more complex than Lila's. Lila had gone from one apartment complex to a similar (although more spatially isolated) apartment complex in another town; Tina had moved with her mother from a block of rooms, shared with her grandmother, above a cluster of businesses on a busy Detroit street corner, to an apartment complex in Roanoke.

Tina's map was similar to Lila's: an anonymous square in a block of apartments. I'd already interviewed Lila when I talked to Tina and was beginning to wonder whether their maps weren't just reflections of the anonymity of apartment dwelling (mobile and displaced kids were more likely to live in apartments than in single-family homes). But as Tina continued, I realized the issue was more complicated: Social class played a big role in how apartments were experienced, as well as in shaping mobility.

Tina had come to Roanoke from Detroit after her mother, a clerical worker for a large service-sector corporation, had been transferred (part of the widespread shift of jobs from highly industrialized regions to nonunion states like Virginia, a bleaker part of the new information age economy). In a sense, Tina had already been mobilized in an abstract space of corporate rationality. When she and her mother initially arrived in the city, the corporation apparently helped them find dwellings in one of the more expensive apartment complexes in the city. Tina quickly developed a consciousness of economics and its role in the restriction of pleasure:

> I moved from Detroit to Roanoke, but I moved to Roanoke County. I lived in Happyfield. But then it was too expensive there because it cost $475 for two bedrooms [*Sighs*]. And when I started there I went to Greenberg School, and that school cost too much too. And then I moved over here.

Apartment dwelling per se didn't produce the bleak map of her neighborhood as a maze of boxes; the nature of the apartments, their small affordances for children's activities and their lack of connection to surrounding neighborhoods were shaping forces. By contrast, as Tina explained, Happyfield, the expensive luxury complex, had offered a variety of activities:

> If I could choose a place to live in Roanoke, I would choose Happyfield. But I would put their rent down. Because there was a playground there. There was a fire camp there. No, actually there was two playgrounds. And they had a volleyball court where you could hook up [a net]....They had a pool there, and they had an activity room for the kids at Happyfield. And it was

fun. There used to be a lot of hills where you could sled over there. Like we had the blizzard? I was sledding all day long.

For most of the last year, Tina had been living in a cheaper apartment complex on a busy street in the area around the school. It was a kind of "liminal space" (Zukin, 1991), partly commercialized, partly domesticated by the Tupler area's reform movement. Tina said little as she drew her map and apologized for her drawing skills: "That's not how big my house is; they're town houses....That's not exactly how it looks" (Fig. 3.4). She stopped when she'd drawn her apartment building, so I asked where she went when she was at home. "Outside," she explained.

"Where outside?" I asked.

"Well, there are some trees," she replied, "and I climb a tree."

"Are there any swings or anything to play on in that courtyard?" I asked.

FIG. 3.4. Tina's Roanoke Map.

She described it for me: "There's a yard in the back. There's grass right here. We have like a little yard, and then we have stairs, downstairs, and then there's a big parking lot, like right there. And then there's one right there, and I roller-skate right here, and there's a big thing right here."

I had to keep asking her questions to get her to draw, but her verbal descriptions of the landscape were impersonal. She talked about the general characteristics of the apartment complex, not her particular activity space:

Every house has like a little place of its own next to it [a backyard]. And every time the house always has stairs, and the stairs go like that; and then half of the side is ours, and half of the side is theirs. And then there's a big thing where you put your garbages, right there....When I go roller skating, there's some, that's like, that's the sidewalk. And there's like a sidewalk there too. So I just go like that around. And then there's a street that connects over here. We go—like it's supposed to be longer, and I go like that?—go like that and turn; there's a little thing right here, and then I turn, go back turn in here, go around that, and then I go and turn.

I asked her to draw the surrounding streets and tell me what they were. She only became interested when I asked her whether she went to any of the stores on the busy street in front of her apartment:

I go by myself to the store. Harold's store across...When my mom goes washing, I usually stay home. And then when I finish playing outside, I walk to the laundrymat [I ask her to draw it]. This is the laundrymat right there....Then it's Harold's store right there, but they closed up. And then there's a bar. And there's a pawnshop right here.

Tina described settings in abstract space, not spaces lived in or used. This point didn't become clear to me until I asked Tina where she'd live if she could live anywhere.

"Detroit!" she answered loudly.

I asked her why.

Because my *family's* there!! Because I like it! Because it's boring over here! There's nothing to do. Over there we had a rock field. But now they've changed it into a tire station....And we used to have rock fights, and we used to ride our bikes over there. There were bumps—they used to have *dirty alleys*, and I liked them. We used to go through them, and we used to bump—like there were a lot of rocks there, and we used to jump up. And my cousin's cousin, he got on the back of my bike, and we turned around by Celmark, because my house was on Celmark and Oakton; it was right on the corner, like it is right now, and we used to go like that. And it was my grandma's apartment. My grandma lived on this side, I lived on this side, and we had a great big yard.

"You want to draw all that?" I asked.

"Want me to?"

"Sure."

"This is *much* more easy to draw!" Tina said, and she began drawing with much more enthusiasm than before (Fig. 3.5). Again she drew where she lived, but this time she narrated as she drew, without any prompting from me:

There was a diamond really there [i.e., a diamond-shaped window on the door]....This is where we lived. That's where my grandmother lived, that smaller apartment. There were stairs going up like that. A hallway right there. These are doors right here....That's the backyard. Goes all the way over to here....And there was a beauty shop right here [i.e., below the apartments]. It had a great big door with—like there was diamonds on each door for the restaurant door [next to the beauty shop]. This [the restaurant] was on the corner, and there was a corner door like that....There's a window right here. I thought we should've had a drive-through. And there was my grandma's porch door right here. And that had no windows. She used to have her porch sales there. And we had base-ments and all too. Like, my grandma, she had an upstairs; it's kind of a kids' room, because she used to babysit. She still babysits. She walks down, and she walks down. There's one step of stairs, and then one step of stairs, and then you got to there; and then you turn around, you go straight, and you go down those steps, and you get to the, you get to the basement door. Then you get to the basement door, and you walk up two steps, and you, you—I mean, okay, you walk down all those steps, and then you walk down those steps right here; then you, see, then you turn, and you still have to walk a couple of more steps, and then you turn, and there's the basement door. Then you go inside and you walk up those steps; then you go back to this hallway and you go up to my house, and then through my house there's a back door right *there* and then you walk through those doors and you—there's plenty of ways you can get to my house! Like you could go through here, through my grandma's house and through the doorway and to my door....You could have gone through here, through the basement, and then you go to the other basement on that side, which is their basement....Right now there's a girl living there [showing me on the map]; she has three or four workers. She has one daughter. There's a girl here, she has one worker—actually two workers. And she has two kids....When I couldn't get in, I usually went into the beauty shop, went out through here—my grandmother's door was usually open—I went out through there. I had my keys, I had my door keys; and I went right through there. When I didn't have a key, after the beauty shop, then I went inside....And then I would scream Grandma in Spanish. And the next door neighbors would go, "Who is she screaming at?" We have, it's goofy. And from here you could go through there, and that connects to there. You go up the stairs, and *then* you'll be by the register in the restaurant. It's goofy.

Once the topic shifted to Detroit, the home Tina pined for, her discussion became animated; the names of streets and institutions entered into her talk. She detailed specific relationships and activities

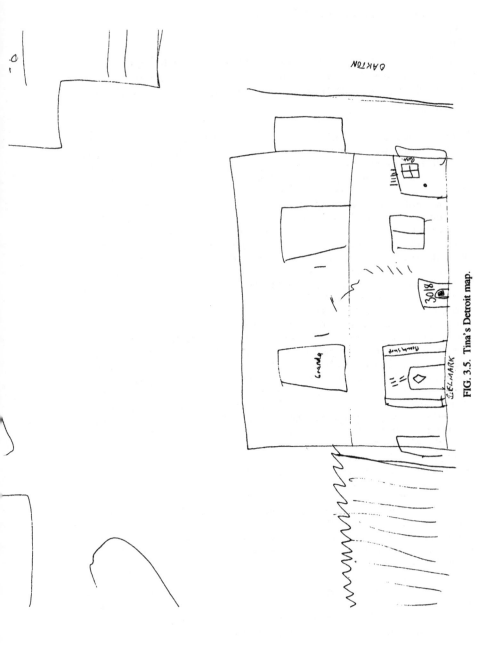

FIG. 3.5. Tina's Detroit map.

112

and explained their meaning for her. The patterns of movement she described became much more extensive and involved. Her talk, and what she described, took on the characteristics of the embedded kids.

School on the Move

Desiree was the only mobile student I interviewed (although probably not the only one in the school). When I asked her how long she'd lived in Roanoke, she explained:

> I moved here only—maybe two or three years ago. But I *mainly* lived in—before I was born, my mom and my dad lived in Charlottesville. And then, when I was born, like a little baby. Uh, they, me and my dad and my mom, we moved to Countryville [a rural area] with my grandpa, because he wasn't doing so good. It was a tremendous house. It had an upstairs—and the upstairs was like a full house. It had a kitchen, a sink. And it had bedrooms...and then downstairs had the same thing....Two bathrooms, yeah, two bathrooms. And they both had showers in them. The downstairs had one. . . .
>
> Our house was like on a hill, and when you go down there, there was the lake. And we could go swimming there all the time. The reason why we moved was because my dad, he had a disk removed, out of his back, and he couldn't mow the big yard anymore, and Pop Pop, he couldn't either. And so we had to sell it.

The family then moved to Roanoke, where Desiree attended a succession of schools as her parents moved from one apartment to another: "See, I went to Russell, then I went to Niles, then I went to Cleaver, then I went here." According to a General Accounting Office report (General Accounting Office, 1994), such mobility is not uncommon. In a national sample, 17% of third graders had attended 3 or more schools since first grade; and of kids from low-income families like Desiree's, 30% had changed schools frequently. Such mobility, coupled with the differences in pedagogy from one school to another, created problems:

> Russell, it was easy too. And Niles, it was like *real* easy. And then when I went to Cleaver, I mean I was like in the third grade, and I was in a third- and fourth-grade class? And, but they had a regular, just third-grade class, but they put me in the third- and fourth-grade class, because I had to take another one, and then, but then I was doing like some of this—'cause I'm in fourth grade now, but I had a fifth-grade English book, and a fourth-grade math book and stuff. And when I came here to finish third grade, I was, I was, I had, I was higher, I had more higher skills than anybody there. And they were going to take me to fourth grade, but they decided not to.

As Desiree explained, "Really, I should be in the fifth grade, but see my birthday is like the 11th month, and my dad just decided to hold me back one year....I want to be in the fifth grade so bad! I want to hurry up and finish school!"

Desiree already knew that she would be moving to yet another school next year:

> When I go to fifth grade, I'm not going to be here. I'm going to go to Monclair, 'cause it's—'cause—I *did* go to—well, I went here, but from, but when I moved? To be able for me to go here, I would have to—my dad would have to take me and drive me to and from school. 'Cause the buses, they didn't go down there? But my dad said that next year he would transfer us from this school to Monclair, 'cause it's a whole lot closer, plus my dad can't drive a car anymore. It'll be easier because we can walk there and stuff.

The good thing about the move to come was that Desiree would be going to school with the other kids in her apartment complex. I asked her how she ever ended up at Thurber if she were in the Monclair catchment area:

> Well, I *moved* here [to her present apartment], I moved from [Farewell Estates, Lila's apartment complex], that's near where Shirley and them people live. And, but then we had to move because the lease there or whatever got too high, so we moved. My dad—when I was younger we had to keep on leavin' schools, so my dad wanted us to finish at this school. . . .

This constant movement, driven by family events and economics, pushed Desiree to an apartment complex at the far end of the segment of the attendence zone contiguous with the school. When I asked her to draw her neighborhood, she located it with reference to a big factory nearby and then drew a sparse set of features relevant to her activity (Fig. 3.6).

> That's like the room...[a factory] is across the street, where they make toothpaste and stuff....I can't draw....Then these are the apartments across the street....And then, in the middle, it's like the courtyard....That's like the sidewalk. And then it's got like these benches and stuff. . . . They got the benches there and stuff. And I go over there and play volleyball or something.

Did they have a volleyball net set up, I asked. "No, see there's like, one person will be on this side [*Pause as she draws*]. A person will be on that side, and another person will be there. Just hit it back and forth [across the sidewalk]."

As Ward (1978) remarked, "Children colonise every last inch of left-over urban space...ingeniously...seize every opportunity for pleasure" (p. 210).

Like Lila and Tina, Desiree didn't label the streets or describe her itinerary of activity through neighborhood space. Nor did she identify

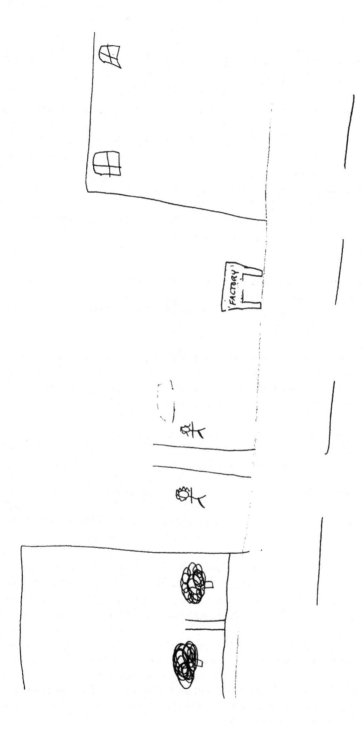

FIG. 3.6. Desiree's map.

spaces or friends by name, as Cicily and Doug had (although there were lots of kids in her apartment complex, she said). Unlike Doug and Cicily, but like Lila and Tina, she moved through the area on foot rather than on a bike and went to a local grocery for her dad on occasion. Although Cicily occasionally rode down to the grocery store, Desiree was the only kid who actually bought things for her family and could talk about relative prices: "It's—well, some of the things [at the local store] are cheap. But some of them are—well, you could go somewhere else and get them for a better price."

Her friendships, which were limited to other kids in the apartment complex, were defined by the economic flows that had brought her and other families there. When I asked her to describe her "neighborhood," she referred to the area of the apartment complex as she answered:

> Well, sometimes, me and my friends, we walk up around the block; sometimes I ride my other friend's bike up there, because I don't have one. And we go around the block. Well, I would call that, like this whole area where everybody lives.

Desiree's mobility around the city, although much more limited than Doug's, like his was oriented around spaces of consumption. Unlike Doug, however, it was not consumption through *buying* that Desiree engaged in; rather, she *rented* spaces and commodities:

> Well, when we had a car, we went up to this—it's called Putt-Putt, and we used to play all sorts of games up there. And we used to go there. And we used to rent videos, well, movies, from Blockbuster, video games and movies. 'Cause they have a bigger selection than this other one that's near my house. But since we can't walk all the way up there—I personally do not feel like it—they've got this other one called Color Video. It's a small one, but it's—I mean, it's, all the movies, almost all of them we've seen. But there's some of them that we haven't seen that we get there.

Desiree had a desire for motion, physical bodily freedom, similar to Cicily's love of all-night skating. But unlike Cicily, the realization of this freedom remained a distant hope. She wanted desperately to go to an amusement park. When I asked her what she'd ride on, she responded:

> The roller coaster! I've *never* been in a roller coaster, ever! Except when they had the fair [she refers to a small carnival set up near the civic center for a week each year]—you didn't really go upside down or anything; it just like went up, and then it turned like that. They had it like going up, and then whoosh, straight down. I lost my stomach, but it was fun. I rode it like twice. Two or three times.

SPACES FOR BODIES

When Lynch (1979) summarized his work on kids' conceptions of the material environment, he commented, "How rarely we heard discussions of a playing field, or of a school" (p. 104). Instead, kids focused on spaces that could be reworked for their own uses. Lynch suggested this was partly because kids' "space was controlled by adults and their time controlled by adults" (p. 107). Kids weren't responsible for spaces or for the performance of activities recognized by a community as legitimate and necessary for their families' or communities' well-being. All this seems consistent with what I found in my mapping interviews with fourth graders. They had no real engagements with their parents' activities (except for Cicily, who stayed overnight when her grandmother was babysitting). They participated in corporate culture only as consumers. They had no access to genuine public spaces. Although their different histories and trajectories created different relationships to neighborhood space, they all shared a marginalization vis-à-vis adult life.

Of course, this estrangement was not always the case. Ward (1978) quoted an older European who described his trajectory of activity at age 4:

> Not as a chore, but as an eagerly desired pleasure, I was fairly often entrusted with the task of buying fish and bringing it home alone. This involved the following: walking to the station in five to ten minutes; buying a ticket; watching train with coal-burning steam locomotive pull in; boarding train; riding across long bridge over shallows separating small-boat harbour (on the right) from ship's harbour (on the left), including small naval base with torpedo boats; continuing through a tunnel; leaving train at terminal, sometimes dawdling to look at railroad equipment, walking by and sometimes entering fisheries museum; passing central town park where military band played during mid-day break; strolling by central shopping and business district, or, alternately, passing fire station with horses at ease under suspended harness, ready to go, and continuing past centuries-old town hall and other ancient buildings; exploration of fish market and fishing fleet; selection of fish; haggling about price; purchase and return home. (Albert Parr, quoted in Ward, 1978, pp. 10–11)

The level of responsibility described in this story may not have been typical for kids in the past; and it's true that in many cases young children were integrated into adult-centered community activities in harsh and exploitative ways. But one consequence of deindustrialization, the collapse of neighborhood-based commerce and the concentration of consumption in island-like malls and shopping centers; has clearly been the evaporation of kid's space in the social life of the city. As Ward (1978) put it: "We have accepted the exclusion of children from real responsibilities and real functions in the life of the city" (p. 206).

Some neighborhood organizations may be able to create islands of meaningful activity for kids (McLaughlin, Irby, & Langman, 1994), but I was not aware of the kids from Thurber participating in such groups. In Roanoke, the transformation of the neighborhoods, the different ways they had been emptied out or domesticated, left kids without a locus of embodied, locally meaningful activity. Their pursuits were often solitary: spinning around skating rinks, dreaming of roller coasters, ogling commodities at the mall, or sitting in front of their televisions. Although the kids didn't mention it much in their interviews, the school played a key role in this general process of regulating and circumscribing embodied activity. In the next chapter I explore the school's "body work" and its implications for kids' understanding of themselves and others.

4 Intersections of Bodies and Spaces at School

Though the body may appear to be where we are most individual, it is also the material form of the body politic, the class body, the racial body, and the body of gender. The struggle for control over the meanings and pleasures (and therefore the behaviors) of the body is crucial because the body is where the social is most convincingly represented as the individual and where politics can best disguise itself as human nature.

—*Fiske, 1989, p. 70*

It should be a commonplace that what we know of the world we know through our bodies, but the implications of this idea are far from obvious. Bodies aren't simple objects defined by a surface of skin—they're intersections through which organic and chemical flows circulate; and except in extreme cases they're always augmented and extended in some way, from the wearing of clothing to the use of tools like computers. Bodies are also inscribed with complex social markers like gender, race, and social class, and the meanings of such inscriptions often change as bodies age, and also affect *how* bodies age. Economic and political forces, along with organizational fields, shape bodies, instill in them certain dispositions, and most important, situate them in flows of activity that move them physically in certain ways and connect them to distant activities spread across space and time (Nespor, 1994). In order to understand life as experienced through the body, then, we must look at the processes—some of them at least—that organize people in space and time.

In some parts of childhood, bodily movement itself organizes space and charts the shapes of pleasures and pains. Kids value settings for the possibilities they allow for bodily play and performance. When the Thurber fourth graders drew maps of their neighborhoods, they drew spaces they inhabited bodily—houses, yards, parks—and described their days as itineraries of embodied play and activity. Their greatest pleasures were bound up in performances of physical exuberance that

119

might strike adults as ordeals. Cicily's favorite place in the city, as I mentioned in the previous chapter, was the roller skating rink where she and other kids skated every Saturday from:

> Seven at night to seven in the morning....Big kids, big kids'll fall asleep, but the ones in between, they'll like drowse a little bit, and wake up, and go skate. And the smaller, the smaller ones, like my age or something like that—or the little bitty ones? They may go to sleep. But my age, my age *always* stays up. I don't know why, but they always do. One or two or five may go to sleep, but not all of us. The middle-age kids they drowse around, they go like that, but they'll just get up, skate. But the teenagers and stuff? Ohh, they're sleepy....Ten teenagers, maybe throw up. But the rest of them, I'm sure they won't.

The only adults there, she told me, were the ones who worked there.

> But some people, they sneak and they go to sleep, because there's like corners and stuff you can go in. And the boyfriend and girlfriend! Woooo! They have, uh, boyfriends and girlfriends, stuff like that? They have the girl sittin' on the boy's lap, and she be sleepin', and he be having his head up against the pole, and they'd be like that [*Laughing*]. This one lady, if she catch you [*Yelling*] "Get up!" But she never holler at me because I never go to sleep.

Already, Cicily inscribed embodied differences to distinguish kids her age, 9 years old, from teenagers. She and her peers stayed awake and active, while the teenagers puked and slept, their bodies already beginning to fail them. For the teenagers, the body had become sexualized, and the focus of the event appeared to be the opportunity it presented for dating. For Cicily the function was pure bodily action. When I asked her why she liked to skate so much, she replied: "It's just a way to get free! Free! In my kind of way, [to] do anything you want."

This was a peculiar freedom, of course. A skating rink in the middle of the night may seem a confining place to adults, and Cicily herself was immobilized there, dependent on adults for rides to the rink and back to her home. Within this observed space, however, no one could tell her to go to bed, wash, eat, stay quiet. The rink was one of the rare public spaces where a 9-year-old girl could be on her own, without parents or siblings. The setting focused attention on her body, and she took obvious pride in bodily control, fending off sleep and exhaustion while others threw up or dozed in awkward postures.

School had a different set of body meanings for kids. As Lucy once exclaimed to me near the end of a school day: "It's almost time to get out of school. That means I'll get to play outside anytime I want. And I won't be stuck in a stupid windowless room without going outside."[1]

---

[1]Aside from bathrooms, there were no windowless rooms in the school, but windows were set rather high in the walls, and seated students could not look out them.

Inside is a space of control and constraint, outside (at least by comparison) a space of expression and movement. Bodies as well as physical structures define the divide: Inside-the-body becomes the space of control and intellect, and the exterior of the body, its extensions and emissions, become uncontrolled spaces, celebrated by kids and suppressed by adults. Except for places like the skating rink (and then only at special times, like the all night skate), the bodies of kids Cicily's and Lucy's ages were increasingly subject to control and regulation. As they got older, the spaces of their lives began to be defined not only by their bodies and embodied activities but also, increasingly, by the positions of their bodies in the formal, abstract space of bureaucracies and markets. In the words of Lefebvre (1991), "spaces of the body"—people's actual ways of moving through the world—are replaced by the "body in space"—the body rendered as a visual display or text readable to an outsider's gaze.

This distinction between the body as a generator of space and the body as an object in a space defined by administrative or technocratic practices is similar to the contrast de Certeau (1984) drew between experiencing a city from the top of a skyscraper and experiencing it from the "ground level," as a pedestrian. On the street, he suggested, the tempos and rhythms of a walker, the detours, improvised routes, stops, conversations, and interactions "actualize the possibilies" of the formal city grid to create spaces of the body. The city is a multisensory bodily experience, not something consumed in a look, but something felt, smelled, heard, and tasted as well as seen. We grasp it not as a totality, but as an unfolding journey: The walkers' "bodies follow the thicks and thins of an urban 'text' without being able to read it" (p. 93). Instead of looking at the city as a representation, a map, walkers, like Cicily at the skating rink or the golf course, *create* spatialities by their paths and itineraries.

From the top of a skyscraper, on the other hand, the city looks like a tableau in an abstract space, a "planned and readable" city (de Certeau, 1984, pp. 92–93). People appear as discrete, interchangable objects moving through the terrain. One body looks much like another to the unaided eye. This focus on bounded, individual bodies, as G. Rose (1993) pointed out, is a selective one: "Bodily processes which transgress the boundary between inside and outside the body—childbirth, say, or menstruation—are ignored," as are "bodily passion or desire" (p. 31).

Along with passion and desire, the view from the top of the skyscraper ignores how activity is improvised and negotiated, how people's acts are grounded in limited and partial perspectives that unfold and develop in time. It ignores, in short, the qualities of bodily experience that shape everyday life. In their place, still speaking metaphorically, the high-rise dweller focuses on a static landscape seen from a distant vantage point. And the more accustomed we become to looking at things from such a vantage point, the more inclined we are to think of them as if they really *were* just like static images. To quote Bourdieu (1977): "In taking up a point of view on the action, withdrawing from it in order to observe it from above and from a distance, [the outside observer] constitutes practical activity as an *object of observation and analysis, a representation*" (p. 2). We begin to treat people, things, and activities as detached objects or visual tableaus to scrutinize and observe at a distance, rather than as things to get close to, to become involved with.

I want to suggest that school is fundamentally about sending kids up the elevator to the top of de Certeau's skyscraper, turning them into Bourdieu's detached observers. A key part of the process is the regulation and control of their bodies. Bodies, of course, are always both social and biological constructions—they are "made," as Haraway (1991, p. 208) put it, rather than born. My focus is a key transformation in *how* they are constructed and how their relationships to spaces are constructed. Kids are taught to control and regulate their bodies in ways acceptable to adults. But more important, as kids grow up, the body ceases to be acknowledged as a primary tool for mediating relations with the world. It never vanishes, of course, but it is devalued in importance and replaced by language, literacy, and other forms of communication. In the process, kids are spatially redefined. Instead of living primarily in their immediate, local settings (albeit settings shaped by distant processes, as described in the previous chapter), their lives are distributed across space and time. Their experiences begin to take place in the abstract spaces defined by written texts and media representations. And school plays a fundamental role in this transformation. It defines regions of space and permissible forms of behavior within these spaces. It tries to suppresses bodily movement and expression and to define appropriate bodily orientations. It helps code bodies as having gender, race, beauty, grace, ugliness, and stink.

These processes don't begin in the fourth grade, and they presumably continue long afterward. In this chapter and the one that follows I partially trace the contours of the fourth- and fifth-graders' movements across forms of embodied experience and representation-mediated experience: from spaces of the body, the main focus of this chapter, to bodies in space, the focus of the next chapter.

REGIONALIZATION OF SCHOOL SPACE

In elementary schools, the spaces of teaching are defined by students' bodies. Having exclusive control of a bounded physical space is an important part of a teacher's identity within the school. For example, the Chapter 1 teacher at Thurber fiercely resisted giving up her self-contained classes and in fact wanted to pull kids out for even larger blocks of time. Having exclusive control of a physical setting and a well-defined group of students was synonymous for her with being a teacher: Working in another teacher's classroom made her feel "like an aide." But teachers' frames of reference, the "spaces" of their practice, were not just their physical classrooms, but also their students' bodies, considered as bounded containers of attributes and behaviors (cf. McLaughlin & Talbert's 1993 arguments that students are the "contexts" of teaching). At one meeting, for example, with just the three of us present, Mr. Watts remarked to Mrs. Court how ill behaved her students had been at an assembly (held when she wasn't at school):

Mr. Watts:	They were an interesting crew....It was interesting to me; I'd never noticed it before. And I hate to even say it, because it's sort of like you label kids? But we were waiting in the multipurpose room for them to come down, and nobody was saying very much. There was no need to say get quiet or any of those things. And all the other three classes are just kind of sitting there, looking at one another, kind of laid back. Fourth grade comes in and—it was like a hell storm had come through. I couldn't believe it!
Mrs. Court:	I'm so embarrassed.

No one thought Mrs. Court, or any teacher, *caused* "their" kids' misbehaviors. This way of talking implied instead that misbehavior was a natural attribute that spurted out of kids unless teachers trained them to hold it in, or were nearby to suppress it (I had to point out that the kids may have been unusually excited because fourth grade was leading the assembly that day). Mrs. Court felt responsible for the way her kids had acted, even though she hadn't been present at the event. Similarly, when she left me in charge of her class for even a minute they would usually start talking or wandering around. I'd worry that Mrs. Court would upbraid me for failing to manage them—but she was never upset with *me*. Instead, she'd apologize to me for their behavior.

When a teacher's space is defined by the bodies of his or her students, the kids' bodily behaviors become the focus of attention. Teachers are held responsible for the noise and movement their kids produce rather than for what they know. The maintainance of calm and quiet serves as the index of teaching "success." Denscombe (1980) pointed out that noise emanating from a classroom is taken to indicate the teacher's lack of control and a concommitant absence of learning. By implication, students who are noisy are thought to be engaged in illegitimate, nonschool forms of activity.

The lunchroom at Thurber was a scene of constant struggle over sound and motion by means of which differences between adults and kids were given body-based meanings. Noise and movement in the lunchroom were tightly monitored and suppressed. "Misbehavior" (which was quite common) resulted in the imposition of "silent lunches." During the 2 years I was in the school, this aspect of lunchtime seemed to be a flash point for student–faculty relations. For example, several fourth graders working with me on the newsletter wanted to do a story on the school and decided to interview Mr. Watts:

Lila:	What's the hardest thing about this school, and what would you do to change it?
Mr. Watts:	The dining room is the hardest thing about this school! Is there any question about that? Doesn't everybody know that? Hmm?
Sheila:	There's not enough space—
Mr. Watts:	Well, that's not the point!
Sheila:	At Happy Park [an elementary school in a more affluent neighborhood] they have a *stage* in their dining room.
Mr. Watts:	Where is this? At Happy Park? That is kind of fun.
Effie:	And they have areas where you can eat at.
Mr. Watts:	The biggest problem for me is—
Sheila:	We're loud.
Mr. Watts:	Loud! Yes. And we've got to solve that problem. We're going to work on it.

As Woods (1978), Everhart (1983), Cusick (1973), and others have noted, what kids value most in school are opportunities for interactions with peers. Silent lunch and no recess period severely reduced these opportunities at Thurber. As Lila, a fourth grader, explained, "What I like best is when we get to talk to other people. And what I like worst is when they turn the lights off and we can't talk. And when we have, uh, silent lunch." Some of the fifth graders I worked with bitterly complained of the silent lunch policy, as in this exchange from a conversation near the end of the 1992–1993 school year:

Lucy:	One thing that's boring about this school, is they don't let us talk good. They just make us be quiet all day.
Jan:	[*Thinking she was referring to her teacher*] Why does she do that?
Lucy:	That's what Mr. Watts makes us do. He makes us sit down and shut up at lunch. When we have to work all day, and he knows that we need a break like teachers do. He sits there and pigs his butt off while we have to sit there, be quiet, and only get a few minutes for lunch.

When parents complained about the silent lunches, Mr. Watts gave a hard-line response:

> When they [the kids] don't behave I'm going to put them on silent lunch. That's the bottom line....I'm sorry. We really don't mean to offend anyone. But...bad is bad, and we've got to make them pay for it. 'Cause that's one of the things we talk about all the time here....Life has choices, it's full of choices, and with every choice there comes responsibility. If we don't take the responsibility, then we're not teaching them properly.

Both Lucy's and Mr. Watts's explanations of the silent lunch emphasized the boundary-maintaining function of the policy, its use for differentiating kids from adults. In Lucy's version, the silent lunch policy unfairly denied what she saw as a commonality between adults and kids: the need to have a break and to talk. In Mr. Watts's version, adults had to take "responsibility" for kids (or their bodies) and suppress external expressions of affect, passion, or excitement. Kids had adult rights to speech only when they displayed idealized (male) adult traits of silence, circumspection, and motionlessness.

In Shilling's (1991) words, the organization of school space "reflects societal and legal rules which view children as subordinate to adults" (p. 32). The details of this subordination vary. Heath (1983), for example, described an elementary school in the South where certain activities were bounded and localized to specific places and times within the classroom. On the one hand, as Heath argued, this fact reflected White middle-class spatial practice (African American kids, by contrast, might appropriate a location for many different activities or move these activities across sites). On the other hand, the regionalization of classroom space represents the institutionalization of adult control through spatial practice. What Heath described is one of the strategies Foucault (1979) identified for "distributing individuals in space" (p. 141)—the creation of partitioned "functional sites" (pp. 143–144) that increase the efficiency of supervisory control. In Heath's study, teachers saw kids who came to school unaccustomed to acting within its spatial system as lacking in manners or self-control rather than as simply having different ways of behaving.

As kids grow older, schools' spatial practices generally become more constraining. Spaces are increasingly "ranked," pupils are assigned to specific, fixed places, and so on (cf. Foucault, 1979, pp. 145–149). Willis's (1981) study of boys in a working-class English school supplies a picture of a system in which space is used to tightly regulate students' bodily activity:

> In a simple physical sense school students, and their possible views of the pedagogic situation, are subordinated by the constricted and inferior space they occupy. Sitting in tight ranked desks in front of the larger teacher's

desk; deprived of private space themselves but outside nervously knocking the forbidden staff room door or the headmaster's door with its foreign rolling country beyond; surrounded by locked up or out of bounds rooms, gyms and equipment cupboards; cleared out of school at break with no quarter given even in the unprivate toilets; told to walk at least two feet away from staff cars in the drive—all of these things help to determine a certain orientation to the physical environment and behind that to a certain kind of social organization. They speak to the whole *position* of the student. (pp. 67–68)

Willis's description doesn't entirely apply to Thurber. Kids didn't sit in rows and usually had some freedom of movement within the room, but they still couldn't go to the bathroom when they wanted, or stand and walk around without a reason, or talk loudly and gesticulate in a way that might attract the teacher's attention, or go to the teacher's lounge and get a soft drink, or decide to go outside after lunch if it was a fine day, or go into the room of a teacher other than their own. As in this scene from my fieldnotes, kids moving from one teacher-dominated space to another (from classroom to lunchroom or classroom to library) were expected walk in single file, facing forward, in silence:

Waiting outside Mrs. Jumpers's classroom for her kids to get back from lunch. Mrs. Kelvin is marching her kids to the class after lunch. As they came to the short flight of steps that separate the library level from classrooms on the third floor, one of the kids lunged down the stairs, skipping the last two steps. Mrs. Kelvin yelled at him and made him come back out of the room, walk up to the top of the stairs, and *walk* down again "one step at a time." The boy went back up the stairs and almost around the corner ("That's far enough," Mrs. Kelvin calls out, maybe thinking he was off down the stairs). As he went down the stairs again, Mrs. Kelvin tried to narrate his motion for him: "Walk, walk, now one, two, three—all right, I said one step at a time." He had taken two steps at a time again, and Mrs. Kelvin made him go back again. This time he went step by step until the last two, which again he took as one. Mrs. Kelvin made him go back again and walk down step by step. "Very good," she compliments him. A little while later, she lets Frasier go to the bathroom. "Walk, Frasier." He looked over his shoulder until he thought she wasn't looking and then sprinted for the bathroom. "Frasier," Mrs. Kelvin called out, "come back here. Go back in the room. You'll have to wait till later." After this the fifth graders move down the hall toward the lunchroom, lurching, jumping up steps, talking to each other. Much the same kind of behavior that Mrs. Kelvin's kids were reprimanded for.

As Lucy explained, sometimes whole classes were made to display their bodily submission as punishment for an individual's infraction: "This school is very weird, okay? You know what they…this class is really weird. This whole school is. You know why? If one person talks, in the hallway, the whole class has to walk up and down the steps, five times!"

CIVILIZING BODIES

Step-walking pedagogy and the bathroom stroll are good examples of tactics used to discipline kids' bodies. They focused on suppressing exuberance, speed, the display of affect, in a word, the "childish" uses of the body. As Barrie Thorne (1993) pointed out, the first things an adult notices in working with young kids are their "playful uses of their bodies, their little experiments in motion and sound" (p. 15). But school squeezes out these experiments. Thorne saw them only on the playground, and I saw them only rarely outside transitional spaces. When I took kids out of the room, either to work with them on a class task or for interviews, they seemed to explode physically and dart into spaces usually forbidden to them. They wanted to run down the halls, slide down the stairway handrail, and begged me to let them ride the elevator. Walking silently was anathema. Even when I got them to a work space, I could barely control their movement: They would rock and spin in the chairs, hop up and down, try to kick each other or play fight, or jump up and dance. All this energy was bottled up in the classroom. "Growing up," as Thorne (1993) suggested, might be seen as a "process of reigning in bodily and imaginative possibilities" (p. 16).

Growing up, however, has not always meant what it means now. The reining in of the body that takes place in elementary school has historical roots in the progressive tightening of bodily control throughout European society from the 16th to the 18th centuries—the regulation of body functions such as farting, pissing, spitting; the development of "manners" and "civilized behavior." Shilling (1993, pp. 164–167) summarized Elias's (1978) analysis of this process in terms of the "socialization," "rationalization," and "individualization" of the body.

Socialization refers to the "hiding away of natural functions" (as in the example of farting discussed shortly), *rationalization* to the development of "self-controls" which defer gratification and the immediate expression of emotions or feelings (as in the silent lunch and its emphasis on talking quietly or not at all; Shilling, 1993, p. 164). Although the socialized and rationalized body is now taken for granted, Elias (1978) showed that it is a relatively recent innovation. And as Bourdieu (1977) pointed out, it is far from innocent. One of the most powerful ways for social orders to shape the dispositions of their members is to "embody" principles of social practice by emphasizing the "seemingly most insignificant details of *dress, bearing*, physical and verbal *manners*" [italics origianl] (p. 94). This is a kind of:

> implicit pedagogy, capable of instilling a whole cosmology, an ethic, a metaphysic, a political philosophy, through injunctions as insignificant as "stand up straight" or "don't hold your knife in your left hand."...The whole trick of pedagogic reason lies precisely in the way it extorts the essential

while seeming to demand the insignificant: in obtaining the respect for form and forms of respect which constitute the most visible and at the same time the best-hidden (because most "natural") manifestation of submission to the established order. . .. The concessions of *politeness* always contain *political* concessions. (Bourdieu, 1977, pp. 94–95).

Kids are taught to raise their hands to speak rather than blurt out what they know or think, to line up single file and move as a disciplined group up and down the halls, to sit quietly and focus their energies for long periods on things on paper, and along with their teachers in elementary school, to regulate their bowels and bladders and learn to eat in a narrowly prescribed time and space. As Gramsci (1971) put it approvingly, "Studying too is a job, and a very tiring one, with its own particular apprenticeship—involving muscles and nerves as well as intellect" (p. 42).

Gramsci to the contrary, the effect of socialization and rationalization is not to create a unity of "intellect" and "muscles" but to create the image that they are separate. Silence and motionlessness are treated as necessary requirements for the work with representations—reading, writing, math—which lies at the center of school learning. Such bodily practices are taken to signal that the body has been conquered, melted away to leave mind and intelligence. This process is what Shilling (1993) called *individualization*—the acquired perception of the body as separate from the mind and self:

> Individuals tend to conceptualize themselves as separate from others, with the body acting as the container for the self or, as Wittgenstein puts it, "an empty tube which is simply inflated by the mind" (Wright, 1980: 11)....People come to construct an "affective wall between their bodies and those of others."...Smells, sounds and actions come to be associated more and more with specific individuals rather than with the species in general (Duroche, 1990). Distance came to be created between bodies, and the flesh of humans became a source of embarrassment. (Shilling, 1993, pp. 166, 167).

This idea of the body as a bounded container (critical to the idea, noted in chapter 1, that teaching is an internal capacity of teachers) pervades popular discourse. E. Martin (1994), in her study of immune system imagery, argued:

> The portrait of the body conveyed most often and most vividly in the mass media shows it as a defended nation-state, organized around a hierarchy of gender, race and class. In this picture, the boundary between the body ("self") and the external world ("nonself") is rigid and absolute. (pp. 51–53)

This boundary between the body and the world doubles as a boundary between childhood and adulthood. The bounded, individualized body is a historically specific ideal of *adult* embodiment. As European styles of manners and bodily dispositions changed to require greater and greater bodily control and suppression, the amount kids had to learn, and the embodied distance between kids and adults, increased.

Consider one example Elias (1978) discussed: farting. Sixteenth-century texts advised readers that "retaining wind" is unhealthy. Farting, even in public, was *prescribed*, not *proscribed*, and youngsters were merely advised to fart quietly or to cough to cover the sound. Two hundred years later, however, similar texts define flatulence in company as impolite (with or without noise) (Elias, 1978, pp. 130, 132). Nowadays, of course, the inappropriateness of farting in public is considered so basic that it doesn't rate mention at all.

Elias (1978) argued that this privitization of farting is one aspect of the historical process of regulating the body which has created a "profound discrepancy between the behavior of so-called 'adults' and children. The children have in the space of a few years to attain the advanced level of shame and revulsion that has developed over many centuries" (p. 140).

The 9-, 10-, and 11-year-olds I worked with had clearly not reached the adults' "advanced level," but they *were* conscious of adult sensibilities. In one of my last interviews with the fifth-grade group, I offered to serve as a conduit and carry their views to the teachers:

Jan:	You're going to be gone [to middle school next year], beyond the reach of the teachers—but if you want to tell me anything that I can take back to them, about what they should do, uh, from a student's perspective. What kind of changes they should make—what you thought about—
Lucy:	Okay!! *You* should be mean to the teachers!
Helen:	Oh, I like Miss Jumpers—in a far-off, *very* far-off way.
Neal:	This is my, this is my—
Lucy:	Don't fart at the teachers.
Helen:	Miss Jumpers has made two people go out of the room for that.
Neal:	She's okay, but sometimes she's real flaky.
Helen:	She gets stupid at times.
Lucy:	Don't fart at the teachers! They cannot stand the smell.
Helen:	Miss Jumpers uses the air freshener every time somebody lets one. Goes right by, Sh-sh [*Mimics getting sprayed in the face*]. Shower freshness! [*Kids laughing*] [*Sings*] "This deodorant helps keep odor away!"

What would have been acceptable behavior from an adult in the 16th century is barely tolerated from children now (and the discomfort such behavior causes adults can be a source of merriment for kids). Over the centuries the body and bodily functions have been progressively restricted as "the positive pleasure component in certain functions" is suppressed "more and more strongly by the arousal of anxiety" or by making this pleasure "private" and "secret" and associating it with "displeasure, revulsion, [and] distaste" (Elias, 1978, pp. 142–143).

By the age of 10 the kids could already look back on their earlier lack of bodily control—in the following example, Lucy's peeing in her seat—though not yet with the shame and revulsion Elias described.

> *Lucy*: Oh! In kindergarten, Miss Pollard she pulled my hair and made me pee in my seat! [*Laughter*]
>
> *Helen*: [*Laughing*] She made her pee in her seat.
>
> *Lucy*: I had to use the bathroom—
>
> *Helen*: My teacher never would have done that; my teacher used to bring her puppy in and let us play with it. She had big hair though—
>
> *Lucy*: Uh, Mrs. Pollard, she goes [*In a monster voice*] "You can't go!" I started to cry—
>
> *Helen*: My teacher was like 21. She had big hair!
>
> *Lucy*: —and all at once I started to pee.

In Lucy's anecdote, the teacher exerts a specifically bodily control over students, and as a child, Lucy's response is bodily: She loses control of her bladder. At the same time, Lucy and the others used a body-centered vocabulary to describe Mrs. Pollard and other teachers: Adults had "big hair," scary voices, and exaggerated physical features. Kids didn't simply express dislike for Mrs. West; they inscribed their dislike in their depictions of her body:

> *Helen*: That old lady was so wrinkled you could fit Niagara Falls in one of those wrinkles. [*Laughter*]
>
> *Lucy*: She dug her nails in my back!
>
> *Helen*: When I had a cut on my arm? She stuck her nails like that, and she would *pull* you around the room.
>
>   . . .
>
> *Earl*: Oh, what about Mrs. Boggs?
>
> *Lucy*: Mrs. Boggs is like this [*Makes a weird face*]
>
> *Helen*: She's got so many wrinkles [around] her eyes.
>
> *Lucy*: Mrs. West.
>
> *Helen*: She's so old and wrinkled she popped her eyes out of her head.
>
> *Earl*: Her teeth are yellow. [*Laughter*]

The kids' descriptions invoke what Bakhtin (1968), in his work on the 16th-century writer Rabelais, described as the canon of the "grotesque body." "The grotesque," he noted, "starts when the exaggeration reaches fantastic dimensions"—wrinkles big as Niagara Falls—when "attention is given to the shoots and branches, to all that prolongs the body and links it to other bodies or to the world outside" (pp. 315–317)—the long fingernails and eyes bulging out of the head. This is the 16th-century body that Elias (1978) described, one that might fart and piss unselfconsiously. And like Elias, Bakhtin (1968) described the "civilized" successor body in which extensions and orifices have been withdrawn or closed off:

> The new bodily canon...presents an entirely finished, completed, strictly limited body, which is shown from the outside as something individual. That which protrudes, bulges, sprouts, or branches off...is eliminated, hidden, or moderated. All orifices of the body are closed. (p. 320)

This civilized body is a schooled body, one that stays silent, walks in line, keeps its hands to itself, and doesn't get out of its chair and walk around the room. Rose (1993) argued that this image is also gendered, that the classical body is one which has lost its "vulgar and feminine orifices and excretions" and replaced them with an "enlightened masculine mind...clearly separate from and untainted by its body" (p. 77). And Sibley (1995) and Corbin (1986) have suggested that this body is class specific, a bourgeois or middle-class body supposedly free from the sweat, smells, bodily urges, and needs of poor people or the working classes.

The consecration of this bounded, classical body at Thurber—the attempt to produce quiet, studious kids with socialized, rationalized, and individualized bodies—played a key role in shaping the meanings of genders and in defining the differences between kids and adults and between African Americans and European Americans. A basic tool for orchestrating these distinctions was the organization of space and activity within classrooms.

ORGANIZING BODIES IN SPACE

The problem of organizing bodies in classroom space is usually examined from the teacher's perspective, as a problem of controlling students and managing activity. But from a kid's point of view, the classroom is a negotiable terrain. There is surveillance, but it is hardly suffocating. I was always surprised and a little nervous that students would casually engage me in conversations when I was in the room, regardless of what the teacher was doing. But teachers and observers simply can't monitor much of what students do (cf. Alton-Lee, Nuthall, & Patrick, 1993). As a result, kids snatched little stretches of time and space for their own purposes, usually for talking to their friends (cf. de Certeau, 1984). Talking, however, was constrained by the organization of their bodies in the room. Kids weren't allowed to move their desks, and they couldn't get up and move through the room at will. Desk arrangements were a key component of classroom management systems. One of the teachers' main tactics for controlling students was to move them physically—temporarily into the corners (for "time out"), or out into the hall (for a stern chat), or for longer times, by physically moving their desks away from those of others.

Desks were one of the few spaces kids could claim as their own within the classroom, although the claim was not absolute: One of the worst humiliations a teacher could inflict was to force a kid to empty his or her desk. At Thurber, the desks were movable tables with metal legs, plastic tops, and little cubbyholes underneath, which kids filled with enormous amounts of clutter. The desk height was adjustable, although in Mrs. Jumpers's fifth grade all the desks had been assembled at a standard height: For some smaller kids in the class, the desk surface was shoulder high, and they had to stand up to work. In Mrs. Court's class, the desks were at varying heights, although the tallest kid didn't always have the highest desk.

The arrangement of desks in the classroom was of great importance to kids as well as teachers, since it determined whom they could interact with on a regular basis during class. Different teachers arranged kids differently. Mrs. Peel moved desks around every few weeks and claimed that she paid no attention to who ended up near whom; Mrs. Jumpers assigned seats and tended to segregate boys and girls. In Mrs. Court's room, kids argued strongly that their desks should be arranged to allow collaborative work—face to face or side by side, rather than in rows. As Desiree explained: "You can't play games by yourself; you can't do everything by yourself." Another student said, "[In groups] things go faster and you don't have to do everything by yourself." "If you don't know how to spell a word and there's people in your group," Lila added, "you can spell the word without having to walk all around the class asking people." Cicily argued that four desks, two side by side facing two other desks, was the perfect arrangent: A "fifth person wouldn't have anybody else to work with." Mel reduced this even further and claimed that the kids should work in pairs, side by side; that way you wouldn't "have nobody else crowding you and going under the table and kicking you."

These debates about the proper distribution of bodies in classroom space became a focus of activity in Mrs. Court's fourth grade. Once or twice a week in the fall, I worked with a team of kids trying to determine how the class should be physically organized and how kids should be arranged at their desks. The kids developed several models for organizing class space which were notable more for what they suggested than for their practicality. If traditional seating arrangements (the chairs-in-rows model) were designed to maximize the teacher's ability to keep an eye on students and command their attention, the kids' models of desk arrangement turned this notion around. One plan, for example, called for all the desks to be arranged in a square facing inward, allowing the students to look at one another. When I pointed out that the teacher was nowhere in their plan, they said, "Well, she can be in the middle." Although this arrangement may sound like a variant of Bentham's early-19th century, surveillance-oriented "Chrestomathic" school (Markus, 1993), where the teacher sat in the middle of a 12-sided ring of students, Bentham's teacher had six monitors to help him watch students. In a single-teacher classroom, the ring arrangement had the opposite force of the Benthamite design (cf. Foucault, 1979): Instead of allowing the teacher to look in all the kids' faces and monitor the class in a single glance, thereby accomplishing an "invisible omniscience" grounded in a spatial organization that allowed "central and complete inspection" (Bentham, quoted in Markus, 1993, p. 68), Mrs. Court, in her students' plan, would have become the object of surveillance in a situation where her back was always turned to at least some kids.

Not surprisingly, this plan was rejected. The kids' next idea was to arrange the desks in clusters, much as they had been, but with a critical change. Up to this time, the clusters had consisted of two desks facing two other desks, perpendicular to the front of the room. Kids had only to turn to the side slightly to look at the teacher, and the teacher could easily command their attention. In the new plan, the kids would be in clusters of five in a cross pattern. The student in the middle desk would face a friend (with a second friend facing the same direction on her right), but the student behind her would face the other direction, as would the other student on her left. The cluster would really combine a group of two with a group of three facing the other direction. The orientation of the clusters in the room, however, was such that at least one group in each cluster would always have its back to the teacher and to the front of the room.

All these plans turned out to be unworkable for the teachers. After arranging the room their way one Friday, the fourth graders returned the next Monday to find their seats rearranged. Mrs. Court explained to me that she just couldn't stand the new arrangement, so she'd put the desks back in groups of four or five and had not really looked to see "who was sitting with whom."

The kids were upset with the change. Glenn, who'd been telling me just a few days earlier how much he disliked the old seating arrangement, said, "This is terrible!"

"But you didn't like the way it was," I reminded him.

"This is worse," he replied. "I can't work with Lila and Kerri," the two African American girls he was now to be seated with, who pretended not to have heard and didn't look at Glenn.

Cindy, who was good friends with Kerri, heard Glenn and responded with her own complaint when she realized she was facing Karl and Doug. "I can't work with boys!" she cried. "Boys are stupid; I don't want to sit with boys." She punctuated her comments by giving Karl a couple of kicks in the shin, but he, like Lila and Kerri, refused to acknowledge the insults.

Mel scoped out the arrangment and tried to figure out a pattern. "I bet it's two boys and two girls at each table," he told me, but I pointed out that one grouping had three boys, including Felix. "Felix doesn't count" [as a boy], Mel informed me. "Felix messes with his sisters' dolls." (Actually, Felix was simply one of the two boys in the class who liked to interact with girls.) The other boys tried hard to separate themselves from girls. Several responded to the new desk arrangement by trying to define the sovereignty of their desk space now that it was in territory shared with girls. They cut cardboard strips to a size they could wedge into their desk openings to create doors with "Warning Keep Out" written on them. Mel and Glenn even tried to set up borders around their social space by starting a kind of club. They had little cardboard badges reading MMD. Glenn couldn't remember the meaning, but Mel explained that MMD was Mel's Mad Dogs. Each had a little card reading "That is the Question." After a few weeks, Mel presented me with one and explained—quite loudly, as he was sitting in the middle of the room and I was in a corner, and everyone was supposed to be working—that if someone asked me "To be or not to be" (the group's password), I was to show the card in response rather than answering verbally.

Some of the fifth-grade boys were just as adamant as the fourth graders about keeping the genders separated. In Mrs. Jumpers's room there was already some segregation. A group of six girls worked at a table in the back of the room, while the other groupings in the room had both boys (always in the majority) and one or two girls. When I was talking to Alf and Duane, they began to tell me whom they'd like to sit at a table with them:

Jan: No girls?

Alf: No.

Duane: They're the mongooses. They already got a table of their own.

Alf: Yeah! All the girls get to sit beside each other.

Duane: I know, we don't like their kind.

Alf: The back table's always loud, and that's where they sit, and Miss Jumpers never moves them.

Duane: They go [Makes stupid noise].

Jan:	How come they get to sit together?
Alf:	'Cause she likes them; she's a girl. If she was a man teacher she, he'd let the boys do it.
Duane:	[*Laughing*] "She."
Alf:	*He'd* let the boys.
Jan:	Have you ever had a man teacher?
Alf:	Yeah, second grade I did.
Duane:	No. I had mongooses.
Alf:	[*Laughing*] Mongooses.
Duane:	And roaches.

When the fifth graders went on field trips, they would divide themselves into groups segregated by race and gender, as they did in the lunchroom—unless they had been given assigned seats in punishment for misbehavior.

Often when I'd walk into the cafeteria to eat lunch with the fourth graders, kids would call out (much to the dismay of the cafeteria aides, the "lunch ladies," as the kids called them) and ask me to sit with them. The boys would always frame this in terms of gender solidarity. As Mel put it one day: "This is the boys' table. Sit here. You can sit here or here."

Iggy added: "You can't sit at the girls' table."

"What happens to me if I sit at the girls' table?" I asked.

"You turn into a girl."

Sheila, who'd been listening to this exchange, countered and said of the boys: "That's the crybabies table." I took a seat with the girls anyway and didn't turn into a girl—nor did the boys hold it against me (or even seem surprised). As Moore (1994) pointed out, following Bourdieu (1977), "Symbolic meanings are not inherent in the organization of space, but have to be invoked through the activities of social actors" (p. 76). *Had* I sat with the boys, I would have reinforced or consecrated the gendered meanings of the tables and of the act of sitting at a particular table. Sitting with the girls strategically reconstructed the link between gender and seating, although not as it would have had I been a fourth grader. My sitting at the girls' table probably just announced that I was claiming the adult's privilege of refusing to play the game.

BOUNDARY WORK

The seating patterns are just one illustration of the boundaries between boys and girls already entrenched by the time they reached fourth grade. Kids not only insisted on the differences but suggested that adults were involved in their creation. Mel assumed that Mrs. Court had purposely divided girls and boys; Alf and Duane insisted that Mrs. Jumpers favored girls by letting them sit together and that a male teacher would have allowed the boys the same right.

Much research on these kinds of gender divisions uses gender as an explanatory variable and treats gender categories as if they were stable and well defined. Findings take the form of categorical statements about how members of a gender behave in a given domain of activity. Sheldon (1993), for example, echoed an influential line of thought that extends far beyond sociolinguistics when she suggested that "male speech" is "competition oriented, or adversarial" and "female speech" is "collaboration oriented, or affiliative" (p. 87).

One problem with such accounts is that they obscure how gendered behaviors vary by race (Stack, 1991), class (Stacey, 1990), and the social organization of activity. Whyte (1983) and Reay (1991), for example, described girls as cooperative in all-girl groups but more competitive in mixed-sex groups. Eder (1990, 1993; Eder, Evans, & Parker, 1995) showed that competitive ritual insulting, once thought to be a male proclivity, is common among some working-class adolescent girls (although the insults function differently among girls than among boys). Eder's (1990) point that "females do not share a single style of speech" (p. 83) could probably be extended to males and to most forms of action.

Those who explore variations in the actions and experiences of members of different social groups—whether difference is framed as gender, class, culture, race, or language—take for granted what should be a focus of inquiry: the practices that produce and maintain difference. Instead of asking how often and in what groupings boys and girls do certain things, we must ask how the meanings of gender get created and maintained; how actions come to be gendered; how action sequences come to be recognized as, say, adversarial as opposed to cooperative. Barrie Thorne (1993) suggested that gender is more an ongoing accomplishment than a simple attribute (cf. Connell, 1987). Thorne pointed out that much research producing statements about "male" and "female" behaviors has focused on activities within same-sex groups (e.g., Hughes, 1988; Lever, 1976). Thorne argued that encounters *across* gender lines, encounters she called borderwork (cf. Rosaldo, 1989), play an equally key role in gender constructions:

> [G]roups may...interact with one another in ways that strengthen their borders. One can gain insight into the maintenance of ethnic (and gender) groups by examining the boundary that defines them rather than by looking at what Barth [1969] calls "the cultural stuff that it encloses." (Thorne, 1993, p. 65)

Thorne's point is that we must look at how oppositions such as male–female are constructed rather than taking them for granted or using them as explanations. Such thinking does not deny biological differences between the sexes, but as Connell (1987, pp. 80–81) pointed out, biology is not sufficient to distinguish genders. Instead, markers such as dress and manners become important tools of distinction.[2] Gender becomes a kind of performance or construction that draws on the body as a resource for meaning-making, even as it shapes the body's meaning (Butler, 1990, p. 139).

To the extent that forms of bodily engagement—running, skating, talking, and so on—are suppressed at school, as part of the socialization of the body Elias spoke of, performances of gender become more like displays. The body serves as a visual tableau, something to be looked at rather than something heard, felt, or smelled. Kids begin moving into the position of de Certeau's (1984) observer atop a skyscraper, focusing on visible totalities. In concrete terms, importance is increasingly attached to visible signs of gender, race, age. Kids begin to worry about their physical appearance. Lila, for example, interviewed Tina about the latter's body worries, her sense that people made fun of her:

> *Lila*:   What do you think about yourself that is very embarassing?
>
> *Tina*:   My weight.
>
> *Lila*:   How much do you weigh?
>
> *Tina*:   200.

In fact, Tina weighed nothing near 200 pounds; she was not even particularly chubby. Yet her worries about appearance led her to stop wearing her glasses; which meant she could barely read some of the class material and had to painfully hunch over her desk with her face to the page. Performances of gender through displays of dress and physical appearance were not, however, the only body-focused gender performances in which kids engaged. Many layers of meanings were added through performances of physical aggressiveness such as chase games and fights.

CHASE GAMES

Thorne (1993), studying playground activities, pointed to chase games as activities that "dramatically affirm boundaries between girls and boys" (p. 68). Chase games at Thurber were uncommon simply because unstructured outdoor activity was uncommon. But they did happen, at least among the fourth graders (Mrs. Jumpers's fifth-grade class wasn't

---

[2]This emphasis on external markers is a consequence of socializing the body, discussed by Elias (1978): When bodily functions are hidden away or suppressed, they can no longer serve to differentiate individuals, and dress and deportment become increasingly important.

allowed outside to play during the time I was with them in the spring
of 1993) and always on the blacktopped basketball courts. Kids would
shout out the frame for activity; boys would chase girls; then a girl would
get tired and shout, "Girls chase boys." The chase seemed to be played
as a variant of freeze tag; once caught, kids would stand motionless until
the direction of the chase shifted. There was little tackling or rough
activity, perhaps because nobody wanted to fall on the hard surface, but
probably also because the teacher was always present and monitoring
activity confined to a small space. I saw no boy-chase-boy or girl-chase-
girl variants, and it was not the case; in contrast to Thorne's (1993)
findings, that the girls were less rough or "far less bodily engaged" than
were the boys (p. 69). Indeed, in the only instance I know of in which the
chase escalated into something resembling a fight, the girls were the
aggressors. This happened on an unusual day when Mrs. Court was
meeting a parent during the lunch period, and the kids were outside
under the supervision of another teacher. I didn't see the fight myself
but heard about it from the kids, two of whom, Shirley and Brenda,
decided to write a newsletter report on the event and conducted these
taped interviews with their classmates:

Shirley: Glenn, we would like to ask you questions about what happened at the playground.

Glenn: Well, I would describe it as obscene. I mean, what I saw was
a bunch of girls just ganged up and started yelling things like
"we're going to beat up the boys; they're wimpy" and stuff like
that.

Shirley: Can you tell us exactly what happened, like from the beginning?

Glenn: Well, I, along with Karl—a few girls were coming towards us
and we just walked away. And that's it. Karl *tried* to hit one of
them, but that was it.

Shirley: Do you know *why* Karl tried to hit one of them?

Glenn: Well, he was probably just mad.

Shirley: Do you know exactly what a girl did to Karl, or was he just
mad because other girls were picking on the boys?

Glenn: I think it was because other girls were picking on the boys.

Shirley: Thank you....Okay, Karl, could you tell us exactly what happened on the playground?

Karl: No.

Brenda: You were trying to threaten a girl or a girl was trying to
threaten you?

Karl: Well, yeah, I tried to punch Effie.

Shirley: Why did you want to punch her? Were you mad because the girls were chasing after the boys or because she was just picking on you?

Karl: Picking on me.

Shirley: Do you know exactly the words she said?

Karl: Not exactly.

Shirley: Can you tell us a little bit of what she said?

Karl: "Boys are wimps. I'm gonna beat you all up."

Shirley: Do you know exactly why she said that? Was it because the other girls said it?

Karl: I guess.

Brenda: Okay, Cicily is our next person. Can you tell us about what happened on Friday at the playground, please?

Cicily: First, we were playing the Chinese game. It was boring. So I said—this is the usual game we play; girls chase boys, and boys chase girls—so I said, let's play that. We all went over there, and said, "Girls chase boys, and boys chase girls." And then somebody, I just all of a sudden heard somebody say, uh, "Girls *hit* boys," and I didn't even see who it was. So I just got out of the group, when they said, "Boys hit girls, girls hit boys." And then I saw that some of these people, we was getting in line, was beatin' up Mel; they was kickin' his butt. I felt sorry for the boy, but I didn't get in it because I'd get in trouble too. I just didn't pay no attention to it; I just stayed out of it.

Shirley: Hold on, Cicily, why didn't you go to the teacher and tell her what was happenin'?

Cicily: Why didn't I go to the teacher and tell her what was happening? Because I thought she knew! 'Cause Miss Engels, she was helping them, right, and then everybody started fighting and stuff so I got out of it. And I thought Miss Engels, she had looked up. And I thought she was going to say something. And then she said, "Get in line." And I didn't get to tell her nothing. So she said, "If you have anything to say, write it on a piece of paper, and give it to the teacher." So that's what I did.

Shirley: Was this outside or inside?

Cicily: When I did what?

Shirley: When you took a piece of paper to write what happened.

Cicily: It was inside.

Like most events among the kids, this fight had no simple reading. It seems in some ways to be the kind of gender borderwork Thorne (1993) discussed. But we can't assume that an interaction is entirely about gender divisions simply because it involves boys and girls differentiating themselves. Shirley, Effie, and Cicily were African Americans; Glenn, Mel, and Karl were European Americans. The event was as much racial as gender borderwork. And there was also, both in the fight and in the interviews about it, some adult–child borderwork going on. Shirley mimicked a common teacher speech style by asking her interviewees to describe exactly what happened and then to explain their motivations and the motivations of the other kids.[3] She also invoked the ideas that teachers are responsible for kids' bodies and that kids should concede this responsibility by telling teachers when events like this unfolded. Cicily described the flattening out of bodily practice in inscriptions when she recounted the teacher's command to "write down" what happened. The teacher herself was described as responding to the fractious body play by enforcing bodily routinization: making the kids get in line.

The incident suggests that the meaning of fighting and physical threat in general were tightly intertwined with the meanings of gender and race. In the remainder of this chapter, I focus on the ways kids and adults alike read physical encounters through lenses of gendered and racialized meanings. Fights were not always about issues of gender or race; but whatever their immediate causes, they became parts of the narratives of masculinity, femininity, and race relations that shaped public definitions of kids' motivations and identities in the schools. Indeed, the very definition of a physical encounter as a *fight* depended on the possibility of making sense of it in such terms.

FIGHTING AND BORDERWORK

Among the kids I worked with at Thurber, fighting played a major role in defining what it meant to be a boy or a girl in mixed-sex encounters.

Fighting had a slippery meaning. As labeling theorists long ago pointed out, what counts as a transgression and who becomes a deviant or criminal are social constructions (Becker, 1963; Ditton, 1979). An action becomes a *crime* and its author a *criminal* not by the intrinsic character of the action, but only when a network of people, rules, and procedures impose, broadcast, and maintain these definitions. Similarly, what counted as a *fight* at school and who was taken as a *fighter* depended more on what happened and how people acted before and after the fact than on the act itself.

---

[3]Shirley's line of questioning was interesting in other ways: She was considered a behavioral problem and was being referred for evaluation as "emotionally disturbed." In these interviews, she demonstrated her ability to take the teacher's position and use interrogation methods and questioning strategies that teachers had undoubtedly used with her.

As I came to understand it, a *fight,* in the kids' sense, was a *sequence,* usually of three steps: taunting or threatening, a physical encounter, usually a shove or a punch, and talk and boasting after the fact. A lot of taunts and threats never led to physical attacks, and not all physical attacks were followed by talk or boasting. Without all three elements, however, an encounter was not considered a fight. For example, Neal, a quiet fifth grader, had taken a punch from and then knocked down another kid in the hall one morning before class. The event was brought up in one of my group discussions later in the day.

Helen:	He slammed JW today!
Neal:	He hit me right here, I picked him up and threw him.
Helen:	Didn't really pick him up. He grabbed him by the waist and just went [*Makes crashing noise*]. That little boy landed like this [*Laughs*].
Jan:	Did you get caught?
Neal:	No.
Helen:	Yeah, he got caught, but he didn't get in trouble.
Neal:	We didn't get in trouble.

The same students who referred to some incidents in which one kid merely shoved another as *fights* didn't call Neal's encounter a fight, and Neal didn't either. The definition of an event as a *fight* depended on others to observe or to serve as an audience for a participant's taunts, boasts, or complaints, and Neal hadn't prefaced his actions with taunts or followed them with boasts.

In most cases, the relevant audiences for taunts and boasts consisted of other kids. Adults were either too quick to read playful punches as real aggression or too slow to recognize the potential seriousness of events. One day, for example, I was in the office before school began, talking to Mr. Watts:

An African American girl comes in and says that Wayne hit her on the bus. "Well, what did you say to him?" Mr. Watts asks her.

"Nothin'," she replies. "Just 'Hi, Wayne.'"

"Do you think he likes you?" Mr. Watts asks. She's stone silent, eyes averted. "That's not what you wanted me to say, is it?" Mr. Watts says to her. She remains silent. "What Wayne is this?" Mr. Watts asks.

"Wayne from Mrs. Richards's room," she replies.

"Wayne —?" Watts asks. "That seems out of character for him." The little girl starts to go away. "I'll talk to him," Watts tells her. "Sometimes they go a little crazy in fourth grade." After she leaves, he turns to me and says that they're "always telling on each other. If I took it all seriously, I've have them all in here."

Here, Mr. Watts seemed to dismiss the seriousness of the event at first, and to read it into the peculiar gendered narrative of boys hitting girls because they like them. The little girl, not finding an audience willing to accept her frame for the event, simply left. Without such a narrative frame, even events of relatively severe violence, let alone a punch on the bus, could escape the label *fight*. At Thurber, however, fighting did not usually result in a lot of physical damage. There are obviously cases where kids of this age do others serious harm (e.g., Children's Express, 1993); but at Thurber, shoving rarely progressed to punching, and the punching never went on long enough to be physically conclusive. In large part this was because there was no recess, and there were few transitions such as room changes to give students space for fighting. The fights that did occur took place in gym, in the lunchroom, or in the halls in the morning before the beginning of class. As these were all spaces monitored by adults, the whole economy of physical encounters depended in a sense on the presence of teachers and the certainty of their timely intervention.

Adult surveillence allowed the kids who initiated physical encounters to get in the most punches before the encounters were broken up. As a result the wildest and most aggressive kids, the ones most willing to accept the teachers' sanctions and the resulting boasting rights, acquired reputations as fighters. One of the most notorious fifth-grade fighters, for example, was a small boy named Eddie whom almost any other boy in the fifth grade probably could have overwhelmed in an extended encounter. What made his reputation was his willingness to throw the first blow in almost any situation, even with the certainty of being caught and punished by teachers.

Fights in school thus depended on an audience not just to observe the encounter but to listen to and appropriately interpret the verbal performance of the fight. Concepts of gender were central to audience interpretations, but they were not used in formulaic ways. Kids worked and reworked the links between fighting and gender categories in the process of constructing masculinities and femininities.

Fighting and Femininity

Thorne (1993, p. 103) has suggested that a preoccupation with drawing sharp contrasts between boys' and girls' cultures may have diverted attention from instances of girls making threats and fighting. As a result, most research on fighting among girls has focused on "deviant" groups (e.g., Campbell, 1984; Davies, 1984) and has suggested that girls who fight are atypical or unusual. As should already be clear, this was not the case at Thurber. Many encounters I saw involved or were initiated by girls, and some kids suggested that fighting was at least as common among girls as boys:

Jan: Do girls get in as many fights now as boys?

Earl: Yeah.

Helen: Oh, god! Yeah! Probably more!

Earl: Boys try to stay out of trouble.

This is not to say that fighting and aggressive behavior meant the same thing for boys as for girls: Fighting among boys was a way of constructing masculinities, but girls who fought were not necessarily considered masculine or tomboys. The following anecdote, based on fieldnotes, illustrates how girls could link fighting and physical strength to notions of femininity, at least in mixed-sex interactions.

I was in the library looking for one of my graduate students when I saw a couple of groups of fifth graders working with the encyclopedia and a CD-ROM encyclopedia. Their teacher had given them a "Desert Scavenger Hunt" worksheet, which had questions such as "What is the average day and night temperature" in such and such a desert, and "Where is the Mohave Desert located?" The kids, working in groups, had to find the answers. One of the groups consisted of Sondra, Rona, Molly, Elwood, and Sissy (all European American, except Molly, who was African American). Sondra, a tiny, studious girl from a religious family, seemed to be the group leader. She was seated at a table working with encyclopedias, while the others circulated around the table.

Elwood and Rona waited near the CD-ROM player for a turn. To use the electronic encyclopedia, kids spelled out words and then did title or word searches. Elwood was trying to get the answer to a question about common desert flowers, but when he finally got his chance at the computer, he slowly typed "Desertflower," did a title search, and came up with nothing. Rona, who'd been waiting impatiently, struggled with Elwood over the control device and finally pulled it away from him. Elwood lunged for it, but Rona shoved him back so hard he almost fell. The two sat down, and Rona typed "flower" and hit Title Search. Up on the screen popped *The Flowers of Evil*. "Huh?" She opened the file and found a paragraph discussing Beaudelaire and *Les Fleurs du mal*. She and several other kids stared at it a minute until they realized it had nothing to do with desert flowers; then somebody said, "My turn" and took the control from Rona. Elwood and Rona went unhappily back to the table.

Sissy scolded them upon their return for not helping. "We were trying to get the answer to one of them," Elwood protested, but Molly informed him that they already had that answer. Rona then realized she didn't have her copy of the handout, and she started digging around through the books and the other girls' papers. This angered Sissy so much that I thought for a moment she was going to punch Rona. "It's not here!" Sissy shouted at her. "You took it over to the computer!" She bounced an encyclopedia volume across the table at Rona.

Sondra, who was sitting between the two of them, said to Sissy, "Now be nice." She picked up the book and handed it to Rona and said prettily, "Would you please put this away for me?"

Rona, however, turned away with a mean look on her face and did not acknowledge Sondra. Sondra got up and returned the book to the shelf herself. While she was gone, Molly shook her head and said, with a mixture of pity and wonder, "Sondra's so nice."

Sissy curled her lip: "It makes me sick!"

Meanwhile, Elwood continued to seethe from his ill treatment at the girls' hands. He vented some of his rage against me by trying to force me to give him an answer. Looking up at me suddenly, he asked: "What's the answer to number 6?" Question number 6 asked, "What is unusual about the Mesquite tree?"

"I don't know," I replied truthfully and tried to remember something about mesquite trees.

Elwood looked at me glumly and insisted, "Yes, you do!"

Molly saved me by informing Elwood, again, that "we already got *that* one."

To get away from Elwood, I went around the table to look at what Molly was doing, and so I missed part of an exchange between Rona and Elwood that ended with Rona saying: "You say if I hit you again you'll knock me into the Stone Age? I'd like to see you try."

The girls all heard this and laughed at Elwood, who got furious. He turned to Molly and said, "I'll hit you with a chair."

Molly didn't even look up from her work: "I'll take your head off. You don't mess with women like me."

The other girls broke into laughter again. Sondra looked up and told Elwood in her calm, serious way that "women can be a lot stronger than you think." The other girls agreed, and Sissy and Molly swapped tales about women doing things like picking up cars to rescue babies. None of them seem to take Elwood's threats seriously. Instead, they countered by defining their bodies as powerful and potentially violent, although their main example, women using superhuman strength to protect babies, drew on traditional images of women as caregivers.

Threat and violence were wrapped up here with a conception of femininity not as vulnerable and needing protection from boys, but as physically self-assured. The girls referred to themselves as women in responding to Elwood and invoked a concept of adult femininity that seemed to come into play mainly in response to boys' aggressive acts.

Adult femininity, however, was tensely connected to other gendered narratives employed by the girls.

Sexuality was one of these narratives. In the interview leading up to the following exchanges, Lucy had been taunting Helen about liking particular boys. The boys she named were not, in fact, ones Helen liked. Several were notoriously unattractive, and Helen was clearly becoming irritated by Lucy's jibes. When later in the conversation I attempted to follow up a topic Helen had raised, Lucy seized the opportunity to embarrass Helen, and Helen manipulated the topic into a reprisal against Lucy. Although I have edited the transcript for reasons of space, the escalation of taunts into a physical encounter unfolds clearly here (I address the striking use of pop culture imagery in this exchange in the next chapter):

Jan: You raised movies Helen. What kind of movies do you watch?

Helen: Horror movies.

Earl: What kind of movies do we watch?

Jan: Horror movies? Like what?

Duane: Rap movies, rap movies.

Lucy: You want me to tell you what she told me at lunch? She told me she watches rated X movies!

Helen: I said my *dad* watched them—

Lucy: No! You said you watched them—

Helen: —*and* I was talking to Muffy, so I don't think it was any of your business!

           . . .

Jan: What about you, Neal? You've been quiet over there.

Helen: Have you ever seen the movie *Mad Max* Lucy?

Neal: Oh yeah, I liked that one.

Earl: That was a scary movie, man. That was weird!

           . . .

Helen: I'm gonna get a motorcycle Lucy. I think I want to get a motorcycle Lucy. I'm gonna get a motorcycle, a badge, and a gun, and I'm gonna come after you Lucy! [*Laughter*]

Lucy: [*Untranscribable; unclear because Helen is talking so loudly*].

Helen: When I grow up, I'm gonna get a motorcycle, a gun, and a badge, and I'm commin' after your butt.

           . . .

Lucy: She [*Helen*] kisses Barney!

Helen: Lucy,

Jan: Lucy—

Helen: I'm gonna make you kiss the floor in a minute.

   . . .

Duane: Here's what Lucy's gonna be saying—

Lucy: [*Puts her mouth on the microphone*] Helen's a dog! Helen's a dog!

Helen: Hey Lucy, let's put it this way; after I hit you, you're gonna be going, "Helen's gonna knock me out!"

Lucy: After I finish with you—

   . . .

Helen: Lucy, you couldn't touch me.

I'd been trying, without success, to stop Helen and Lucy from baiting each other, but at this point I gave up and ended the interview. As I got up to take the group back to class, Helen lunged at Lucy and punched her on the arm. I got between them, but once we were out in the hall, Lucy punched Helen in the shoulder and then ran down the hall to the classroom where her teacher saw her and scolded her for running.

This argument has to be understood first as a situated performance by the two girls for an audience that included me and two boys, Earl and Duane. When I later interviewed Lucy and Helen without these boys around there was no conflict between them although they were not close friends. As a situated performance, the argument seemed to be about the narrative construction of Helen's femininity, and in particular the sexualization of this narrative by Lucy. Lucy taunted Helen about whom she supposedly liked and about her supposedly watching X-rated films. Helen's response was to invoke a male body and reframe herself in an explicitly male narrative drawn from the Australian movie *Mad Max*, in which evil bikers and leather-clad cops battle each other, and women characters function mainly as targets of male violence. It is a narrative of control and in another sense a narrative of maturity and (male) sexuality: both in terms of the content of the movie (Helen inserts herself into an adult, powerful role), and because the movie itself is an "adult," R-rated film. Lucy's response to Helen's attack was to try to infantilize her by linking her to Barney, a dinosaur who hosts a popular television show for very young children.

Fighting and Masculinity

The overlap of sexuality narratives and maturity narratives also appeared in the boys' attempts to construct gendered selves. Boys had two ways of performing masculinity. One was fighting, which I'll examine in a moment. The other was a public preoccupation with sports. Boys could claim masculine identities among their peers by allying themselves, though popular media products, with hypermasculine sports allies distant in space and time. I discuss this process in greater detail in the next chapter, but in a nutshell what I mean is that a public preoccupation with sports was an assertion that a boy was a member of an indisputably male domain, an assertion made plausible by the continuing dominance of men's sports in the popular media and by the boys' refusal to talk with girls about sports, even when girls knew demonstrably more about the subject than the boys did. Actual participation in organized team activity was much less important in establishing masculinity than constant talk about it, in part, perhaps, because girls were as likely to be as active and as proficient as boys in team sports such as basketball. But sports talk was also important because boys could use it to define their masculinity without direct reference to girls. In the following short exchange, Duane's declaration of sports-love is clearly offered as an alternative to the other kids' talk about boyfriends and girlfriends.

Lucy: You're going together?

Helen: No! I'm not going with him.

          [*Everybody talking at once*]

Jan: All right, I know that's a big deal, and probably more important to you than math [which is what I'd been trying to get them to talk about]—

Chorus: Yeah!

Earl: My girlfriend don't like me no more.

Duane: I like basketball!!

If aligning themselves with sports was a way for boys to establish their masculinity apart from girls, fighting was a way to construct localized masculinities that depended in part, for the fifth-grade boys at least, on relationships with girls. Among the fourth graders, only two boys, Wally and Felix, would admit to "liking" girls. Both were stigmatized because of it, although girls talked pretty openly about which boys they liked. Among fifth graders, by contrast, it was acceptable, even status enhancing, for a boy to have a girlfriend. The following exchange was prompted by the fact that Earl had been forced to go to a company picnic with his mom instead of to his girlfriend's birthday party.

Helen: I think today we should talk about girlfriends and boyfriends, considering Earl forgot his girlfriend's birthday!

Earl: We'd have to leave Duane and Neal out of this conversation.

Helen: Yeah, yeah.

Earl: No! We can't talk about that, we have to have everybody in the conversation.

Helen: Well, they've had girlfriends.

Duane: I have!

Helen: [*To Neal*] Have you ever had a girlfriend?

Neal: [*Speaking in a distorted nasal voice*] No.

Helen: No wonder, you're ugly.

Jan: Be nice here!

Duane: I don't want a girlfriend!

Helen: See, he'll still be in the conversation, he don't want a girlfriend.

Earl: Well, for good reason too! 'Cause they drive you crazy. And you've got to watch what you say in class. You can't act up.

Duane: I don't want to end up like that.

Helen: He's a girl.

Earl: He can act up all he wants to; around the girls, he can hate everybody too! [*Pause*] But when you've got a girlfriend, you've got to watch out!

Helen: You've got to learn to fight better too, Earl.

Neal: That's a big decision.

Earl: I know how to fight already, but I just don't like to.

Helen: [*Sarcastic*] He don't like to hurt nobody.

In this conversation, Earl's behavior was constrained in a seemingly contradictory way by his relationship with a girl. Having a girlfriend meant that he had to act better, but it also meant he had to be ready to fight. A boy who didn't have a girlfriend could "act up" and engage in insults and play-fighting with other boys without necessarily precipitating a sequence of events that would turn it into a "fight." Having a girlfriend, however, defined an additional audience for public, physical encounters, and as an audience of "strangers," the girls reduced the flexibility of interpretive frames and made it more difficult for boys to redefine encounters as nonfights. Acting up or acting hateful in the presence of a girl became more problematic, as such actions much more easily became defined as fights.[4]

---

[4]In fourth- and fifth-grade boys' talk, the absence of predatory sexual attitudes commonly reported in studies of slightly older boys (e.g., Mac an Ghaill, 1994; Willis, 1981) might reflect a displacement of such attitudes into comments about representations or imagined spaces (e.g., girls and sexual situations portrayed on television; see chap. 5.)

Having a girlfriend could also increase the likelihood of a boy's fighting because boys were expected to protect their girlfriends and retaliate for insults or attacks. Just which offenses required a response was something negotiated, however. In the next exchange, Helen tried to position Earl so that he'd be compelled to fight in response to another boy's harrassment of his girlfriend:

Helen: JW hit your girlfriend on the leg, twice, with a match.

Earl: When?

Helen: On the bus.

Jan: This was coming back from [the field trip]?

Earl: Coming back or going?

Helen: Coming back. He hit your girlfriend on the leg with two lit matches.

Earl: Lit matches? He wasn't sitting beside her though.

Helen: He was sitting behind her.

Earl: Sitting behind her.

Helen: And I was sitting in the same seat with her, so I should know.

Earl: You ain't lyin' are you, just to get me to beat him up?

Helen: No, I'm not lying.

Duane: Helen, so was Alice.

Helen: I know; Alice got hit in the back of the leg with them too. And so did I.

Earl: It wouldn't hurt that bad, would it?

Helen: Yeah.

Neal: Yeah, fire hurts, you know.

Earl: I've been burnt by a glue gun fire and stuff.

Duane: I cooked marshmallows over a candle, burnt my fork!

Helen: On your legs? You don't shave your legs. It's more painful that way, believe me!

The exchange produced an occasion for Helen to differentiate boys and girls bodily and to position herself within a femininity defined in terms of physical vulnerability and weakness in interactions with boys. She could insert herself, along with the other girls, into a gendered narrative with the somewhat unwilling Earl as protagonist. This construction of vulnerable femininity was merely a strategic one, however, and was by no means the only way girls positioned themselves, as the library encounter with Elwood, Molly, and the others demonstrated. Helen herself strategically altered her positioning. As Moore (1994) suggested, "Individuals can refuse the construction of gender as it is presented, they can approach this construction deviously or ironically, they can refer to it endlessly, but do so against its purpose, against the grain" (p. 82). In the following exchange, part of the conversation quoted earlier in which Earl talked about problems with his girlfriend, Helen suggested he send the girl something "romantic":

Earl: I was going to, but I said, no, that's not boy's stuff.

Jan: Not what?

Earl: Not boy stuff yet.

Jan: When does it get to be?

Helen: Please! I've had—Earl—I've had more romantic *dogs* than you.

Jan: When does it get to be?

Earl: Uh, 15 years old.

Helen: Earl! I've had more romantic dogs than you. [*Laughter*]

Earl: You are really mean, Helen!

Helen: Well, excuse me!

Earl: The bathroom's right down the hallway.

Helen: I could throw you from here to the bathroom.

Earl: [*Sarcastically*] Oh! Wow!

          . . .

Helen: Earl, let's put it this way; I've had dogs that were more romantic than you. I've had *fish* that were more romantic than you.

Earl: I've had *pigs* more romantic than you.

Helen: You wouldn't know; you've never been my boyfriend.

Earl: And never would be!

Helen: Yeah, I know. I never want you to be either. I like older guys, not younger guys. More experienced older guys.

When Earl attempted to reconfigure the narrative of masculinity—to suggest that behaving "romantically" toward a girl was a form of mature masculinity but would violate forms of boyhood masculinity—Helen attacked the notion that there was anything like the latter. Earl, she said, was no more masculine than a dumb animal, and when he protested, she further taunted him by threatening him physically. Helen defined older, more mature "guys" as desirable and associated maturity with both romantic desirability and potency as a fighter.

Boys and girls, then, shaped differences by strategically inscribing bodily vulnerabilities and potencies. When faced with physical threats, girls could define themselves as strong; but they could also strategically portray their bodies as weak and vulnerable to shape their relationships with the boys (e.g., shaved legs as opposed to unshaved ones). The boys, on the other hand, had to carefully balance the need to portray their bodies as potent, especially in contrast to the girls, with the need to avoid actual confrontations that might lead to fights.

These strategic engenderings of bodily meaning took on new overtones as kids began to contemplate the move to middle school. Secondary schools were not only larger than elementaries, with more student-controlled spaces; they were also more academically and socially differentiated. Kids were tracked and had to deal with five or six teachers a day rather than with one. Cliques based on modes of consumption became more prominent. As kids came to see mind and body as separate, the different meanings attached to them further differentiated genders (Shilling, 1993):

> *Helen:* I'm signing up for the same classes as four other people [in middle school]....I'm not going to take pre-algebra.
>
> *Jan:* Why not?
>
> *Helen:* Because I want to be able to have fun. The in- crowd—see, me and three other girls in my class, and Earl knows one of 'em, personally, [*Laughter*] we're in the, we *are* the in-crowd....
>
> *Jan:* How come the in-crowd girls aren't going to take pre-algebra?
>
> *Helen:* 'Cause some of the in-crowd girls are—
>
> *Duane:* Stupid!
>
> . . .
>
> *Earl:* Muffy's not that stupid.
>
> *Helen:* Yes, she is. I wrote her paper for her!
>
> *Neal:* Yes she is!...She's got a bolt loose in her head.
>
> *Jan:* Which paper did you write?
>
> *Helen:* Oh, I write the paper and then she copies what I write. I did that for her whole contract. I don't know why. Oh, well, she passed and I passed. I guess I'm smart!
>
> *Jan:* What makes [someone] a part of the in-crowd. Is it how they act? How they dress?
>
> *Earl:* Both of them. . . .

Helen: How they act and how they dress. You got to dress like this. *[Pinches her blouse]*. Silk.

   . . .

Jan: Are the boys going to take pre-algebra next year?

Earl: And fail.

Neal: I want to get out of school, I'm taking it.

Earl: I like science!

   . . .

Helen: I hate math.

Duane: I like PE!

In this exchange, boy–girl was mapped onto smart–stupid or mind–body, although not without some tensions. Helen would never have called herself stupid, but she claimed she would avoid the hard classes to stay friends with all the "in" girls who were dumb. And although Earl and Neal wanted to take difficult academic classes, Duane still fancied himself an athlete and seemed uncertain about what courses he would take. My point, then, is not that girls and boys automatically assume particular positions within body discourses but that these discourses play a major role in their thinking and self-formation in childhood and early adolescence.

EMBODYING RACIAL OTHERNESS

Gender was not the only dimension of difference kids formulated through their bodies. Race, at least in some contexts, seemed to be articulated through a body-based language. The discourse of race was muted in public—race and ethnicity were not addressed in the classrooms I observed—but this "silencing" (Fine, 1991) was accomplished with the complicity of the kids themselves.

For example, I was once talking with a group of fourth graders—Cicily, Carol, Dot, Lois, Glenn, Mel, Beavis, and Rufus—who were working on a newsletter project: a survey of the activities, musical styles, foods, and so forth, that kids in their room and other classes liked. I'd thought it would be interesting to compare students from different ethnic backgrounds, so I suggested adding a question asking students to circle which "race or ethnic group" they belonged to: African American, White, Asian American, Hispanic American, or Other. Dot read this and squinted up at me, "What's that mean?"

"You're Asian American," her cousin Lois explained.

"Yeah, you're Asian American," Cicily echoed, talking to Dot, "But you're not, Lois."

Lois looked at her, puzzled. "I am too!"

"No," said Cicily, "you were born in the United States."

"Well," I said to Cicily, "her parents were from Laos; her heritage is Asian. It's like with an African American, they're not from Africa, but their heritage is African."

"My great grandma," Cicily replied emphatically, "I saw her when I was five, and she was real old; she's dead now. She was born in South Carolina!"

"So you're not an African American?" I asked.

"No!" she replied, very serious.

"Would you rather I say 'Black?'" I asked.

"No! That's black," she said, pointing. "Your bag is black."

The kids laughed. "She's brown," said Mel.

"What am I?" asked Glenn. "My grandmother was Irish."

"I'm Irish too!" Cicily insisted. "My great grandmother was part Irish."

Glenn just looked at her. "I'm just going to take that question off the survey," I said.

"It has nothing to do with the rest of the survey questions," Cicily pointed out.

"Well," I responded, "neither does whether you're male or female [another question on the survey]. The questions are just there to give some idea of what kind of people were responding. But I'm going to take that question off 'cause it's obviously going to cause some problems."

I don't think the fourth graders actually would have had trouble classifying one another by race or ethnicity, but they weren't fluent enough in the discourse to counter Cicily's objections to the categories. In fact, among the kids I got to know in fourth grade, racial rhetoric—at least in my presence, and it may have been muted for my benefit—was uncommon. Sybil once called Iggy, a light-skinned African American, a "honkie White boy"; Effie protested in the cafeteria about having to sing "Shenandoah." Doug had sung the first line as "Shenandoah, I love your daughter," and Effie exclaimed, "I don't love no White man's daughter." But when kids openly spoke in racialized terms like this, their class-mates invariably reacted with mock outrage (mock in the sense of exaggerated facial expressions and voice pitches) and shushed them. The others' difficulty in responding to Cicily's objections also suggests that they weren't really sure how to explicate or defend racial categori-zations.

The fact is, I never saw the kids, except in the instances I discuss here, use race or ethnicity as explanations for behaviors, performances, tastes, or attitudes in their conversations with each other or with me. It may be, as Holmes (1995) argued, that younger children (she studied kindergarteners), especially children who've interacted with kids from other ethnic groups in collaborative settings, show little racial or ethnic animosity. She suggested that such cleavages arise in later elementary school and secondary school. Yet even older kids don't necessarily adopt static definitions of ethnicity (cf. Heath & McLaughlin, 1993, p. 24). Instead, they seem to use attributions and invocations of race and ethnicity as strategic resources for making sense and shaping identities in particular situations or when dealing with particular topics.

Thus rather than trying to get kids to talk about race and ethnicity in an interview context, I looked for situations or topics in which they might raise the issue themselves. Among the fourth graders such situations were rare, but among fifth graders, at least among European American kids,[5] racial discourses emerged, almost always in the context of talk about physical violence or bodily injury. Sometimes the references were disguised, almost hidden. For example, in this exchange Duane and Alf (both European Americans), began to fantasize about which of their friends would excel at particular sports:

Jan:	Do you feel like you write better or you know more math? Or more science?
Duane:	Know more basketball!
Alf:	I know baseball.
Duane:	Bo knows more baseball!
Alf:	Alf knows baseball; Duane knows basketball.
Duane:	Jerry [a big European American boy] knows football.
Alf:	Yeah, really. JW [a small European American boy] knows soccer. [*Pause*] Who likes hockey? Who, who, who would probably be a good hockey player?
Duane:	Me.
Alf:	Noo—
Duane:	I got my own skates!
Alf:	Instead of you—I do too! Uh, how about, Thurman [an African American boy]? He's tough. And then how about—
Duane:	Benny [African American].
Alf:	Clarence [African American].
Duane:	Barry [African American].
Alf:	Naw, Barry's too little, he'd—he'd get scrunched.

---

[5]Although I interviewed a number of African American fourth graders, none of the parents of African American fifth graders gave me permission to interview their children. I talked to them but not on tape.

What struck me, but only as I transcribed this tape, was that Alf reserved the sport most commonly known for fighting—hockey—for African American boys although of all the sports mentioned I believe it is actually the one in which African Americans account for the smallest percentage of professional players. This implicit distinction—that African Americans were more violent and tougher than European Americans—was made explicit in other situations.

In a group interview with fifth graders, as I was setting up the microphone, Helen showed me a scab on her elbow and began telling me this story:

> *Helen*:   I used to do a job...in the office. And I was going down there, to do my job, and I was walking down the hall, and this boy that didn't like me came up behind me, and he asked me what I was running from. And then he took his arms and he bammed them into my back—and I landed on the marble floor, and, well—
>
> *Neal*:   —Broke your elbow—
>
> *Helen*:   [*Holding out her arms*] One arm's bigger than the other one.

The other kids in the room, Lucy and Neal, began to collaborate in the story.

> *Lucy*:   She [Helen] came, uh, in the classroom, and she was screaming and crying. And [her teacher] said, "What's wrong?" and she showed her her arm right here? I think?
>
> *Helen*:   Uh-uh. Right here, my elbow.
>
> *Lucy*:   She showed her and—
>
> *Helen*:   —She said, "Well, I don't know if it's broken, but I think it is."
>
>   Then I went downstairs and Mr. Torgersen [the PE teacher] says, "Well, it's broken" [*Laughs*]. He just like, didn't care. He goes, "Who did that?"
>
>   And I said, "Bruce."
>
>   And he said, "You all was into it in PE, wasn't you?"
>
>   And I said, "Well, not really."
>
>   And he said, "Let me look at it." He pulled it out. [*Makes sounds of being in pain*] And then he goes, "Yep. It's broke." He's not a nice guy. But, see, it's [her elbow] bigger than the other one right here.

There was a lot of body play going on here: Helen boasting of her injuries and showing her scars (later in the conversation both Neal and

Lucy would also talk about past injuries), portraying adults as either ineffectual or even adding to her pain by jerking the broken arm. At the same time, the theme of the discussion began to shift from bodies, to bodies and race. Bruce, the boy who knocked Helen down, was African American.

Helen: You can tell, they don't keep discipline on Black people in this school....They don't do anything if they hit you or somethin'—cause Bruce got suspended for a couple of days, and they told me he was gonna be suspended for at least two weeks: three days.

   . . .

Helen: But, like, the Black people in this school, they don't treat 'em like, like they treat everybody else....'Cause if they do somethin', they go down there and they just get talked to. Now, if one of us does somethin'—like, we got into a fight in the lunchroom. Calling each other names. And we had to go into Mr. Watts's office, write down a list, make up, and then if they—

Lucy: I put mine in the desk—

Helen: —Mine's ripped, but it's in the desk somewhere.—but if they do something like that? They get in fights on the bus? All they do is say, "Well, don't do it again. Go to your class." And if we do something like that, then, it's like, "Sorry, you're suspended," or "You got to go to ISS [in-school suspension]."

Neal: I think this school's got a little racism in it.

Helen: Yeah. This school has a lot of racism!

Neal: For one reason—

Helen: I could say a few more things about it—

Lucy: Mr. Watts—

Neal: Benny [an African American boy] gets accused every time—like JW [a European American boy] was, uh, doing something, and Benny got accused of it and he didn't do nothin!

Helen: And the teacher says "Benny! Stop talking!"

          And he goes, "I ain't doin nothin!"

          And she says "Don't lie to me! You were talking!" And he doesn't say anything. And so—

Neal: There's another time, too! Benny's on the computer and JW way over here doin' something. And she turned around and told Benny to go to time out!

Helen: I know; she's done that a lot.

Neal: I think she is racist! Sometimes I do!

Although the comments of the kids flowed together, they advanced different arguments: Helen claimed that African American kids weren't disciplined harshly enough, while Neal thought his teacher unfairly punished African American boys for infractions others committed. What binds the two arguments together is the notion, which Helen embraces and Neal attributes to his teacher, that African Americans are different, their bodies less classical, less well controlled than those of the European Americans. Some parents shared this view. Mrs. Grigsby, whose daughter played on a girls' basketball team organized by a neighborhood recreation center, complained about how big and rough and physically punishing the African American girls on the teams from the recreation center in the Farewell Estates area were.

The image of African Americans' bodies as dangerous took on additional meanings as the kids began to contemplate leaving Thurber for middle school. The fifth-grade interview group—all White, working-class kids from the neighborhood around the school—had interacted with each other in bounded spaces for anywhere from 2 to 6 years. Some had known each other since preschool. Within their circle, languages of the body such as fighting and gendering were means of distinguishing selves and establishing domination. Middle school disrupted this situation. As kids approached the teenage years, they gained access to multiple identity-defining networks, through school-based tracking practices, through participation in sports or other extracurricular activities, through activities centering on forms of popular culture, through workplace experiences, and so on (Eckert, 1989; Gaines, 1991). Secondary schools reshaped the spatial and temporal organization of their bodies. Kids from Thurber would find themselves placed with students from other schools (and from other social classes), and their time together would be fragmented into multiple class periods. And since middle schools contain more transitional and student-controlled spaces than do elementary schools (e.g., hallways during class changes), kids would be more likely to interact with students of different ages. Gradually they would grow more mobile and independent from their parents in their activities outside school. As these spatial and temporal organizations of bodies change, the connections between gender, fighting, and race probably change as well.

For one thing, the slight opening up of spatial horizons kids experience allows for longer and more serious fights to take place. Kids entering secondary school routinely experience what Delamont and Galton (1987) called "fears about the building" (p. 238), fears that their childish, unsocialized bodies will be exposed by the older kids in the unsupervised spaces of the school. "The recurring themes are: larger children bullying smaller ones, victims being forcibly immersed in a polluting container (lavatory or rubbish bin), or humiliated by nakedness" (Delamont & Galton, 1987, p. 240).

The fifth graders told similar tales, some of them apparently inspired by teachers, and pointed to the best years of school as being those when they were the oldest within the building:

Neal: Only thing [their teacher] tells us is that middle school is scary.

Helen: Yeah, "middle school is scary."

Neal: No it's not, just higher-level thinking.

Helen: You think middle school is scary; wait till you get to high school.

Duane: Wait till you get to college.

Earl: College! Dang!

Neal: College is not scary. . . .Eighth and twelfth grades are the funnest grades there are.

Helen: I'm getting out of that house as soon as I can.

Earl: You really think so?

Helen: College is probably the funnest.

Earl: Fifth, eighth.

Neal: Fifth, eighth, and twelfth. Twelfth you get to dump the sophomores and everybody into the garbage cans.

Tales of expected victimization at the hands of older kids in middle and high school were already common. But unlike Delamont and Galtons's (1987) British research, race was a key element of the European American kids' anxiety. Depending on where they lived, kids at Thurber would go to one of three middle schools: Buffer, Steele, or Pounder. Buffer was the old middle school for the European American neighborhood around Thurber; Steele Middle School, Pounder Middle School, and Williams High (the high school most of the Thurber students would attend), were situated in or near African American residential areas and had predominantly African American student bodies. All three had been designated magnet schools to encourage attendance from outside their catchment areas, but their historical associations and locations continued to stigmatize them in the minds of the European American community:

Jan: What middle schools are you going to?

Lucy: Buffer.

Duane: I went to Steele today. [In the spring, fifth graders visited the middle schools they were assigned to for the following year]

       . . .

Lucy: What was it like?

Duane: I almost got knocked over by an eighth grader.

Helen: That was smooth Duane.

Lucy: How?

Helen: Get in their way.

Duane: I saw a fight.

Helen: Who? Did you know them?

Duane: I don't know.

Helen: Okay. Was it good?

Jan: Did you choose to go to Steele?

Duane: No. I don't want to go.

Neal: His mom doesn't want him to go either.

Jan: Why not?

Duane: I want to go to Buffer.

Helen: Steele is—[*Everybody starts talking*] really, *really* rough.

Lucy: That's where this boy got shot....This boy got shot there, he got there; his cousin shot him. His cousin shot him just 'cause—I don't know.

Duane: I want to go to Agnew [middle school in the predominantly European American county].

Jan: You want to go to Agnew. Why?

Lucy: That's a good school.

Earl: You can get beat up there.

Lucy: No, you can't.

Jan: Agnew?

Helen: You can get beat up anywhere.

Duane: My cousin, my cousin's cousin hasn't.

Helen: You can; believe me you can. I know some people who have. Course they probably had smart mouths, knowing the people I know.

Jan: So Agnew and Steele and Buffer are all Grades 6, 7, and 8.

Duane: Pounder [middle school].

Helen: Don't even talk about Pounder. You don't want to get me started on Pounder, Man.

Jan: . . . Pounder is?

Earl: Tough.

Helen: They bring guns! And knives.

Earl: They do in the colleges too!

Helen: Not all of them.

Lucy: Do they bring knives and guns and everything at Virginia Tech?

Helen: My ex-boyfriend is—14, or 15 or 16. And he carries a knife about that long [*Hand about a foot apart*] on him every day.

Earl: Crocodile Dundee.

Helen: And he always carries three little pocket knives. I don't know why. Let's put it this way: He has metal spikes on his shoes. That'll tell you how rough Pounder is.

. . .

Jan: So anyway, Pounder is the rough school? Steele comes after that in terms of roughness and then—

Helen: Buffer is sort of last

Lucy: Buffer is a good school; that's why it doesn't have bad people goin' there, like killin' people.

Helen: Lucy, I wouldn't say that it don't have bad people! [*Lots of people talking at once*] Lucy I encourage you to go to Pounder. I strongly encourage you to go to Pounder. You'll get mauled. [*To me*] Buffer, it doesn't have *as* much violence; they had a riot.

Earl: They had a riot?

Duane: LA riots!

Helen: Yeah, they had a riot. Two kids got in a fight and then all of their friends started in and then the whole school was against each other. My brother went up there. . . .

. . .

Neal: Williams High School—It used to be terrible, but it's not as bad as it used to be. There used to be guard dogs on every door.
. . .

Lucy: [*Incredulous*] Williams?

Helen: Williams.

Earl: My brother had to go to that school.

Helen: Pounder is close to the same way.

Earl: He got in a *lot* of fights.

Helen: You take a knife or a gun, or you literally can get killed.

Earl: No, they'd take the knife from you and kill you with it.

All middle schools were dangerous, the kids agreed, but they constructed a hierarchy of danger paralleling the proportion of African Americans in the schools. Earl's invocation of "Crocodile Dundee" when Helen described her ex-boyfriend's knife supplied a visual reference for the knife, but it also suggested a narrative for making sense of the situation. Crocodile Dundee, the Australian backwoodsman in the film of the same name, was shown in television advertisements for the film being confronted by a young African American mugger on a dark New York City street. The mugger flashed a switchblade knife, but Dundee appeared unconcerned: "That's no knife," he said. "*That's* a knife," whereupon he pulled out a foot-long hunting knife, and the mugger fled. Earl's invocation of the image carried with it the racial imagery of the advertising clip: The kids in the conversation were all White, the "rough" schools they were talking about were predominantly African American, and it was the African American kids they feared.

These attitudes seemed to come from parents as well as older siblings. When Duane's mother told me that she wanted him to go to Buffer instead of Pounder (and then to Smith High instead of Williams High), she explained:

> I was debating on Pounder; let him to go Pounder, because Pounder feeds into Williams. But, uh, you still hear about the Blacks. So I'm still concerned about that. Nothin' against them, but, you know, until he has to go through it, and I don't know if he will go through it. You know, the domination stuff.

Doug, although only a fourth grader, had already been coached in attitudes towards the schools: "I'm gonna be here in fifth grade. Then I'm goin' to Buffer. Then I'm not goin' to Williams High....I'm not going to Williams! My mom don't want to see me there, because there's *guards* guarding the gate and stuff!"

Not all European Americans shared this view of the school. Alf, who lived near Pounder and would inevitably be going there, insisted that it was a good school because it was a magnet school. For most of the kids, however, especially those who lived near Thurber and far from Steele, Steele and its African American students were defined not just on the basis of embodied experience: The most dangerous and fight-ridden community spaces these kids had experienced, in fact, were the church day camps some attended during the summer. (As Earl explained, "Well, they don't *allow* fighting or anything at church camp. But if you get caught, you just sit on the bench for a couple of minutes, and then you get to go back out and start beating up people again.") Rather, the meanings of school spaces were shaped through representations, many drawn from the media, none from the school curriculum, that allowed the kids to organize their environments.

5 Intersections of Kids, Signs, and Popular Culture

Ethnography must re-define itself as that practice of representation which illuminates the power of large-scale, imagined life possibilities over specific life trajectories. This is "thickness" with a difference, and the difference lies in a new alertness to the fact that ordinary lives today are increasingly powered not by the givenness of things but by the possibilites that the media (either directly or indirectly) suggest are available.

—Appadurai, 1991, p. 200

By suppressing some bodily functions, regulating others, and focusing activity on the use of representations (reading, writing, mathematics), schooling at a place like Thurber was supposed to produce a tight link between a specific kind of body—the adult, male, European American body (and remember, I speak of a "body" not only as physical form, but as all its attendant techniques and dispositions)—and specific activities, such as the manipulation of written or printed representations, which come to be defined as "intellectual." As we saw in the preceding chapter, embodied meanings did *not* disappear; age, gender, race, and physical threat remained potent resources for meaning-making. But school-sanctioned uses of representations were squeezed into a classical, rationalized body, one that would be silent, still, self-contained, or, when group work was required, would stay in one place, keep its voice down, take turns in talking.

This segregation of bodily experience from what counts as official, rewarded, institutional experience depends on a kind of "magic," as Lefebvre (1991) called it, a "spiriting-away...of the body," a shift from "the space of the body to the body-in-space" (pp. 201, 202). Thinking and knowing in this decorporealized space are defined as ways of looking from a distance upon the world rendered as a representation in books, paper, film, or television—the view from the skyscraper described in the previous chapter. In Mitchell's (1988) terms, we come to regard the world as an "exhibition":

162

a world more and more rendered up to the individual according to the way in which, and to the extent to which, it could be set up before him or her as an exhibit...not...an exhibition of the world but the world conceived and grasped as though it were an exhibition. (p. 13; cf. Gregory, 1994)

This rendering of the world is what Lefebvre (1991) meant by "abstract space"—"a space dominated by the eye and the gaze" (Gregory, 1994, p. 392). History is not where you live, but in a set of novels about characters from the past; English is not everyday communication, but classroom-based writing and reading; math is not what you use to shop or save, but algorithms applied on paper. Learning is something you do at your desk, in your classrooms, with texts. Some teachers at Thurber would periodically try to give kids back their bodies by letting them perform stories or by taking them outside to walk a mile so they could *feel* the distance. But even when kids were taken bodily into historical settings, on fieldtrips to places like Appomattox, for instance, their interactions with these settings were mediated through films (which they watched in visitors' centers) and commodities (which they purchased in the souvenir stores). From my notes on the Appomattox field trip:

> The kids raced to the bookstore when they saw it. Once inside, all of them except two African American kids, Bruce and Alice, who I think were broke, began grabbing stuff to buy: coins, fake Civil War money, postcards, little flags (North and South). Some spent more than $10 (they were told to bring no more than $5). Alice, sounding like an adult, said aloud to no one in particular:
>
>> All these people are buying toys; they're not even going to want them tomorrow. I got better things to do with my money. I mean, if there was something I wanted I'd get it, but there's nothin' here. I thought there'd be cheaper stuff anyway, like a quarter or something.
>
> Outside everybody showed each other what they'd bought. One little girl was surprised to find she'd paid $4 for some black and white cards and envelopes. Her friend said, "You bought something, and you didn't even know what it was?"

The trouble is that school does not, and probably never did, monopolize the definition of the "world as exhibition" for kids. School knowledge—school-based literacy, math, science—can't slip uncontested into the vacuum created by the school's attempt to deny embodied experience. It has competitors, one in particular which also mediates activity through representations and defines experience as an act of looking on a display. This competitor, "popular culture," has some advantages over school culture. It is more widely disseminated and easily transportable; it is tied more directly to kids' core concerns, issues such as gender, sexuality, race, violence, and power. Finally, in a time when kids' spheres of activity are more and more segregated from those of adults, popular culture is open to appropriation and use by kids interacting with peers, while school-based representations still often presume interactional systems containing both kids and adults. The end result may be, as Willis (1990) suggested, that school-centered systems of representation:

> will become almost totally irrelevant to the real energies and interests of most young people and no part of their identity formation. Common [popular] culture will, increasingly, undertake, in its own ways, the roles that education has vacated. (p. 147)

School occupies about 6 hours a day, 180 days a year for U.S. kids, but on average they spend 4 hours a day every day watching television and more hours playing games with, reading, or shopping for the artifacts of popular culture. For the kids I worked with, at least, the intensity of engagements with popular culture were certainly greater than with school-based activities. For example, when I talked to Felix, a fourth grader, about what he did outside school, he insisted that he read only when he was grounded and that he only got grounded when he back-talked his mother or hit his sister. I asked him why he'd hit his sister:

> She gets on my nerves. Like she sings these baby songs, and I might say "Sis, stop it." And she keeps on bugging me while I'm playing Nintendo, SuperNintendo. 'Cause we, I made a rule in the house: Anybody that goes upstairs and bothers me or talks near me when I'm playing Nintendo, they will pay the price. Even my parents. I told them that....That's the rule. And most of the time when I'm playing is when they have to be all busy. 'Cause then I don't have anything to do, and they won't let me go outside....I have Mario World All Stars, Ken Griffey Jr. Baseball League, Mortal Kombat, and Alladin.

Some writers have suggested that kids like Felix are enslaved by video games and spend all available time playing them (Sheff, 1993). Felix, however, loved to ride his bike and to play outside with friends. Nintendo, an indoor occupation centered around the manupulation of representations, was only part of a complicated network of social and material relations that structured his experience. This exchange followed the statement I just quoted:

> Jan: When you're playing SuperNintendo, do you have to read instructions to learn how to play them, or do you just start playing them?
>
> Felix: Well, when I first get the game, I've learned how to play them. 'Cause they're out in the malls, and you get to play them, and then I'll learn all of the moves. Like, in All Stars? The only time when I learned how to erase was like a couple of days ago,

and I've had that since January [the interview took place in late April]. So I learn by myself.

Jan: You learn by yourself just through trial and error?

Felix: Uh-huh, except in Mortal Kombat. That I learned from Michael and Bob. 'Cause they rented it a couple of times. They're pretty good at games. When they get 'em, they beat 'em—well, not the first time, but they beat 'em when they rent 'em. And then they teach me how to play, and I buy them, and they buy them.

Jan: So you play them sometimes at the mall, at the video arcades?

Felix: Yeah, that's how I learned how to play—well, not the video arcades. Video arcades it's harder because you have different controllers.

Jan: So where do you play them at the mall?

Felix: Like, in toy stores and stuff; they have sort of like a TV now; they set up a game, and then you get to play them. At Toys "R" Us they do that. At Toys "R" Us they do that with the *new* Nintendo, not the old ones. The new Nintendo, Sega Genesis, Gameboy, and SuperNintendo.

Here, Felix's involvement with SuperNintendo, which appeared at first intensely private, begins to look more complicated. Seemingly local, private activities, like local settings and neighborhoods, are powerfully connected to distant settings through increasingly dense economic and cultural ties—so much so that the very distinction between "global" and "local" relations is called into question (Giddens, 1981; Harvey, 1989; Soja, 1989). Massey (1993) suggested we need a "global sense of the local" (p. 68) and an understanding of local "places" (and activities) as "articulated moments in networks of social relations and understandings" spreading out in regional or global "spaces" (p. 66).

Trying to account for Felix's Nintendo work in this sense we can note, first, that it clearly depended on an international corporate network to produce and distribute the video games. Nintendo Company Ltd. is the largest toymaker in the world, a dominant force in the video-game industry. Its products, in one third of American households (Sheff, 1993), are produced at the intersection of corporate hierarchies, the abstract spaces of global finance circuits (Allen & Pryke, 1994), and software programming environments (Sheff, 1993).

Second, Felix's involvement depended on the existence of stores like Toys "R" Us, which controls one fifth of the U.S. toy market and makes one fifth of its profits from Nintendo products. Such stories share the 19th century department stores' privileging of vision over bodily engagement:

A department store's fixed prices altered the social and psychological relations of the marketplace. The obligation to buy implied by the active exchange of bargaining was replaced by the invitation to look, turning the shopper into a passive spectator, an isolated individual, a face in the department-store crowd, silently contemplating merchandise. (Crawford, 1992, pp. 17–18)

Thus Walter Benjamin (1978) recalled the city of his early-20th century childhood as a "theater of purchases...an impenetrable chain of mountains, no, caverns of commodities—that was the town" (p. 40; cf. Zukin, 1995). But in that theater, local productions, so to speak, still predominated. By the late 20th century, on the other hand, Toys "R" Us and other superstores tie together global networks of consumption organized around the act of looking.[1] Looking, itself, becomes an elaborate, media-driven social construction. According to Gottdiener (1995), "Entrance to the mall means the actualization of consumerist fantasies that are primed by years of conditioning deriving from exposure to advertising and the mass media" (p. 95). Television characters and toys based on those characters inspire feature films and video games. Kids interact, then, with systems of representations and material products that connect different forms of popular culture. Doug, for example, told me:

Doug: I always like going to Toys "R" Us.

Jan: What do you do there?

Doug: Look for Power Ranger stuff. What else?

Jan: Power Rangers. Now, what are they? Are they a TV show or what?

Doug: A TV show.

Jan: When do they come on?

Doug: Don't you know anything!?

Jan: No, I don't know much.

Doug: Channel 8, on at 7:00 in the morning and Saturdays at 7:30.

Jan: . . . You get up that early and watch them?

Doug: Sometimes I get up at 5:00.

---

[1]Global in more than their finance and production networks. *The New York Times* (Eliott, 1994, p. D6) reported that the advertising firm D'Arcy Masius Benton and Bowles conducted an international "New World Teen Study" to "quantify teen-agers' cultural attitudes" and "consumer behaviors." In the words of an agency executive, the survey was to "test the hypothesis that this is the first generation uniquely tied together around the world because of media." "What's fascinating is how cohesive they are," the executive added, referring to the teenagers' attitudes. (For anecdotal corroboration, see Brooks's [1995] short article on youth culture in the relatively closed society of Iran, and for more scholarly perspectives see Amit-Talai and Wulff, 1995.)

Jan: Why?

Doug: I don't want to miss *Bonkers*! Or, uh, *Sonic the Hedgehog*, or *Merrie Melodies, Goof Troup, Ghost Busters*—uh, that's it.

Jan: What's your favorite?

Doug: My favorite power ranger is the Green Ranger! Tommy! Uh, I don't know why I like them; they're just cool! They got all these Megazords, Dragonzords, Ultrazords—the MegaDragon-Zords.

The Mighty Morphin Power Rangers, like many pop culture entities, are globally distributed systems. Tied in with a television program that was rated first among 2- to 11-year-olds in the United States at the time of my fieldwork, the dolls are produced by the Japanese megacorporation Bandai. The largest conventional toymaker in the world, Bandai has the dolls assembled in piecework shops in Thailand where workers earn around $5 for a 13-hour workday (Thais assemble Power Rangers, 1994; Power Rangers workers pay investigated, 1994). The dolls are then marketed at the same malls and toy shops as the SuperNintendo games Felix coveted.

The role of such commercial establishments in mediating Felix's patterns of use is a third aspect of his involvement with Nintendo. The stores allowed him to play the games and begin to become proficient with them (or to rent and practice them). The process is perhaps a bit like trying on clothes, except that clothes presume a social and aesthetic sphere of relations in which they'll be judged as appropriate or not. Hence trying on clothes is always an incomplete experience, to be validated only in later social engagements. The games, on the other hand, are self-contained experiences; playing them at home is the same as playing them in the stores.

Finally, these networks of relations shape kids' interactions with peers and parents. Peers become information resources and sources of expertise. Parents, meanwhile, as I suggested at the end of chapter 2, become instrumentalities for obtaining toys and games. As Ward (1978) wrote: "Modern urban life in fact exposes the young to the cornucopia of consumer desires while progressively denying them the means of gratifying these expensive wants except through the munificence of parents" (p. 147).

Kids work out an impressive array of tactics for inspiring such munificence. Responding to Lila's question for her "How to get your parents to give you what you want" story, Felix explained:

> I give them the puppy-dog look. I beg. I'll be bad till they give it to me. I do lots of different things. I give them my money [*Laughing*]. I try to give them my money so they'll buy it for me. And when I don't have my money with me, I tell them, "Buy it for me, and I'll repay you back."

In addition to providing money, parents must supply the time, space, and privacy necessary for mastering the game. As Felix explained, mastering a game can be a slow, practice-driven experience. He said he learned by himself (or occasionally with friends), but to understand this learning it is necessary to consider the complex network of people, institutions, and things intersecting in his interactions with Nintendo. And that means we have to reconsider what it means to learn.

POPULAR CULTURE AND KID-BASED "FUNDS OF KNOWLEDGE"

The idea of learning that drives formal schooling is bound up in a spatial metaphor: transfer. School is considered a special space in which students are endowed, as individuals, with abstract, context-independent skills and knowledge. The experience of schooling is said to produce qualitative and quantitative changes in what and how they know. This learning is supposedly internalized and stored somewhere inside the kids' bodies. Upon leaving school, they supposedly carry these capacities and deploy them in concrete activities in other spaces. These notions, of course, presume the individualized, classical body examined in the previous chapter. As Rose (1993) pointed out, the "bounded body and its role as simple container of rationality both contribute to the idea that we are socialized by internalizing lessons which the 'outside' world teaches us when we act in it" (p. 77).

This concept of learning rests on a notion of space as a formal, homogeneous medium composed of interchangeable fragments. Differences "that come from nature and history as well as those that come from the body, ages, sexes, and ethnicities" are ignored (Lefebvre, 1979, p. 289; see also Lave, 1988). School knowledge is grounded in a particular context presumed to be universal: the abstract space of advanced capitalism. We've already seen an example of this conception of space in the business-in-the-school project, in which difference was recognized only in terms of quantities of standard, measurable assets, and the assets themselves were treated as possessions of discrete individuals who could unproblematically exchange or expend them.

But just as the kids' possessions proved to be inextricably woven into family-based and other forms of meaning—to be situated in a complex landscape of social relations rather than flowing freely through an open plane of abstract space—so everything we learn is grounded in particular spaces in the highly differentiated terrain of everyday life (Lave, 1988; Newman, Griffin, & Cole, 1989). And to complicate things more, as I've argued earlier, spaces are themselves "articulations" of intersecting networks beginning and ending far beyond their immediate boundaries.

So what does it mean to say learning is "situated" when situations are themselves confluences of widely distributed streams of activity? It means we need to talk of learning in terms of network or webs of association. We can begin by looking at an approach I talked about briefly in chapter 1, Moll, Tapia, and Whitmore's (1993) use of a construct from economics, the "fund," to characterize household systems of knowledge in "communities" of interacting adults. They defined *funds of knowledge* as:

> The diverse social networks that interconnect households with their social environments and facilitate the sharing or exchange of resources, including knowledge, skills, and labor essential for the household's functioning, if not their well-being. (p. 140)

Kids obviously participate in these networks, although perhaps marginally. For example, Neal, a fifth grader, told Lucy and me about boating on the weekends with his and another family:

Neal: It's a boat that's got these two metal things around it full of air, so it can float. It has a motor and it goes up to like 40 mph.

Lucy: You better be holding on!

Neal: I did that once and I was standing up and went full throttle.

Not a profound example, but it does show Neal engaged in a valued, multifamily activity in a way that shaped his sense of identity as a member of the group (and in the telling of the story shaped his identity for Lucy and me). I suspect every kid at the school was, like Neal, a participant in these kinds of networks.

By focusing *only* on households, however, Moll and his colleagues ignored other funds of knowledge that kids draw on, some of which may be extremely important for understanding how they make sense of themselves and their environments. Along with Lave and Wenger (1991), Moll, Tapia, and Whitmore (1993) seemed to be interested only in networks or communities that are composed of humans or animate entities and are dominated by adults who engage in face-to-face interaction or communicate directly with each other. They did not address the nature of communities that include inanimate or nonhuman elements, have kids as central participants, or are spread across time and space and link people through mass-distributed images or representational spaces. Yet it is this latter type of community that is becoming increasingly important in kids' lives. Felix and his Nintendo game are one example. Consider also this strip of conversation about computers among Earl, Duane, and Lucy.

Duane: I work with him [Earl] on computers sometime, at his house....We're gonna type up stories and stuff.

Earl: Yeah, I type stories, and sheets for, uh, new clubs, for people to fill out. And I put like—

Duane: I wrote a story, but the printer was broke!

. . .

Earl: See, my printer was broke. The first one I got for Christmas was broke, and my mom—kind of messed it up. So we took that one back to Sears, I mean to J. C. Penny, and we got *another* one for the one we had and hooked it up. And finally we got one that works....See my mom—now she goes to the stores, and she gets this PC—personal computer idiot's guide to, uh, DOS or Windows or whichever one. Right now she's workin' on DOS....She doesn't understand it. We're trying to program games in, and we're messing them up....Like Commander Keen to the Rescue! . . .

Jan: Have you ever taken a course, or has she ever taken a course?

Earl: . . . She's taken a course; she got a 52-, 53-, 54-page thing that my printer printed. She reads through it and—there's her course....She's taken a computer course at work. They made a new computer course for personal computers at home—and they're working on that. They *did* have what's called moon-lighting. It was a weight loss thing. My mom was in that. She joins all that stuff that they have at work.

Jan: Do you ever get to use your computer at home for your schoolwork?

Duane: No.

. . .

Jan: What are you all writing stories about?

Duane: Things we like to do.

Earl: I just think up stuff; I got one heck of an imagination.

Duane: So do I.

Jan: Is it stuff for school? Or just stuff you like to do?

Duane: Stuff we like to do.

Earl: Like to do....I like to write stories! I like to write!

Duane: Imagination stirs you!

Earl: But I don't like to write things that the teacher assigns us, unless it's—sometimes I like it, but usually I like to make up my own stories.

Jan: Why's that better?

> *Duane*: You get your own free time.
>
> *Earl*: Yeah, you get your own free time, and you can add stuff that you want to put in there. When she gives you an assignment you have to write exactly what she tells you. And I like to let my imagination run wild [*Screams*].

Earl's computer use was at the intersection of a family network (he was learning with his mother, who was taking computer classes), a friendship network (with Duane), and various commercial networks (the games and software he bought). Everyday life is made from such articulations. In this case the three networks blended together to create a heterogeneous fund of knowledge that connected Earl and his friends to distant and unknown groups of kids (who would also be fashioning identities in interaction with games and computers) and shaped their relationships to one other in the immediate environment. In the next exchange, for example, status and connection within the local group are partly shaped by engagements with elements of such funds:

> *Earl*: Hey, Duane...I know how to, uh, how you hang like that so you don't kill yourself and fall on Prince of Persia on my, uh, computer.
>
> *Helen*: You do?
>
> *Jan*: What's Prince of Persia?
>
> *Earl*: It's a game where you get a prince, and he's trying to get to this girl, and you gotta jump over the top of things and you gotta jump up and grab the ceiling; it'll fall down on top of you, and you got to get a potion to get your life back.
>
> *Helen*: I don't know how to hang on.
>
> *Duane*: You gotta—
>
> *Earl*: And you jump over—
>
> *Helen*: How do you hang on?!
>
> *Earl*: You jump over things and fall down; you get stuck on a spike, and it shows the blood and everything! You fall through stuff; uh, you fall down and you're smushed.

To paraphrase Moll et al. (1993), this kid-based fund of knowledge connected kids in ways that facilitated the exchange of information and shaped lines of friendship and identity. As the example suggests, many such funds of knowledge are articulated through the mass media, which allows kids to overcome their relative immobility in physical space (see chapter 3). They can then participate in a widely distributed set of social relationships connecting them to other people whom they may never meet in person. Once, talking to Alf and Duane about which of their classmates they saw outside school, I asked:

Jan: You ever interact much with the Black kids?

Alf: Yeah.

Duane: Yeah, I got a friend.

Alf: I got a lot of friends that are Black.

Duane: —he goes to Williams.

Alf: I got Barry, Eddie, Benny, Thurman.

Duane: I got a boy named Adam.

Alf: I got Dave Justice and Ron Gant! My friends [*Laughing*].

Duane: I got Ryne Sandberg—oh!

Alf: I got Bo Jackson! And Frank Thomas.

Duane: I got—

Alf: I got Michael Jordan.

Duane: I got Larry Johnson and Muggsy Bogues—the whole Hornets team.

Alf: I got Alonzo Mourning and Shaquille O'Neal.

Duane: I got Dell Curry. I got, I got—uhhhh—Scottie Pippen.

Alf: I got Jordan.

Here the local and global, the embodied and represented, were artfully combined. After quickly exhausting the Black classmates with whom they were on speaking terms, Duane and Alf, both avid collectors of sports cards, began naming African American sports heros. Alf began the play with Justice and Gant. Duane, who was a basketball enthusiast, made a false start with Sandberg (a European American Chicago Cub), and Alf trumped him by dropping two names from the other Chicago baseball team (Jackson and Thomas, who played for the White Sox), for good measure throwing in a Chicago basketball player (Jordan). Duane, probably thankful to get away from baseball, named two players from his favorite basketball team (Johnson and Bogues, who at the time both played for the Charlotte Hornets), and so it went. Spatial relations and distributed networks influenced the selection of cultural images the kids worked with. Both Justice and Gant, at the time of the conversation quoted here, played for the Atlanta Braves baseball team. Kids in Roanoke could be fans of an Atlanta team because its owner, Ted Turner, broadcast its games on his television superstation TBS, part of the standard cable package in the Roanoke area. The fact that Duane and

Alf then went on to talk about players for various Chicago-based sports teams reflected the fact that these teams were broadcast by the other cable superstation, WGN in Chicago. The Charlotte basketball team got mentioned as the professional team based nearest to Roanoke and thus most closely covered by the local media.

The boys used a language of possession to describe their relationships to both the local classmates with whom they interacted and their distant heros. Sports heros became part of a virtual community scattered across time and space. Media represenations define new "social settings that include and exclude, unite or divide people in particular ways" (Meyerowitz, 1985, quoted in Poster, 1990, p. 44). The media distribute these representations across space and allow kids to construct identities, selves, and social relations.

To follow the logic of these media-entangled, spatially distributed kid-based funds, however, we need to reject the practice of focusing on kids' places in adult-dominated communties of practice, of conceptualizing kids' spaces and actions only in terms of their relations to adult space. These assumptions stand out, for example, in the way Rogoff (1994) distinguished between schools and informal learning situations:

> In informal learning situations, children participate in inherently valuable community activities with some support from adults; in schools they are segregated from the mature activities of the community—the goal of the few adults present is to constitute a community of learners around the children's interests in ways that will involve them in meaningful activities connecting with the skills and values of adulthood. (pp. 213–214)

Rogoff's basic point is reasonable: Learning depends on meaningful connections to ongoing, relatively stable systems of activity. What's problematic is her seeming assumption that such systems are necessarily adult centered, that adults are always the central participants of communities of practice. As Thorne (1993) suggested, such an adult-centric view may fundamentally distort our view of kids' lives:

> [S]ocial scientists grant adults the status of full social actors, but define children as incomplete, as adults-in-the-making....[But] there is much to be gained by seeing children not as the next generation's adults, but as social actors in a range of institutions....Children, like adults, live in present, concretely historical, and open-ended time. It distorts the vitality of children's present lives to continually refer them to a presumed distant future. Children's interactions are not preparation for life; they are life itself. (Thorne, 1993, p. 3; see also Kelly-Byrne, 1989, pp. 252–253)

Kid-based funds of knowledge are made up of heterogeneous networks of people (adults and kids) and things (representations and technologies). I do not suggest that adults are excluded, but instead of assuming that the activity within the networks focuses on stable adult spaces of practice, I want to look at kids as the central participants, *exchanging, invoking, inhabiting,* and *appropriating* adult-produced representations that circulate through the spaces of popular culture. Engagement with popular culture is a fundamental social activity in the United States, perhaps second only to work in the amount of human energy people allocate to it (cf. Poster, 1990, p. 47). Yet in spite of the recent surge of interest in integrating cultural and educational studies (e.g., Giroux & McLaren, 1994; Giroux & Simon, 1989), young kids' uses of pop culture remain little-researched. Instead, attention is focused on critiques of products, analyses of producers, or studies of young adult or adult users. My aim here is to look closely at elementary school kids' uses of popular culture and in the process to examine concepts of community, identity, and consumption.

EXCHANGING POP CULTURE

You first notice popular culture in the school in its visible manifestations: shirts and caps with corporate logos, comics and cards passed about before school in the morning—popular culture in objectified, manipulable forms: commodities. As we saw in chapter 2, the kids had difficulty understanding objects purely as items for exchange. Commodities, "objects outside us," as Marx (1967) defined them, always have both use *and* exchange values: Comic books can be read and (in theory) resold. These values are not intrinsic qualities of the things but instead characterize the forms of practice within which they circulate (cf. Baudrillard, 1981).

As Appadurai (1986) wrote: To understand "things" we have to examine the conditions under which they "circulate in different *regimes of value* in space and time" (p. 4). The meanings of things "are inscribed in their forms, their uses, their trajectories. It is only through the analysis of these trajectories that we can interpret the human transactions and calculations that enliven things" (p. 5). The question is not "What is a commodity?" but "What sort of an exchange is a commodity exchange?" (p. 9). Appadurai answered this question by suggesting that "the commodity situation in the social life of any 'thing' [is] the situation in which its exchangeability (past, present, or future) for some other thing is its socially relevant feature" (p. 13).

In some situations the exchange value of popular cultural products seemed to be a primary if not exclusive interest. I regularly heard conversations like this one from my fieldnotes:

In the morning, before class, a couple of students, Ruben and Bucky, are comparing basketball playing cards. Bucky says he's got a Christian Laettner worth $1 and a Larry Johnson worth $2. He shows the latter, encased in hard plastic. Ruben says he's got a Shaquille O'Neal. Bucky tells Ruben that in one pack of cards he got a card "of a girl! A whole girl in a bathing suit." Bucky somewhat furtively pulls a stack of cards out of his bag to show Ruben.

Cards were a way to display wealth (although the occasional girl card might have its use values). Kids didn't often boast about clothes or other items that might signify wealth, but the dollar values, and implicitly the commodity status of cards, were often mentioned:

Standing in the hall before classes start one morning, I'm talking to Esmeralda when Ruben interrupts us and starts showing me his baseball cards and telling me how much they're worth. He has one, an error card of Nolan Ryan [a card with flaws in its manufacture, thus rarer and more valuable than ordinary cards], that he says is worth $29. He says that he's going to send it to Ryan, get it signed, and then it'll be worth $600. He regales me with tales of other expensive sports cards he owns.

As Appadurai (1986) suggested, the same objects can move in and out of commodity status. For these fifth graders, comic books were things that could be read or packed away for later sale:

Helen: We read comic books, horror books—

Duane: No! Whenever I buy a comic book, I put it in a case!—

Earl: We don't read books; I don't read books.

Duane: And I don't read it! I don't touch it!

Jan: You just collect them like cards?

Helen: I'll read it and put it in the case.

Earl: See, my book is TV.

Helen: That's what I do. I got a Heathcliff; I traded in all my Archies for Heathcliff.

Earl: Heathcliff—he's a heap of cliffs.

Duane: I got X-Men.

Helen: I don't have any of those.

Earl: X-Men—

Duane: I got X-Men first edition. And I got—

Helen: I got 2001 the first edition. Expensive.

          . . .

Duane: I got a New Defenders, first edition.

Jan: You don't read 'em, you just collect them?

Duane: I read 'em when I get 'em, but if they're in like a little bag thing
          I don't take them out.

Helen: I read, I read all mine.

The focus on exchange did not mean that items such as comics mattered only in a narrow economic sense. The previous conversation, for example, clearly hints at gender constructions woven into cultural tastes, with Helen describing humorous comic books and Duane and Earl favoring action heros. As Crawford (1992) suggested, commodities are strategic resources for shaping identities:

> As culture, leisure, sex, politics, and even death turn into commodities, consumption increasingly constructs the way we see the world....Consumption hierarchies, in which commodities define life-styles, now furnish indications of status position more visible than the economic relationships of class positions....Moreover, for many, the very construction of the self involves the acquisition of commodities. If the world is understood through commodities, then personal identity depends on one's ability to compose a coherent self-image through the selection of a distinct personal set of commodities. (pp. 11–12)

Which things the kids collected could also be important. If the monetary exchange value of the commodity was all that mattered, there would have been no bias against "boring" things, but there was:

Duane: I like Marvel comics: X-Men.

Alf: [*Laughing*] X-men. [*Singing*] Superman.

Duane: I hate Superman!

Alf: I know, that's boring. Everybody collects that. Spiderman too.
          Batman.

If objects were resources for constructing identities, discrimination in their selection was critical; kids never simply collected the material thing. Along with the things people buy, they buy the images, statuses, and meanings the things suggest. As Slater (1987) noted, "The greater part of consumption is the consumption of signs" (p. 457). The small and easily transportable sports cards that boys especially coveted make an interesting case. Instead of investing in a single character (such as Superman), boys could invest in a sport and all the meanings attached to it.

This phenomenon reminded me in a way of my own childhood. When I was in the fifth grade and had just moved from the country to a working-class neighborhood in Tulsa, Oklahoma, I played little league baseball, went to minor league games, listened to major league games on the radio, and collected baseball cards. But being a participant, playing on a team, was the core activity. The team provided the social network within which I could use baseball cards and spectatorship to shape my identity. Cards wouldn't have meant much if I hadn't played the game.

Among the fourth and fifth graders I knew at Thurber, however, collecting sports cards no longer seemed connected to playing a sport. Doug, a fourth grader, had a collection that covered several genres, but he seemed strangely unsure of just what he had:

> *Jan*:   Do you collect baseball cards?
>
> *Doug*: I got a whole stack of baseball cards upstairs in my room. I got two collector's items. Some Batman. Some other. Ninja Turtles. Ninja Turtles 2. I have, um, two collectors' baseball cards. I have some NASCAR. I got a lot of baseball cards. And some Batman cards.
>
> *Jan*:   What do you do with them?
>
> *Doug*: Leave them in a box and keep them stashed. I don't do anything with them.
>
> *Jan*:   You said you had some collectors' items, what are those?
>
> *Doug*: Two of them.
>
> *Jan*:   Who are they?
>
> *Doug*: I don't know.
>
> *Jan*:   How do you know they're collectors' items then?
>
> *Doug*: My grandad bought them for me. And one of them's the Sox, and another one is, I think, New York Yankees.

Possessing cards and talking or displaying them to others seemed to give the boys feelings of mastery over the domains depicted in the cards. To have a representation of something was in a sense to have the thing itself. As I suggested in the previous chapter, boys collecting sports cards consumed the masculine and virile images attached to the sports. This was true even when they knew little of the games themselves (and although girls probably participated more in sports than the boys did, I met only one girl who collected cards, and she was *not* active in sports).

In my interviews with fifth graders, Duane pleaded with me through the first five discussions to let him talk about basketball and often signaled his displeasure with my neglect of it by simply shouting out the names of basketball stars. Finally, I gave in, and he came to our next meeting with a card of the basketball star Larry Bird.

> *Jan*:   You collect those?
>
> *Duane*: Yeah! Worth $6!

. . .

Jan: How long have you been collecting basketball cards?

Duane: Since I was 5.

Jan: Since you were 5?

Earl: Uh-uh!

. . .

Jan: So what do you do with them?

Duane: Collect 'em!

Earl: Collect them.

Helen: Keep them; put them in plastic cases.

Earl: Sell them. Pick them up and show them to people.

Jan: Where do you sell them?

Duane: Sell them?

Jan: I mean, I know they have like—

Earl: Go to Hobby USA and sell them.

At this point the discussion began to wander (much to Duane's dismay) to other hobbies such as computer games and to discussions of other collectibles. Finally, Duane had enough and shouted, "Let's talk about basketball!"

Jan: You want to talk about your cards?

Duane: Just players you like.

Jan: Players you like?

As the discussion turned to basketball, Helen got up to draw a diagram on the chalkboard. Duane and Earl joined her, and the rest of the interview session was spent filling up the board with diagrams or more exactly, pictures of basketball courts with zones blocked out. I was a little surprised to realize that none of them knew much about the game. Duane, for example, asked, "Is it six people or five people?" I asked him how long he'd been playing, and he answered 3 years. After a while, Earl, who didn't pretend to be a sports enthusiast, said, "You don't know what in the world you're doing, do you, Duane?"

Helen said, "No, he doesn't. I do!"

At one point, Duane asked me to explain the legend on his Larry Bird card. I read it aloud: "In an event that should have been dominated by sharpshooting guards, Larry Bird ruled the long distance shootoff from its conception. The only pure forward to win the event, Bird showed remarkable range for a 6 ft 9 in scrapper."

Thinking he might not know that guards were supposed to be better outside shooters than were big forwards or that he didn't understand that the three-point competition was part of the buildup to the annual NBA all-star game, I asked him, "What don't you get?" As far as I could tell from his shrugs and questions, Duane didn't understand anything: What a three-point shot was, who Larry Bird was, what a forward was. His engagement with the sport seemed purely that of a naive spectator, for watching a sports event does not presuppose completely understanding it. A person can get the essential meanings of competition, masculine aggression, and force, with an imperfect knowledge of the rules. Indeed, Elias (1978) argued that the rise of sports can be associated with the transformation of these traits from embodied affects to visible spectacles:

> This living-out of affects in spectating or even in merely listening (e.g., to a radio commentary) is a particularly characteristic feature of civilized society. It partly determines the development of books and the theater, and decisively influences the role of the cinema in our world. This transformation of what manifested itself originally as an active, often aggressive expression of pleasure, into the passive, more ordered pleasure of spectating (i.e., a mere pleasure of the eye) is already initiated in education, in conditioning precepts for young people. (pp. 202–203)

The lack of understanding on the part of spectators is *assumed* within the mass media packaging of sports. Sports broadcasts, even those that are televised, have play-by-play announcers to tell viewers what they see and "color" announcers to explain its significance. This is another facet of the world-as-exhibition. Kids learn not to play but to *watch* games:

Jan: When did you all get interested in this?

Alf: When I was probably 2 years old.

Duane: When I was not even born!

Alf: My dad taught me how to play it, I mean, watch it.

Duane: I watched my dad play baseball and football. That's how I got into sports.

In their conversations, Duane and Alf, who didn't know each other well, competed to see who could claim the earliest allegiance to sport: The bigger the fan, the more masculinity he could claim. There was an equation of watching sports with being in good physical shape:

Alf: I know somebody who don't like sports!

Duane: Who?

Alf: Richard. He don't.

Duane: Earl don't either!

Alf: When I first moved in, he didn't know how to play baseball.

Duane: Earl, he likes sports, but he don't want to play them.

Alf: They're lazy, him and Richard. See, that's why he ain't in shape, and Richard, and nobody else is in shape.

Sports cards, then, became emblems of *distant,* disembodied values: power, masculinity, maturity. Sports cards, comics, and video games were links to distant sites of practice. Exchange was a way kids could use distantly produced representations to affiliate themselves to these distant meanings in a local context. But the mere possession of a commodity, as Duane's problems with his basketball cards (his inability to convince Helen and Earl that he knew what he was talking about) suggest, was not always sufficient to produce these local meanings. Kids also had to be able to successfully, that is, persuasively, before an audience of their peers, invoke, inhabit, or appropriate the meanings of popular culture products.

INVOCATIONS OF POP CULTURE

Kids invoked popular cultural forms to position themselves in local settings by connecting themselves to distant sites of practice. Some of Alf's and Duane's uses of sports heros were examples of invocation: a collective, shared reference to cultural products. Invocation presumes an active, participating audience: Duane's basketball talk worked with Alf, but not so well with Helen or Earl. For example, during the bus ride on a field trip, kids grabbed my microphone and recorder and, without anyone ever explicitly defining the frame, began to improvise a kind of music–radio show:

Lauren: I'm gonna sing, "My Boyfriend's Back." [*She sings the entire song*] [*Pause*] Ch, ch, ch, ch—I'm changing the channels: [*Sings*] "It's my party, I'll cry if I want to"—Oh I hate that. I'll change the channel. Ch, ch, ch, ch, ch, ch, ch, ch, ch. Oh! Here goes something. "You are my sunshine, my only sunshine; you make me happy, when skies are gray; you'll never know, dear, how much I love you; please don't taaaake, my sunshine, away...." [*Sings more of the song, then sings, "It's my party"* again; a weather forecast follows*] Now back to Effie, with her song, "Jesus's Will."

Effie: [*Sings the gospel song. Sings "I'm not a superwoman; I'm not that kind of girl"; then hands the microphone to Felix*]

Felix: Okay, this is Snoop Doggy Dog. This is when I was really little. [*Sings*]...Hey girl in the pink dress [Effie], what do you want to be when you grow up?

Effie: A nurse!

Felix: That's a good thing. Hey girl in the blue dress, what do you want to be when you grow up?

Desiree: A tap dancer! I don't know.

Felix: Hey you, in the braids, what's your name? My name is Snoop. What do you want to be when you grow up? I want to be a mother hustler. You better axe some! I want to be a mother-fuckin' hustler! You better ask somebody! Nurr Nurr Nurr Uh! Ah! I see, you got what you wanted....Hey you, what d'ya wanna be when you grow up?...I can't see when you—okay—[*Responding to Desiree's gesture of shock*]—That was in the song!

Desiree: The thing is "What do you want to be when you grow up"—[*Talking to me*] you can't let nobody else listen to it, 'cause he'll get in trouble.

The key thing in these kinds of conversations, which were relatively common when I let kids use the microphone for their own purposes, seemed to be the ability to display an appropriate familiarity with mass media products: whether these were old pop tunes, church gospel, weather broadcasts, or rap. But while some aspects of this event were playlike improvisations designed to amuse others, the kids also seemed to be signifying, by claiming allegiances to particular popular culture products, the roles or identities they wanted to assume in class. Effie, the gospel singer, was a sweet African American girl who constantly managed to get herself in the teacher's doghouse by talking out of turn or showing an excess of enthusiasm. Lauren was a perky, middle-class European American, all sweetness and obedience (until the teacher's back was turned). And Felix, performing the hypermasculinized and wildly misogynistic rap of Snoop Doggy Dog, complete with profanity, was one of two boys in the fourth grade who openly expressed his attraction to girls, a habit which got him labeled "queer" by the other fourth-grade boys. All these meanings depended on the kids' shared understandings of popular culture.

INHABITING POP CULTURE

In addition to invoking cultural forms in this fashion, kids also actively inhabited roles or characters drawn from the media. Earl, for example, in one of the exchanges quoted earlier, spoke of letting his "imagination run wild" when he wrote for himself on the computer. But from what I could tell and see in his writing, his imagination usually ran down paths already laid out by the mass media:

> *Jan*: What are you writing?
>
> *Earl*: It's just a, about, kind of like a movie I watched. I'm kinda writin' a book about it. It's different.
>
> *Duane*: You should put, "Duane, Earl."
>
> *Jan*: [*Reading the title*] "Operation Kill Earl"—is that something you saw on TV?
>
> *Earl*: No, it was really the movie *Toy Soldiers,* but I changed it.
>
> *Jan*: Oh, I've seen that. It's the one about the terrorists trying to take over a school, and the kids—
>
> *Earl*: They save the school. It's bad.
>
>   . . .
>
> *Duane*: —When me and Earl were thinking about that story about the school, getting invaded? We just let our imagination run wild didn't we?
>
> *Lucy*: Oh, where's that story?
>
> *Earl*: I used to make myself dream of the school being invaded and then I'd save it. [*Laughs*]
>
> *Duane*: I know.
>
> *Jan*: Did you show anybody that story?
>
> *Duane*: We couldn't print it. The printer was broken.

Earl and Duane did not passively adopt roles and personae from media products like *Toy Soldiers.* As Earl pointed out, his story was "different," molded to fit his fantasies of gaining distinction by saving the school. This partial inhabitation of media-disseminated roles is apparently common among young kids. Dyson (1994), for example, described second graders' using images, characters, and plot lines from popular cartoons and comics like *Teenage Mutant Ninja Turtles* and *X-Men* to work through issues of gender and power:

The appeal of the X-Men to the second-grade girls seemed tied to the greater role of girls in superhero play....All children familiar with the superhero stories agreed that both girls and boys are on the X-Men team. Moreover, they knew too that, in Sammy's words, the X-Men women are "as strong as men." (pp. 227–228)

As Dyson pointed out, girls were frequently marginalized in X-Men–based play because the romantic relationships between the comic book characters exposed kids taking on these roles to ridicule from their peers (Dyson, 1994, pp. 228–229). It was only through a creative and negotiated reconstruction of the characters' identities and relationships that girls could create a desirable place for themselves within the performances.

But where Dyson (1993, 1994) talked about classrooms themselves as communities, it seems to me critical that the kids she described are working with flows of popular culture that begin and end beyond the classroom. How the teacher structures the classroom can shape what kids can do publicly with these flows (Dyson, 1994), but it is misleading to treat popular culture simply as a peculiar source of curriculum. Earl and Duane were writing a story for their own purposes, not *for* school or *in* school or even in writing formats used or recognized by their teacher. Rather, they were crafting temporary identities out of the resources of a fund of knowledge distributed, in this instance, through a broadcast text (one in which adolescent boys, who were considered behavior problems and sent to a military school, become heros by defeating invading terrorists). Such identity frames circulate through funds of knowledge that connect students, teachers, and everyone else to people, things, and events that are distant (Pred & Watts, 1992). As Paul Willis (1990) suggested:

> Making (not receiving) messages and meanings in your own context and from materials you have appropriated is, in essence, a form of education in the broadest sense. It is the specifically developmental part of symbolic work and creativity, an education about the "self" and its relation to the world and to others in it. (p. 136)

The materials out of which the kids constructed messages and meanings were distributed in stable forms across neighborhoods, regions, and nations by the mass media, which supply "a rich, ever-changing store of possible lives" and also indirectly influence how people act in and make sense of other aspects of social life: "The biographies of ordinary people, thus, are constructions (or fabrications) in which the imagination plays an important role" (Appadurai, 1990, pp. 197–198, 200). Earl and Duane, and the kids Dyson studied, were not mesmerized by the media, but the media articulated ready-made, disposable identities they could pragmatically appropriate. Hall (1989) suggested:

> [O]ne only discovers who one is because of the identities which one has to take on in order to act…I think identity is sort of…like a bus, you just have to get from here to there, the whole of you can never be represented in the ticket you carry but you just have to buy a ticket in order to get from here to there. (quoted in Pred & Watts, 1992 p. 196)

Popular culture passes out bus tickets for identitites. In using them kids move in and out of networks or funds of knowledge organized by video games, comic books, baseball cards, forms of music. Their memberships are fluid, overlapping, sometimes temporary, almost always partial rather than total. Moreover, identities can be means of conveyance across as well as within funds of knowledge. People can transfer from one "bus" to another, detour, circle around, get out, and walk a bit. Is the space of social practice defined by the grid of city streets and the map of all possible bus routes or by the paths and "spatial practices" that "appropriate" space? As de Certeau (1984) asserted: "Space is composed of intersections of mobile elements. It is in a sense actuated by the ensemble of movements deployed within it" (p. 117). To get a better sense of how these movements are orchestrated or improvised, we have to look at appropriations of popular culture representations.

APPROPRIATIONS OF POP CULTURE

The more complex images of community and identity I've outlined suggest that we should look for uses of popular culture different from the clearly bounded, if complex, inhabitations of media-defined roles that characterized "Operation Kill Earl" or Dyson's second graders' performances of the X-Men. This notion goes somewhat against practice in the field of cultural studies, where the focus is usually on genres (horror movies), artists (Madonna), product forms (comic books), or particular texts (the X-Men). Research typically involves studying production practices, comparing and analyzing products, interviewing people about what they think of particular genres, products, or performers; or going with them to movies, rock music clubs, or Star Trek conventions (see, for example, Bacon-Smith, 1992; Becker, 1982; Frith & Horne, 1987; Grossberg, Nelson, & Treichler, 1992; Radway, 1984). These approaches treat popular culture as consisting of well-defined products or practices that people partake of as wholes. And this view may be true as people grow older: Willis (1990), Gaines (1991), and others have shown that by midadolecence, kids often craft their identifies through dense engagements with particular genres (heavy metal music, for example). But the 9-, 10-, and 11-year-olds I worked with had much more fluid if no less pervasive relations with popular culture. I saw them messily using it in school and in their interactions with each other to get on with everyday life.

In these interactions, the genres, styles, and products of popular culture weren't always treated as coherent wholes. De Certeau (1984) noted that the meaning of a representation comes from "its manipulation by users who are not its makers" (p. xiii). But use and "manipulation" don't require that the interaction be focused on the representations (as in the case of Dyson's second graders). People can appropriate elements of popular culture products and move these elements across genre and product boundaries to create situated meanings and fashion identities for particular purposes.

Let me work through a few examples, beginning with one from a dark and stormy spring day when a torrential thunderstorm delayed the buses that took the kids home at the end of the day. As we all waited and the delay dragged on beyond a half hour, the fourth graders I was with became increasingly edgy. I decided to use the time and provide some distraction by doing an extemporaneous interview with Doug and Mel about the upcoming standardized test they were to take. They agreed with each other that the test and all its components were "boring," "stupid," and hateful. Then they reflected on other things they hated:

Doug: I hate storms!

Mel: I hate school!

Doug: Me too!

Mel: I hate homework!

Doug: School sucks!

Mel: And one thing, one thing I hate more than homework, more than school!

Mel &
Doug: [*Together*] More than anything, Girls!

Jan: Why?

Doug: They get on my nerves. One sitting right there [Lauren] gets on our nerves.

Mel: [*Almost whispering*] And girls, they admit things to boys, like they like them and stuff, and that makes some boys upset and stuff. But not me; I just make fun of them and stuff.

Doug: Me too.

Mel: Call them names.

Doug: Me too . . .

Mel: And then when I get like into high school, I'll go skiing and see these ski bunnies, ask them out for a date or something.

Jan: Ski bunnies? What?

Mel: Ski bunnies; I'll ask one out for a date.

Doug: Yeah, they're girls!

Mel: Oh man! Whoo!

Jan: What's a ski bunny?

Doug: It's girls dressed like in a skin suit.

Mel: And bunny ears and a cotton tail, skiing down mountains and stuff. And they walk around in the snow and stuff. Woo! That's when I'm gonna get big in college. I mean, not college but high school.

Doug: The other thing we hate in school, is school! School sucks. But you can make it fun by going into detention.

Mel: That's not fun.

Doug: No! Like—on *Saved by the Bell*.

Mel: You try to get your girlfriend in trouble, then you get in trouble, and you're all alone!

Doug: Then you go to detention and lock it and cut off the lights.

Mel: [*Slaps hands together*] Oh, baby!

Doug: You knocked Shakespeare's book off the table like [?].

Mel: But Kelly wasn't there.

Doug: Mr. Slater moved. Spanish teacher!

Mel: [*Speaking to me and reaching to turn off my recorder*] Okay, this is not *Saved by the Bell*. Thank you very much. You've been most helpful. Ehhhhhh! [*Turns my recorder off*]

All this took place in a carnival atmosphere (Bahktin, 1968). The extraordinary delay in getting away from school, the lightning, thunder, and rain outside, the mixture of kids from other classes milling into the room, me with my tape recorder, the lack of an acknowledged frame for what was supposed to be happening—all allowed the kids to invert the usual orders of school activity, to move around at will, play with friends, and yell out their hatreds. As Lash and Urry (1994) suggested, "Carnival is...a zone in which revellers wear masks; in which they are free to try on a set of masks or identities" (p. 132). The most readily available masks, it seems clear, came from popular media sources. Real girls like Lauren, who had been hinting that she liked Mel, were publicly identified as objects of hatred; but the boys could still assert their heterosexual masculinity (with me, as an adult man, their audience) by expressing lust for media bunnies. All these positions were ingeniously bundled together when the boys fluidly segued to an episode of the teen-oriented television series *Saved by the Bell*, its meaning altered (Hodge & Tripp, 1986) to connect hatred of school with a trip to the detention hall, a trip that then became a sexual encounter with a media babe.

The difference between this phenomenon and the way the kids Dyson (1994) described used the X-Men, or even Earl's "Operation Kill Earl" story mentioned earlier, is that instead of borrowing the framework provided by the popular culture product and asserting meanings within it, the frame here was the situational enactment of widely distributed meanings about masculinity, for which purpose popular culture elements could be pulled from a wide range of unconnected sources. I never could get Mel and Doug to explain exactly where the ski bunnies came from (perhaps *Playboy* magazine), and not until a moment after the exchange did I realize they were talking about a television show (at the first mention of "saved by the bell," I was trying to figure out what bell had rung). Although adults created the representations the boys appropriated, they were not central participants in the fund of knowledge or central recipients of the meanings the boys constructed. As an adult, I was peripheral. Mel's and Doug's brief collaboration with the media imagery developed fluidly and entailed no sustained work with either the genre or the particular episode. Indeed, I never heard them mention the show again.

This easy combination of ski bunnies and television show plots suggests that kids didn't necessarily focus on one product at a time in constructing identities in their peer-centered funds of knowledge. Rather, they could appropriate and detach fragments of popular culture—plot elements and the ski bunny image or simply words or phrases, as in this interchange with fifth graders about their writing assignments:

Jan: Why were you writing about that? Why would she have you writing about "if money grew on trees?"

Lucy: 'Cause she's just crazy.

Earl: She lets us write fun things once in a while; then she gives us hard assignments.

Duane: [*Mumbling*] Stupid assignment.

Jan: What's a hard assignment?

Lucy: What we're doing right now.

Earl: Yeah. We have to write a play.

Duane: That stupid idiot!

          . . .

Lucy: This is a short one.

Duane: "You stupid idiot."

Earl: [to Duane] Okay, Ren and Stimpy.

Duane: "Stimpy, you stupid idiot."

Here Duane borrowed a core phrase from the acerbic Ren, a character on the television cartoon show, *Ren and Stimpy,* to lend resonance and supply force to his characterization of the teacher's assignment. Duane repeated the phrase until Earl acknowledged that he'd understood the intended frame. This exchange was a pointed use of popular culture discourse to make meaning, but not at all *about* the cartoon show.

Interactions in which kids appropriated pop culture elements were not confined to particular genres. Let me return to a section of a group interview I discussed in the previous chapter in the context of fighting and femininity, the exchange between Lucy and Helen after Lucy had angered Helen by telling us about a conversation she overheard in which Helen told another girl that her father watched X-rated videos.

Helen: Have you ever seen the movie *Mad Max* Lucy?

Neal: Oh yeah, I liked that one.

Earl: That was a scary movie, man. That was weird!

          . . .

Helen: I'm gonna get a motorcycle, Lucy. I think I want to get a motorcycle Lucy. I'm gonna get a motorcycle, a badge, and a gun, and I'm gonna come after you Lucy! [*Laughter*]

Lucy: [*Has been talking at same time as Helen, but I can't make out what she says because Helen is talking so loud.*]

Helen: When I grow up, I'm gonna get a motorcycle, a gun, and a badge, and I'm comin' after your butt.

Jan: Come on.

Neal: Time, time.

Trixie: Time out!!

Lucy: I'm gonna get Betty Boop.

Helen: Betty Boop is dead! Betty Boop is long dead; even her voice is dead!

Jan: Come on. Lucy.

Duane: You're gonna be blown to boop! [*Laughter*]

Helen: [*Laughing*] Shut up, Duane.

          . . .

Lucy: She [Helen] kisses Barney!

Here Helen and Lucy drew across a variety of genres and cultural forms to assert interpretive frames that would position them favorably in their conflict. Helen appropriated the image of a violent male movie character. Lucy's response crossed medium and genre to invoke Betty

Boop, the squeeky-voiced 1930s cartoon heroine who was frequently menaced but always triumphed. Neither Helen nor any of the other children found this response strange (although it still mystifies me) but rather treated it as simply ineffective. Lucy pulled from another genre to reply with a jibe that tried to position Helen with Barney the dinosaur, a treacly television star. In this exchange the kids clearly drew not from particular genres but from a general fund of images, roles, and plots distributed through popular media.

It's also clear that many of the images and roles the kids appropriated centered on issues of gender and sexuality. But if boys used popular culture to try on masculine and adult male roles, girls' public appropriations of popular culture seemed more complex. Most of the girls were serious media users. Ora, for instance, was, along with her mother, a professional wrestling fanatic; Carol had a remarkable collection of Elvis memorabilia. But I didn't see, maybe because I was a guy and not an appropriate audience for the girls, a consistent public use of popular culture similar to the boys'. In fact, much of the girls' public uses of popular culture seemed to depend on the presence of boys (e.g., Lauren and Desiree playing along with Felix's Snoop Doggy Dog impersonation). The friction between Helen and Lucy, for example, all but vanished when there were no popular boys in the interview groups. Perhaps this pattern was due to the fact that so much popular culture is directed toward boys, or perhaps it was because boys dominate public space and didn't give the girls a chance. In any case, girls didn't always passively play along. In the event described next, which revolved around an X-Men comic book and provides a useful contrast to Dyson's (1994) work with kids just 2 years younger, Cicily seemingly appropriated a role completely outside the frame of the comic book, that of an adult woman, to disrupt a masculinist appropriation of the comic.

On one of our bus rides back from a fieldtrip, the kids were passing around my microphone and mostly singing songs into it, when Cicily, looking over her shoulder, saw a group of boys (Doug, Mel, Beavis, and Rufus) huddled over an X-Men comic book:

> *Cicily*:   Let me talk into this microphone! [*She grabs it*] These boys, they learnin' at an early age about these stupid comic books! They look at girls! You hear him? He said, "They're pretty babes." They learnin' at an early age. They ain't supposed to be doin' this. That one over there. He lookin' at them too. He turned around and looked at 'em. All these boys, they're looking at the girls in the comic books.

> *Jan*:   They're reading X-Men, right?

> *Cicily*:   No! They ain't readin' no X-men. They lookin' at the girls. See, they have close-ups.

As if to support Cicily, Mel showed me a page with a large picture panel centered on a superhero girl doing a high kick, my first glimpse of the comic since childhood. X-Men premiered in 1963 and by the early 1990s had become the world's best-seller, with a 14% share of the total comic book market and tie-ins with trading cards, a Saturday morning cartoon show, and plastic dolls (Martin, 1994). (For the uninitiated, the X-Men are a group of mutant superheros, male and female; within the comic's narrative, they are students at a school for the "gifted" run by a telepathic mutant in Westchester County, New York.) As Dyson (1994) showed, the presence of women provides space for girls to appropriate meanings (albeit with some difficulty). Girls are said to make up about one third of the Saturday morning cartoon version of the comic (Martin, 1994). But the ways women are depicted allow boys to appropriate the images for rather different meanings:

Mel: Oogah! Oogah!

Doug: Hot Baby! Jean Gray is! [Jean Gray is one of the X-chicks.]

Mel: Dr. Nespor, I got to show you this!

Cicily: They talkin' about them girls! He's talking about that girl right there.

[Boy]:   I can definitely make some money off of these girls.

Cicily: See, they think they can make some money off them stupid ugly girls.

Doug: They show her leg, man!

[Boy]:   Real girl women!

The boys began to argue over which of the X-chicks was prettier, and Mel made a wolf-whistle into the microphone. Cicily spoke: "You heard him whistling about them girls. That's a shame! They need to stop looking at these girls. The teacher shouldn't let them have comic books on the bus!"

The boys, who'd initially been keeping to themselves, ogling pictures of the pointy, conical breasts and high kicking bare thighs of the female superheros, now began to make a public game of it and began to chant, "X-chicks, X-chicks." I asked Cicily if she'd ever read an X-Men comic:

Cicily: Yes I have *read* them. And don't nobody look at them ugly boys [i.e., X-boys]. They got eyes that shoot out rays! They look crazy! But these girls [the X-chicks], they don't care what they look like; they just look at 'em. Talk about X-chicks, X-chicks, X-chicks.

Although it hadn't occurred to me before Cicily mentioned it, it does seem that the male X-Men have more visible abnormalities than the X-chicks (who tend to mental powers or picturesque physical abnormalities). The particular ugly-boy Cicily was referring to was the Cyclops, Jean Gray's boyfriend, who wears a special visor because death rays shoot from his eyes. Before I could pursue Cicily's explanation of her dislike for the X-Men, however, Mel began showing around what to him seemed a particularly exciting picture of a woman doing a vertical split as she kicked someone in the head and thereby produced a superhero crotch shot. Trying to be the good ethnographer, I took a photograph of him with the comic.

Cicily: Shame on you Dr. Nespor.

Jan: What did I do?

Cicily: You're the same! Dr. Nespor likes them X-chicks too!

Rufus: Personally I like Playboy better.

Doug: Ooh, you like Playboy magazine? . . .

Cicily: They talkin' about them women....They need to go home and learn some school work instead of them chicks.

Doug: We study chicks.

Cicily: They said they study chicks; it's their special thing.

Doug: We study chicks! And they are our speciality! And that's why God put us on this earth! We're men!

Cicily: God put you on this earth to work! And to learn!

           . . .

Doug: All we do at school is study chicks together.

It seems to me that Cicily was publicly defining the boys' reading of the X-Men as a statement about their sexuality or an expression of sexism in which women were reduced to representations in the abstract space of the world-as-exhibition. I don't think Cicily was uncomfortable talking about sexuality per se. In any event I'd seen her sit though Mrs. Kelvin's sex education lecture on erections which utilized a life-size picture of a fleshless male body with a detachable penis (so that Mrs. Kelvin could illustrate flaccidity and tumescence with interchangeable members). Cicily asked sensible questions in the class and was at ease with the topic. The boys, by contrast, were plainly uncomfortable, more so when Cicily turned in her seat to make faces at them. And having watched her interact with these boys over the school year, I could not say that she liked any of them. The boys, who had been quietly talking among themselves until Cicily caught them, turned the situation into a game by responding loudly, confirming her accusations, and becoming progressively wilder in their own statements. The transformation of the interaction from whispering among the four boys to a public, tape-recorded performance almost certainly generated some of the carnival-like features of their performances, for example, Doug's claim to be "studying chicks." But although Cicily's outrage may seem comically exaggerated, it was genuine and lasted for weeks. Her reaction focused on how the boys used the comic to ogle the women's bodies. As there was no acceptable place for her in the narrative or imagery of the comic, she broke the narrative frame and appropriated the role of scolding adult ("God put you on this earth to work and learn").

REPRESENTATION AND EVERYDAY LIFE

Both Cicily and the boys were experimenting with adult attitudes and roles, played broadly but not frivolously. Popular culture, in the form of the X-chicks, provided a stage and props (along with other resources imported by the kids, and found items like my microphone) for a performance of adult gender roles. As Heath and McLaughlin (1994) suggested in a very different context, this taking on of roles is a fundamental feature of learning through participation:

> Roles are constituted through combinations of skill, attitude and symbolic means, and the taking on of roles is made posible by the expectation of performance. Participants observe and take part in activities with a sense of fit between their current attitude and abilities and possible roles they may play within a situation or slice of action within an episode. Individuals then *take part* by *taking a part* or role mentally or physically in events that surround them and they now contribute to a resulting performance. (p. 474)

Media spaces, invoked, inhabited, or appropriated in situated interactions, could function as "border zones" (Heath & McLaughlin, 1994, p. 475) where kids looked at their everyday lives and at alternative life ways situated in the abstract spaces of the media.

It may be that images of alternative lives were once (and still are) generated within the embodied community. Tina gave me a rhapsodic description of her life in a Mexican American neighborhood in Detroit, where she'd lived until moving to Roanoke:

> All my cousins would go over; my grandma would be there; she would entertain me with church songs. My mom would be there. And then my dad would pick me up. I usually spent every single day outside over by my dad, because they had a boys' and girls' club over there—which I *can't* hardly find over here. I had a card to get in; I could go swimming. I could

go eating there. In the summer they had lunch for free there. Then, uh, some days like for Halloween they gave you candy. And there was an art room; you could make anything you want. You just had to ask. And then there was—everywhere you go there was a corner store. And I'd walk there. I miss that!...I loved it over there because...my sister's dad, my sister's dad had a restaurant; no, my sister's dad had a *taqueria*, that's a little small place that just sells tacos. And they had a building right next to it. Now they have a store there, a baby store. And my aunt, my *aunt* [pronouncing it *ant*], I'm not going to say "aunt." My aunt had a beauty shop. My uncle had a restaurant, a bakery, and a bar. On all the same street: on all the same street, I could get food, free tacos, free hamburgers, free drinks. I could get half-price on haircuts. I could get free bread. Every time I passed by there, there was this girl—I knew, I knew, she was real short. I'm taller than her now. She, all the time I passed, she'd always run out and give me a small bag with about 20 or 10 cookies inside of there, free. Because my dad—my dad's uncle owned about three places around there. He owned two bakeries; he own three bakeries, but one of them closed down, so now he owns two. He owns one bar. And when he went to Mexico for about a month, my dad was in charge of it. And he had to spend—he got out of work at about 4:00. And all the days, he used to have to go over there to ask if he could, if he could at around 8 or 9, because from night to morning, my mom had me. And then from 4 to about 8 or 9, I'd stay with my dad. Then I'd go to my dad's house. Then on Friday and Saturday, I'd go to my dad's house. That's the way it used to go....There was a big market over here called, not Market Place, but they had like a shopping store right here, a clothes store. Dunkin Donuts. A big store right here. A tire store right here. Toys "R" Us right over here. A *big* plaza over there.

Not surprisingly, Tina told me she'd hardly watched television in that life and could think of the name of only one series she watched regularly. On the other hand, when I asked her if there were any places in *this* town she liked, she replied only: "My room." And when I asked what she did away from school she first said, "Nothing," then added that she *did* watch television:

That's the only thing that's fun over here. I have a color TV....I watch *Saved by the Bell, Full House, Rosanne, Married with Children.* Sometimes I watch *90210,* sometimes I watch *Melrose Place.* Sometimes I watch, uh, *Family Matters.* I watch, sometimes—[*Laughs*]. You don't want to know everything I watch. I could make a list....Oh!! *Phenom,* and *Martin,* and, and, and *Living Single* [*Claps hand*]. Oh, I don't know, I don't know! I like *Phenom* a lot. And I like *Someone Like Me....Fresh Prince of Bel-Air,* and *Blossom. Animaniacs, Tiny Toons, Weinerville.*

Tina's case suggests that the dense engagements of kids with popular culture, which I treat here as a network, a fund of knowledge, are partly determined by their access to other kinds of social networks (cf. Dimaggio, 1990, p. 118). As Lash and Urry (1994) suggested, "For true mass culture, more traditional social, and especially class and family, structures must partly subside, and atomizing, niche marketing and lifestyle creating communication networks must take their place" (p. 134). As we saw in chapter 3, the structure of many modern cities like Roanoke immobilizes kids in apartment complexes or residential neighborhoods devoid of the big city life Tina described (I mean not just the density of her relatives but the businesses, clubs, and public spaces to which she had easy access).[2] In neighborhoods and apartment complexes surrounded by busy streets, kids become dependent on their parents for movement, for access to the world at large. Insofar as they are immobilized in their immediate neighborhoods, representations become the only means of travel allowing kids access to spaces and meanings beyond their localities. A peculiar world-as-exhibition is produced: When I asked fourth graders where they'd like to live if they could live anywhere, a few, like Tina (who wanted to go back to Detroit), named cities where relatives lived. The most common answers, however, were theme or amusement parks—not just somewhere else, but a different sort of space altogether. Desiree's need to get away was almost palpable:

> *Desiree*: I want to be in the fifth grade so bad! I want to hurry up and finish school!
>
> *Jan*: . . . Why do you want to finish school so fast—you don't like it?
>
> *Desiree*: I like it, but I just want to be out so I can stay up late and drive a car. And go to the movies by myself, and stuff like that.
>
> *Jan*: What do you want to do when you finish school?
>
> *Desiree*: Drive a car and go out of town.
>
> *Jan*: Where would you go?
>
> *Desiree*: Florida. Florida or King's Dominion [a Virginia theme park]. I want to go there so bad!

The spaces of popular culture and mass amusement, it seemed, were linked for the kids to promises of physical freedoms, to the "childish" bodily pleasures progressively constricted in school settings. When Carol explained that she'd like to live in Disneyland above all other places, she said that it was "so I could ride all these rides. I wouldn't have to walk around, do this. I could just, you know, ride."

As these kids get older and gain independent access to spaces beyond the school and home, this aspect of their popular culture could change as well. Uses of media are tightly linked to, not independent of, the other social networks and spatialities in which kids engage. I think Tina's case implies that the importance of popular culture is a function of the drying

---

[2]This statement is merely an illustration. To some extent, big cities' decline corresponds to the collapse of the social networks Tina describes (Wacquant, 1995).

up of public spaces for kids her age in urban neighborhoods, but the articulations of bodies, landscapes, and signs might be very different for middle school or high school students. In these schools, students from a wide range of neighborhoods and backgrounds are clumped together (the schools themselves organize neighborhoods spaces differently than do elementaries), and kids become more mobile as they begin to get access to automobiles. Popular culture might then become a strategic resource for marking identities and forging ties across neighborhood, ethnic, or class lines—or for reinforcing these divisions.

These intersections shouldn't be taken as immutable connections but as particular articulations of general flows. As I said at the outset of this book, the problem of inquiry is not to find patterns of intersection that generalize across settings but to trace flows of practice that organize widespread social relations, to expand maps of these networks, and to show how the intersections we begin our analysis with are connected to other intersections across time and space. Coming to the end of this work, I realize how limited my success has been. At best, perhaps, you now have a feeling for how things might be articulated, a sense of the density of the intersections. And perhaps, like me, you come to the end with still more questions.

6   Loose Ends

Ethnographies examine sectioned-out parts of ongoing processes. We may treat these processes as if they had beginnings, middles, and ends, but it's really *our* engagements with the processes that begin and end. The people and institutions we study don't stop what they're doing when we stop looking at them. The meanings people attach to the things we see, hear about, or experience during fieldwork continue to change. I'm reluctant, then, to summarize the events I've written about within an overarching framework. The chapters add layer upon layer to my characterization of the school, and it would be self-defeating now to reduce this hard-wrought complexity.

I'm also reluctant to end by elaborating a theory supposedly arising from my fieldwork. It's not that I have inhibitions about theoretical writings (e.g., Nespor, 1994). But the extended fieldwork at Thurber has forced me to re-examine my usual ways of doing things. The academic world I work in is fragmented into regions that struggle to insulate themselves from one another by adopting increasingly specialized academic dialects, tightly drawing the lines of their professional associations and special interest groups, and narrowing the scope of the audiences for their texts. And one reason for this fragmentation, or at least one of the things that sustains it, is the acceptance of theory as an autonomous field of discourse, along with the idea that "merely empirical" work exists only to provide illustrations for, or as a means of generating, theory.

Theory-as-an-independent-arena-of-discourse-and-practice is a powerful glue for tying together academic networks, but I found at Thurber it pushed me away from people outside academia. The separation of theory (which usually corresponds to writing about other academic texts) from empirical description (writing about what people say and do) inevitably privileges the former and distorts or reduces the complexity of the latter. I haven't abandoned theory but have tried to imbricate my theoretical work with my attempts to show what was happening at Thurber. And now, instead of rearranging my arguments under a coherent theoretical umbrella, I shake them up one last time.

196

Webs and networks, after all, don't have conclusions or codas. Untangle them and you have paths leading outward, moving through other intersections, making more connections. You either follow such paths indefinitely, without benefit of a map, or stop somewhere, usually for more or less arbitrary reasons. What you have at the end is a record of itineraries which you've worked through, and questions and suggestions for future research. What follows is not exhaustive by any means, but I hope it provides a useful model of what you might do with this book once you've read it.

WHERE COULD THIS LEAD?

In chapter 1, I suggested that *pedagogy* had been decontextualized and treated as a virtual system of classroom practice. Instead of looking around to see whether the same process occurs at other schools, we could ask how vocabularies of practice developed by publishers and reformers combine with teacher education programs, school system policies, school organizational practices, and educators' biographies to create and maintain various images of teaching. How do participants in these various networks talk about themselves? Whom do they talk to? Parts of this question are already known, but we lack studies that show the structures of the networks that constitute "teaching": multisite ethnographies of different schools in the same districts, the teacher education programs to which they're linked, the central office administrative policies with which they have to deal, and their relationships to parents and communities.

In chapter 1, I suggested some affinities between the political organization of the school system and the administrative structure of Thurber itself. What are the connections between inter- and intraschool administrative and political structures? The idea of teachers carrying their expertise in their bodies as "embodied cultural capital" (Bourdieu, 1986) defines the politics of pedagogy as an issue of staffing (the distribution of properly endowed bodies around the schools and within a school). We need not endorse this way of thinking about teaching to realize that it points to a need for better understandings of how career, recruitment, hiring, and transfer practices distribute teachers from different backgrounds, levels of experience, ideological perspectives, and fields of specialization in different schools. What do the staffing mobility patterns in schools look like (cf. Becker, 1980). How long do teachers stay at schools? How do they move? How are they recruited to the school division in the first place? What connections exist between teacher preparation programs and school system personnel offices? How do these influence student–teacher placements and hires?

If the meanings of key reform concepts like whole language are not simply matters of philosophical or academic dispute but are empirical questions worked out in the ongoing politics and practices of schools, we might also ask: What are the chains of interpretation within which terms like *whole language* acquire meanings? When does a term get introduced? By whom? Through which channels? Attached to what practices? Connected to what administrative enforcements? It might be useful to do do "life histories" of the term (cf. Kopytoff, 1986) across a given space, a school system, or even a state, to trace the connections between the various sites of definition and dissemination.

How are teachers spatially related to the schools and communities in which they work? Where do their everyday geographies take them, and how often do their paths intersect with those of parents and students? Ogbu (1974) long ago drew attention to problems created when teachers live far from the neighborhoods of their schools, but we still have a poor understanding of how residence patterns distribute people from different backgrounds across a cityscape and how the relations between community and neighborhood activity and work activity are spatialized.

In chapter 1, I explored parents' vertical and comparative perspectives on educational processes and their focus on students' careers across grade levels. Although this parent standpoint may not be universal, it casts an interesting light on schooling, a light obscured by the emphasis on virtual pedagogy, classrooms, and individual schools. For example, in the movement toward collaborative horizontal planning in which teachers from different curriculum areas collaborate to plan courses at a given grade level, little attention has apparently been given to the issue of how teachers at different levels of schooling, elementary, middle, and high school, might collaborate. Parental involvement is presently thought of in terms of binding parents to educators' space–time orientations to school. What might happen if parental involvement meant the opposite—teachers gearing their practice to parents' space–time orientations? Certification structures, teacher education programs, as well as school system structures, separate elementary, middle, and high school teachers. But the obviousness of this separation escapes me; it would seem more logical for teachers involved in a particular curriculum stream from kindergarten to twelfth grade to collaborate. How did the present separate system get ensconced? What ideologies continue to support it? What status hierarchies among teachers place constraints on vertical collaboration both within and across schools? What would it take to get teacher educators thinking of curriculum across the grade span?

Do parents ever organize on a cross-school basis (e.g., in a kind of parents' consumer union)? Under what conditions do parents overcome their fear and reticence to voice concerns or objections to educators' practices? Under what conditions might they more effectively mobilize themselves to become involved in curriculum and teaching at the school system level, rather than at the level of the individual school? What do parents' school-focused funds of knowledge look like and how do they operate?

How do national, state, and regional political movements affect parent activism? I pointed to some striking parallels in the situation at Thurber and the political shift toward political conservatism in the state, but the flows of practice that actually connect larger movements to local action aren't clear. How do the media, churches, political parties, unions, and friendship networks shape parents' and teachers' ideas about pedagogy and curriculum?

What would educational research and theory look like if they were refocused on schooling as a long-term trajectory? This change implies shifting from administrators' and teachers' temporalities (which revolve around the class, the school year cycle), to students' (which include both these shorter cycles as well as cross-year patterns).

Fourth and fifth graders at Thurber, along with their parents, already knew a lot about middle schools and high schools. How do schools get reputations? How are reputations communicated across neighborhoods and maintained over time? How are school reputations related to parents' attitudes toward the school placements of their kids? How do parents form opinions about special schools like the magnet schools?

Many kids move around a good deal. What are their cross-school mobility patterns, and how does mobility alter uses of media and popular culture, access to neighborhood space, and status in school?

How do assessments and grades function as communication between school and community? How do kids' understandings of their grades change as they move from elementary to middle to high school? How do parents interpret report cards? How many parents save kids' schoolwork? For how long? To what end? How do they form opinions about teachers based on their kids' grades and the work they bring home?

How are kid-focused funds of knowledge (or if you don't believe there are such things, think of them as circuits of consumption) held together? How are the various adult roles (as designers and marketers) articulated with the kids' roles? Can we map the production and distribution networks that shape kids' networks? How are kid-based funds articulated with adult-centered community funds of knowledge?

How stable are kid-focused funds of knowledge? Mutant Ninja Turtles give way to Power Rangers, whereas some heroes, like the X-Men, develop effective survival strategies. Corporate marketing and production strategies play a big role in shaping consumption trends, but how are these strategies articulated at the point of impact—the kids? How do kids in different sociospatial locations gain and lose interest in particular cultural artifacts?

Do kids exchange, invoke, inhabit, or appropriate the school-based representations they encounter in their academic work? Why not? Should they? What *do* they do with the stuff?

Although this may seem to be an extravagent suggestion when we know so little about kids' understandings and uses of popular culture, how do teachers understand students' popular culture uses? And because popular culture is not unitary but a complex and heterogeneous network in which adults as well as kids participate, how do teachers, principals, and central administrators use popular culture? What television shows and other materials do they use? How do these activities connect to their understandings of schooling, kids, teaching, learning, and knowledge generally?

The peculiar attitudes of kids vis-à-vis economic logics—confusion from the standpoint of production (chapter 2), but familiarity from the standpoint of consumption (chapter 5)—raise the issue of how kids participate in corporate-financial spaces. This issue could be explored by tracing the histories of kids' engagements with money and work over long periods, perhaps by extending Lila's study of how kids get parents to give them what they want. How and at what points do kids cease to use parents as intermediaries for the acquisition of goods? How do corporate marketing and advertising strategies exploit these patterns of parent–child relationships?

How do preadolescents use cultural products, and how do these uses fit into their networks of friendship and association? Rather than asking kids to talk about popular cultural products or genres, why not study how popular culture appears in their ongoing interactions? The kids I interviewed used comic books and sports cards in what seemed to me peculiar ways (hoarding them as investments, using them to accumulate masculinity by association). How do kids elsewhere use popular culture items? Do traditions of use develop?

How and when do students make the transition from the willy-nilly plundering of popular culture I described to the deep identifications described by Willis (1990), Gaines (1991), and others? What do such identifications mean? Is the emphasis on adolescent or adult users of popular culture an artifact of the relative ease with which researchers can identify and interview such groups? What would studies of their everyday practices involving popular culture (outside of marked events like concerts, parties, conventions, theme parks) look like?

I was struck by the differences in how the fourth and fifth graders at Thurber talked about relationships with kids of the opposite sex. How do the functions of open expressions of cross-gender association or desire change as kids move through the grades? How are are these changes connected to media portrayals, constructions of masculinity and femininity, and gender relationships among adults at the school?

How do meanings of *fighting* change as kids move from elementary to middle and high school? How do the functions of violence within the school change over time? What are the geographies of violence among kids in a region? How is violence spatially distributed?

What does it mean to become embedded in a neighborhood? I treated this as an unmarked category, but there's no reason to assume that people who live in the same house all their lives become embedded in neighborhood space. Different neighborhoods afford people different opportunities for engagement. And as a related question, how do kids' understandings of community identity and community history develop?

How do kids' movements through city and neighborhood space change over time? What public spaces are accessible to kids from different social backgrounds? What uses do they make of these spaces? What geographies do girls and boys, of different social class and ethnic backgrounds and living in different neighborhoods, chart as they grow up? Where do they spend their time? How do they move around? Recall Tina's discussion about life in different apartment complexes: how does social class influence kids' experiences of public space?

In studying bodies and body work, we need also to be careful not to work within received frameworks that focus on how bodies are shaped or regulated. What would maps of kids', teachers', parents' opportunities for bodily exhilaration look like? Can spaces be mapped by the intensities of their bodily meanings and pleasures?

How do schools shape *adult* bodies? The first time I went into a teacher's classroom at Thurber, I resolved to stand up while the teacher stood and to sit only when she sat. By the end of the day, I was in pain. And as Randall Ward, a third-grade teacher in my writing group reminded me, elementary teachers often have no time to use the bathroom and only limited time to eat lunch. There's also a gender division of bodies within elementary schools: the male principal with his private office, private phone, and freedom of mobility; the female teachers with a shared lounge space, a shared telephone in a busy public space, and extremely limited mobility.

What happens in school–business partnerships? Close studies of corporate activities in the area of educational collaboration are needed to examine the ideological functions of such efforts, the uses of volunteerism, the public relations functions of collaborations, and their connections to changing political positionings of corporations.

And what, finally, can be made of the long-term systemic relations between university programs and school practices? I suggested at one point that schools of education promoted a particular image of teaching, but a complicated bit of research would be required to demonstrate this fact. Teacher educators have begun to study the impacts of their own programs, but it would be helpful to study a school system to learn what schools its teachers came from (plotting the waves of hirings, the different distributions of teachers across schools); to compare the major feeder programs; to talk to the teachers about influences. A bit ambitious, perhaps. In the following chapter, I touch on a few ways in which the relationship between my university and the school system shaped the conduct of my research.

7   Fieldwork
as an Intersection

Those of us who study education in our own societies, especially those of us who work for colleges of education, are not so much creating new relationships when we do school ethnography as we are trying to extend and redefine already existing relationships. I came to Thurber burdened with pieces of ready-made identities: the faculty there had known people like me when they were college students, and there were ongoing connections between my institution and theirs. My university, for example, sent student teachers into the school system, and the college of education I worked for was the destination for many of the system's administrators seeking advanced degrees. People's experiences with my college and colleagues—and what they'd heard secondhand—affected how I was accepted into the school and what I learned there. As Weick (1985) pointed out, people study us as we study them, each of us using our familiar categories to make sense of the other (cf. Kondo, 1991).

GETTING INTO THE SCHOOL

The principal, Mr. Watts, orchestrated my access to the school, endorsed my first proposal, presented it to the superintendent for approval; introduced me to teachers, gave me time at a staff meeting to pitch the project, and helped me send letters to parents. Later he made me a member of the school's site-based management committee and its report card revision committee. Without his help the project could never have been undertaken.

I met him for the first time only a couple of weeks before I began the study. In early September 1992, Mr. Watts had approached one of my colleagues at Virginia Tech, Josiah Tlou, a social studies educator, for advice on how to introduce a global education theme into his school's curriculum. Tlou had asked several of us on the faculty to meet with

Watts. I went for a couple of reasons: I had just finished writing a study about what it meant to learn in university programs (Nespor, 1994), and I wanted to work through the question of learning in a radically different setting. I had an inkling my university-grounded concepts would founder in an elementary school and that in the wreckage I could learn about both the theory and the school.

At the same time, I was intent on doing a different kind of ethnography than I'd done at the university, where I'd been an uninvolved outsider. I wanted to create a long-term relationship that would involve me and a group of graduate students working collaboratively with teachers, kids, and community members to explore how city politics, school system ideologies, parent–school relations, and kids' experiences of education came together in practice. I wanted this project to draw at least part of its agenda from teachers, parents, and students and to address them as well as a wider audience of researchers.

When it became clear as the meeting progressed that Mr. Watts was really less concerned with global education than with promoting a whole language curriculum at his school, I thought I'd found a point where his needs and mine connected. In my limited understanding (based on Edelsky, 1991; and Heath & Mangiola, 1991), adopting a whole language philosophy involved re-examining and reconstructing the links between a school and its communities. Whole language approaches, as I understood them, required teachers and students to make their language and literacy practices objects of study and analysis.

I suggested to Mr. Watts that I, and perhaps some of my graduate students, could become partners with Thurber Elementary. We could help teachers and students do the inquiry I presumed they would be initiating, and at the same time we could begin studying community and school system practices that created the contexts within which the school operated. Not expecting Mr. Watts to agree immediately, I told him I'd write a short memo detailing the project and drop it off at his school within the week.

When I wrote the memo, I must have been feeling insecure about the vagueness of my plans, because I tried to hide their ambiguity behind verbiage. The four single-spaced-page memo contained language like this:

> At our meeting you described Whole Language as a major organizing principle at your school. The Whole Language perspective is premised on a reconceptualization of the relations between school language and literacy and the language and literacy of the community. A successful whole language program has to be based on an on-going understanding of language and literacy practices in the community and of the relationships between school and community literacy practices. As Carol Edelsky, a leading whole language proponent explains:

> The Whole Language conception of reading as a transaction between
> a situated reader and a text in a context necessarily acknowledges
> readers' home discourses, schemas, and personal histories (includ-
> ing histories with other texts) as prime contributions on the reader's
> part. It overturns a faith in single interpretations that transcend
> history, the moral excellence of standard dialects, and single canoni-
> cal traditions. (Edelsky, 1991, p. 163)

A collaboration, I suggested, would allow us to study the "literacy,
linguistic, and cultural practices in the community (or communities)
served by the school" and to "work collaboratively with teachers to create
the environment of reflective inquiry critical to the Whole Language
perspective." I explained that the work I was proposing could lead in
many directions, including "tracing out and describing family and economic networks, cultural boundaries and processes"; studying the political, economic, and educational views of parents; doing an
ethnographic survey of literacy practices in the community; doing a
"historical geography" of the area served by the school; doing "time
geographies" of students, parents, teachers; starting "participatory action research" projects with teachers to address issues they identified
as important, and on and on.

Later, one of my colleagues in the teacher education program remarked that he couldn't imagine teachers giving him the time of day if
he sent them such a memo. The language was too academic and the
questions too distant from the everyday concerns of most teachers. I'd
hoped, of course, that my assurances about the openness of the design,
and my promises to work collaboratively with teachers to address their
agendas, would offset the language. This was not the case, but I did get
permission from Mr. Watts to begin working in the school.

Getting access to a school, however, isn't the same thing as getting
access to the people working there. My project was just one in a long line
of programs and philosophies Mr. Watts had embraced. This innovative-
ness made the school especially interesting, and because I strongly
supported much of what was being attempted—whole language, performance assessments, nontraditional report cards, and inclusion of
kids with disabilities—I wanted even more for my fieldwork to be truly
collaborative and beneficial to the teachers. But in the context of the
school's multiple reform agendas, my proposals for collaborative research must have seemed, at least to some teachers, like just one more
time-sucking scheme. The cumulative weight of the innovations left
teachers feeling ragged and overworked. Complaints about meetings
were common in the teachers' lounge by midyear, and one day in January
of 1993, Mrs. Peel asked me if there had been any "resentment" about
my project from the other teachers. Unsure what she meant, I replied
that teachers probably weren't jumping at the opportunity to collaborate

because I hadn't been clear enough about what these collaborations might entail. "I'll *tell* you the problem," Mrs. Peel responded. *"Time"*:

> We don't have any time. [Mr. Watts] asked me to be on a state panel to work on SOLs [that is, to revise the "Standards of Learning," the state's curriculum guidelines], and I told him I just didn't have the time. I normally do a church summer-school program, but I can't do it this summer. I think I'd just be burned out."

Now, time constraints are a generic feature of schools: Most pedagogical economies operate by eliminating temporal slack so that students and teachers are kept constantly busy. This approach forestalls any tactical appropriations of school space for unofficial purposes (cf. de Certeau, 1984, p. xix). But Mr. Watts's willingness to try new things strained the already taut schedules of the teachers at Thurber. His openness to new ideas got me access to the school but at the same time made it difficult for me to find teachers able to consider collaborating.

THE INFLUENCE OF MY UNIVERSITY
AFFILIATION

I also had the problem of defining a viable identity for myself in the school. I was an anthropologist who'd never been a public school teacher. That, along with the fact that I was a professor in the college of education at the only major university in the region, defined a powerful and familiar identity for me centered *outside* the school, in the university. This identification was full of problems. As Sarason (1990) pointed out, in the complex power relationship between universities and public schools, universities control the credentialing of school personnel, and schools exert power inasmuch as they "provide field sites for pre-professional practice....are a source of students for a variety of programs without whom these programs and their faculties could not be justified financially....And...serve as sites for research by university faculty" (p. 65).

The tensions produced by these power relations certainly affect research practice. For example, midway through my first year at Thurber, Mr. Watts began talking about entering the doctoral program in education at my university, Virginia Tech. This possibility added a new identity to my fragile and unconvincing "researcher" persona, that of informant about doctoral programs. Mr. Watts had decided he wanted a PhD rather than an EdD. He was sure the PhD would be "more marketable," that it could "open more doors." But gaining a PhD required a 2-year full-time residency on campus whereas the EdD required only 1 year, and it was unlikely he could get or afford such an extended leave of absence. "What do you want to do with the doctorate?" I asked.

"Work as a supervisor of instruction or teach instructional stuff at a university."

"There's no real advantage to a PhD for that kind of thing. It's really mainly just a status thing among the professors."

"But even if it's only a status thing," Mr. Watts asked, "won't the people making hiring decisions be influenced by that?"

I couldn't answer with certainty, and Mr. Watts was adamant. He told me that he'd recently been to a meeting of public school administrators looking into the doctorate program and that he and the others had decided the 2-year residency requirement was just a "rite of passage that a bunch of old white males want people to jump through for the PhD."

Although this comment might have been meant as a roundabout criticism of *me* as a white male denizen of the ivory tower, I think it's better understood as a reflection of broad, underlying school–university tensions. By requiring that people sever their practitioner links with the public schools in order to become socialized into academia, the residency rule helped reinforce the arbitrary boundary between people who worked in schools and people who worked in universities. My identification with the university made me guilty by association of helping maintain the very researcher–practitioner boundary I was trying to erase in my fieldwork. Needless to say, my attempts at blurring this boundary were not very successful. I offered myself, sincerely and with no preconditions, as a potential collaborator, ready to follow whatever agendas the teachers defined. But as the representative of a powerful institution that directly regulated upward mobility for people like Mr. Watts (inasmuch as it regulated the acquistion of advanced degrees) and indirectly set much of the agenda for what goes on in the schools, I was viewed with suspicion.

The teachers, quite reasonably, kept their distance. I spent a lot of time talking with them informally in the lounge, trying to allay whatever misgivings they might have. But some teachers avoided the lounge, and getting to know the ones who were there didn't necessarily reduce their uncertainty about my professional motivations.

It might seem that this dynamic would have restricted me to working with only the few teachers who actively expressed interest in participating in the project. Mrs. Peel, for example, had had student teachers from Virginia Tech in her classrooms in the school where she had previously taught. This history predisposed her to give me the benefit of the doubt, and she agreed to participate.

In addition, early in the first year of fieldwork, I had written letters to the parents and guardians of kids in the school and had explained that I wanted to do some research on children's literacy and on school–community connections. Among other things, I asked for permission to interview students. I got a smattering of responses from across the school, and to minimize disruption I decided to do the interviews one class at a time, beginning with the room with the highest concentration of permissions, Mrs. Jumpers's class.

My only contacts with Mrs. Jumpers until then had been at staff meetings, on a couple of fieldtrips, and in a few brief conversations in the lounge. We first talked when I stopped by her room to borrow some students' folders for photocopying and to ask her about arranging interviews with kids. She asked who took over my classes when I was at Thurber, and I explained that I'd tried to schedule my courses on Monday and Tuesday so that I could spend as much time as possible at the school.

"It hasn't been enough, though," I whined. "I've been coming here, what, since October? And I still don't know what's going on."

"Oh," Mrs. Jumpers joked, "I've been here two years, and I don't know what's going on. What do you teach?" she asked.

I explained that I taught several courses for graduate students and one for undergraduates, Social Foundations of Education.

She said:

> I think I took something like that, only it was called History of Education or something. All I remember is that we talked a lot about economics and all sorts of things that I remember thinking didn't have anything to do with anything I knew anything about. I remember the professor was a little bald man with a bow tie, and yeah, he talked right over my head. What department are you in, anyway?"

"Curriculum and Instruction."

"So you're in education? But you're an anthropologist?"

As I began to explain, Mrs. Jumpers confided, "That first time you spoke to us [in September]? I didn't understand a thing you said. I understood your name, and after that it was all incomprehensible."

Trying to put a good face on it, I said that one reason it may have been confusing was that at the time I wasn't altogether sure what I was doing myself. I was improvising.

"Yeah," said Mrs. Jumpers, "I do that myself." At this point children began coming into the room, and I left.

The next time I spoke with Mrs. Jumpers she told me more of her experiences with people like me. "Oh," she recalled, with an expression of disgust; "I hated that course [history of education]! Do you go into all that Jeffersonian stuff and all that?"

Oh no, I assured her.

"I didn't learn a thing in that course. My professor talked to the wall all semester, and I didn't have any idea what was going on. I don't know how I got a B."

"Maybe he just gave everybody Bs," I suggested. "I had a professor like that once."

She assured me, however, that many people had flunked. We talked about the fact that the state no longer allowed students to major in elementary education in college. Mrs. Jumpers told me that hers was the last group at her college to have the major and then complained, as if commenting on the worth of the degree, that "none of what they taught me at [her university] has been any use to me at all here. Nothing about how to deal with administrators, how to deal with parents. Nothing."

Mrs. Jumpers's references to an obscure, useless foundations class, her confession that she hadn't understood anything I'd said at our first meeting, and her general trashing of her teacher education program were ways of informing me of the position I occupied in her world: I was a Martian. And in a way, this reaction was unsurprising. Goodson (1993) argued that "foundational" programs like mine—discipline-based studies in the history, anthropology, or philosophy of education—have long been considered "irrelevant" by practitioners:

> This problem of the older disciplines arises in many cases because the scholars working in disciplinary modes often develop their first allegiance to their home disciplines—say history or philosophy. Whilst this is not intrinsically or inevitably a problem it has the effect over time of divorcing such scholars from the world of schooling. This problem is often exacerbated by the fact that foundational disciplines adopt a hands-off posture with regard to schools; added to which, all too often, these scholars have no previous experience of teaching in the schools. (p. 2)

Still, when I explained to Mrs. Jumpers that her class had the greatest concentration of parents who'd given me permission to approach their children for interviews and that I'd like to sit in her class for a few days, observe how the kids talked and interacted, and then, if there were any way it could work in her schedule, take them out for interviews, she readily agreed. In fact, noting that I'd already spent a good deal of time in Mrs. Peel's fifth-grade class, she said, "It's about time....I was wondering why I was left out."

Although I ultimately spent quite some time in Mrs. Jumpers's classroom and even more time in Mrs. Court's room the next year, I had decided at the outset against doing classroom research. Having done such work in the past (e.g., Nespor, 1987a; 1987b), I was troubled by the way it compartmentalized students' and teachers' lives and imposed arbitrary time frames that had no connection to experience or life outside the school. And besides, as Goodson (1991, 1993, 1994) frequently pointed out, a classroom focus is a poor basis on which to build the collaborative relations I was trying to establish: "To place the teachers' classroom practice at the centre of action for action researchers is to put the most exposed and problematic aspect of the teachers' world at the centre of scrutiny and negotiation" (Goodson, 1991, p. 141).

Although I'm less certain than Goodson that teaching shouldn't be scutinized—should we ignore bad or abusive teaching in the interest of preserving good relations with teachers?—I think that scrutinizing "teaching" entails, first and foremost, examining the political, cultural, and economic flows that determine what is possible within classrooms, that shape the identities of the teachers and students who meet there, and that pressure or constrain them to act in certain ways. (See chapter 1.)

I didn't try to explain all this to Mrs. Jumpers, but I did tell her that I wasn't there to observe her or judge her teaching but to get to know her students informally before I began interviewing them. She agreed to let me attend on the condition that I didn't take any notes in her classroom. I spent about every other day in her room until the end of the year. Although most of my work was with the students, I made several overtures for collaboration. Mrs. Jumpers declined these and said she didn't want to "shortchange" the rest of her curriculum.

Working with the fifth grade kids in Mrs. Jumpers's room rounded off my first year of fieldwork. I'd spent a lot of time in the school, if not on the collaborative terms I initially dreamed of, then at least in a way that let me get to know teachers, students, and parents. Still, I didn't want to continue in the same fashion for another year. I wanted to try, once again, to generate some kind of collaboration with the faculty as a whole.

THE END OF MY ATTEMPTS TO COLLABORATE WITH THE WHOLE FACULTY

As my first year of fieldwork wound down, I asked Mr. Watts for time at a staff meeting to talk to the teachers. It would be my first meeting with them as a group since September. I didn't intend to summarize the year's events (most of which I hadn't understood), or to report on my interviews with students (which I hadn't yet entirely transcribed). Instead, I wanted to address conditions that seemed problematic for the school and for the collaboration I hoped to generate. In particular, I was concerned that the school was trying to implement changes without forums or opportunities for the teachers to talk together.

Thus, at a Wednesday afternoon staff meeting in early June, I began a too-long talk in which I tried to suggest that the changes being promoted in the school needed to be connected to broader discussions among the teachers. I acknowledged that one of the comments about my initial proposals had been that they were too vague, abstract, and general, and I wanted to be more concrete now. I pointed to the need for faculty discussion in three areas: organization, instruction, and resource use.

> In talking about it in terms of "organization."...Whole language, whether you want to pursue it, whether or not you want to talk about cross-age tutoring, or social action writing projects where kids engage in things going on in the community, whether you want to make the shift from doing activities to doing whole language. That's a problem of philosophy....And I think a problem in the city is that the attempt has been to kind of impose this from above. What you need is some sort of...teacher forum, whether those are discussion groups or reading groups or whatever you want to call them....All this implies a certain commitment from the administration, not only in terms of moral support, but in terms of time. Which means not doing some things and doing other things in place of them. It fits in with the whole idea of site-based management, which presumes that issues are being generated among the staff and in interactions between the staff and the community. [*Long pause*]

These comments were directed partly toward the teachers and partly toward Mr. Watts. I'd seen that the teachers were pressured by the multitude of agendas flowing through the school, many of which they hadn't chosen. I was also familiar with Little's (1981) research emphasizing the importance of teachers talking to one another. Unfortunately, my suggestion was a tactical blunder. In spite of my efforts to locate the school in intersections of flows across space and time, I'd neglected to examine the history of the faculty and thus was unprepared when Mrs. Tanner interrupted me to explain that they had already tried what I was suggesting:

> Could we talk before you go on?...Well, a million things have been racing through my mind. I probably won't remember them all. All of these things that you've discussed and listed here, they're all things we are aware of and have discussed in the past, and just for the sake of—we just don't have enough *time* to fit in all of these things. I know at the beginning of the year we had teams and reading groups and all of that. I don't know.

In other words, my suggestion of a discussion forum to address the school's multiple agendas was seen as just another imposed agenda—and not even an original one. Before I could respond to Mrs. Tanner, Mr. Watts jumped into the conversation: "We decided not to do it—what was it?—*you* [meaning the teachers as a group] decided not to do it." Mrs. West responded by reminding him that "so many other things were happening at the same time." Even Mrs. O'Brien, who seemed to enjoy all of the multiple stands of activity, acknowledged that the teams and reading groups had been "overwhelming."

Mrs. West's solution was to simplify: "We need to think about maybe selecting *one* thing and focusing on it."

Mrs. O'Brien, trying to support the line I'd initiated, suggested that the problem was lack of coordination among the different strands. "We do these things separately, we're all going five different ways each one of us"—a problem that might be addressed through structural changes.

I suggested that the key was for the teachers to talk things through among themselves and to begin to define their own agendas. Mrs. West countered that even if they did that, there would still be "other things from on high and other goals and objectives that will be placed upon us without us saying yea or nay, that we must have to do."

I wasn't sure whether Mrs. West was referring to demands imposed by the central administration (for example, the standardized testing that ate into time in the spring semester) or to Mr. Watts's reform experiments. I was trying to suggest that for innovations to work, teachers needed to have some say in selecting them and planning their implementation. To Mr. Watts, however, I seemed to say that the teachers should push through change in the school: "Your point," he suggested, "is for *them* to generate their own needs, for them to generate what it is they want to know, where they want to go, and how to get there."

To Mrs. West, on the other hand, what I was saying was irrelevant; whatever the teachers did, overriding expectations would always be imposed from the outside. And for Mrs. Tanner, I was merely telling the staff what it already knew: "We are aware and have discussed and thought about these very same areas." "Well," I asked, feeling a little frustrated and wondering if all the previous discussions she referred to had resolved anything, "do you think there *is* a problem?" She responded: "Well, the entire educational system in the United States has got to change! You know. We don't have enough time! We don't have enough time to be paid to be the professionals that we need to be to do this!"

I didn't have a good answer for her. I agree that the educational system needs changing and that teachers aren't paid enough and lack time to talk to one another and to study their own practice. As Sarason (1990) argued, school reforms generally fail precisely for lack of attention to the point Mrs. Tanner was making: that schooling is a *system* extending far beyond the walls of the school. But in the context of the meeting, her statement worked as a "contrastive rhetoric" (Hargreaves, 1981), a defense of the status quo by describing alternatives as unrealistic or characterizing them in pejorative ways: in this case, defining the only alternative as a change of the whole educational system. Or perhaps Mrs. Tanner was simply evaluating my suggestions according to their lack of immediate practicality and promise of additional demands upon her time (Fullan, 1991, pp. 127–128).

Either way, in retrospect I was clearly naive to assume—unconsciously—that the teachers and I could share a common perspective on the school. Mr. Watts, Mrs. Tanner, and the other teachers were at the center of a whirl that I was looking at from the outside. For them, things seemed to be coming from all directions without discernable pattern. They had no time for the kind of reflection I engaged in (nor access to the kinds of tapes and notes I had). They didn't have the luxury of looking at things from an outside vantage point. There was no organizational slack—no discretionary time or resources—that they could appropriate to explore changes or do the things I was suggesting. Their perspective was focused locally on events in their classrooms or directly affecting their classrooms. Thus my decision to eschew classroom research, in the hope of fostering collaborative opportunities, may have actually reduced such opportunities; the classroom would have been the topic and the setting the teachers would have been most interested in and able to study (cf. Cochran-Smith & Lytle, 1992).

The conversation stalled. After some attempts to salvage it or arrange for it to continue later (I offered to take the faculty out to breakfast every couple of weeks over the summer just to talk about things like whole language), the discussion switched to more pressing and conventional end-of-the-year teachers' meeting topics (The year after my fieldwork ended, however, Mr. Watts did succeed in starting regular discussion groups among teachers.).

The meeting capped a sobering year. At the beginning, I had wanted to shed my old research persona, to begin a collaboration instead of remaining the outside researcher who imposed his own research agenda, collected his data, and carried them back to the university to write reports that no one at the school would ever see. As Cameron, Frazer, Harvey, Rampton, and Richardson (1994) pointed out, an obvious alternative is to acknowledge and work with the agendas defined by insiders such as teachers:

> One of the ways in which researchers are powerful is that they set the agenda for any given project: what it will be about, what activities it will involve, and so on. But...researched persons may have agendas of their own, things they would like the researcher to address. If we are researching "with" them as well as "on and for" them, do we have a responsibility to acknowledge their agendas and deal with them in addition to our own? (p. 24)

But *not* imposing a research agenda can be problematic. In my case it meant I'd come across as a vague time-waster. All my offers to collaborate were deflected. I wanted to hook up to the agendas of the teachers, but the agenda that most faculty in the school embraced was to be left alone—by me, by the principal, by parents, and, for some perhaps, by the kids (cf. Hargreaves, 1993).

It was clear, after this first year, that I probably wasn't going to start any collaborations with groups of teachers, let alone with the whole faculty, so I decided to try a different strategy. Instead of working with several teachers, I would begin the second of year of fieldwork working with just one. I'd spend a lot of time in the classroom but not to do classroom research. The classroom would be my point of entry, a context to begin getting to know the teacher and her kids. Then, over time, I could try to interest them in doing some genuinely collaborative inquiry.

COLLABORATING WITH MRS. COURT

As the the second year of fieldwork began, I approached a fourth-grade teacher, Mrs. Court, to see if she would let me visit her room regularly. She readily agreed, but seemed apologetic about not being as far along with the whole language process as she thought some of the other teachers were. She seemed to think, despite my protestations of ignorance, that I was an expert teacher who knew how to do whole language "right." She talked about going to the Outcomes-Based Education workshops the summer before and getting excited about what she was hearing, of having become dissatisfied with the way she'd been teaching, of wanting to change.

Two weeks into the year this enthusiasm had been severely tested. Mrs. Court told me she didn't know what the kids learned from activities like the collaborative writing exercises. She thought that the class lacked structure, that things hadn't been planned well enough. She wanted to go "back to the books" (i.e., teach out of her textbooks) for a week. At the same time, she asked other teachers and me for help. At one early morning meeting with me and Mrs. O'Brien, she explained:

> The reason I want to just go ahead and do this is because, I told you I wanted help in making my classroom a more whole language classroom, and I'm just going to do things like this, slowly. I do some things, already, but I'm going to allow myself to teach the way I teach and feel comfortable with right now, and then do some of these things. And eventually, it'll come to me better, or it'll be more natural for me, or whatever.

But getting used to a new way of teaching was difficult in a setting where not all the teachers supported the change, where there were few opportunities to talk about such issues as a faculty, and where parents still expected teachers to cover a specific body of material. Although it was fine for me, as a researcher, to spend a few months getting kids to reflect on their patterns of social interaction, Mrs. Court had to deal with their behavior on a daily basis. She was caught between two sets of pressures and expectations: one to teach in a traditional manner and steadily cover material and keep the kids in line; another to open the classroom to risky activities that allow students autonomy and demand flexible uses of time.

Mrs. Court tried to combine the two philosophies for a while but soon found herself in a nether region, not comfortable with whole language, but no longer comfortable with the textbook-based approach used in previous years. The help she wanted was the opportunity to talk with the other teachers, in a sustained and substantive way about what she was doing. But the talks never happened.

I felt frustrated myself and questioned my usefulness when I couldn't help a willing teacher with whom I was regularly interacting. By midyear I was coming to her classroom about three days a week. In addition to my interviewing, I'd become a kind of volunteer, running errands, helping individual students, or working with groups of students. In January, Mrs. Court asked me if I were interested in helping the kids put together a newsletter, something to update parents on classroom activities, to give the kids an outlet for their writing, and to give me a legitimate participant role in the class. I readily agreed and saw participating as a way to give something back to Mrs. Court for her patience and as another way to get to know the kids. In the end, however, the newsletter didn't turn out as planned: Ice storms closed the school and made it impossible for me to meet with the student researchers for about a month. Standardized tests ate into class time. Additional schedule disruptions, bad word-processing software, my commitment to have everyone contribute something to the paper, and my willingness to let groups develop long research projects as part of the newspaper activity delayed our editions so long that after one issue the "newsletter" turned into an end-of-the-year class research anthology. The kids and I had fun doing it, but in some ways it only added to Mrs. Court's worries. It didn't function as the line of communication to parents that she had wanted, and at the same time she felt guilty because she couldn't spare the kids very often to work with me.

The redefinition of the newsletter was also unfortunate because by January the parents, as I described in chapter 1, were becoming especially strident in their complaints about teaching and assessment at the school. Mrs. Court, having a parent–teacher association (PTA) leader's child in her room, often bore the brunt of these complaints, and her confidence further eroded. One afternoon at the end of April, waiting out a furious rainstorm after the kids had left on the buses, she told me: "I feel like I don't know what I'm doing. I feel like I haven't taught anything all year." She felt she hadn't been supported and that there was no unity among the teachers about adopting a whole language approach. She told me she thought she should go back to worksheets, that she needed more guidance through observation or feedback, that there were no sustained conversations among teachers on teaching or assessment (cf. Fullan, 1991, 77–78). I could offer her sympathy and suggestions, but she really didn't want *my* help. She wanted the faculty as a whole to address questions of curriculum and teaching, and there I could be no help at all, my own attempts to foster such a discussion having been failures.

RESEARCH WITH PARENTS

Although most of my time was spent working with kids and teachers, I also tried to get to know the students' parents. I went to PTA meetings, tagged along on fieldtrips with parent volunteers, went to school functions (back-to-school night, field day, etc.) and for a couple of years was a member of the school's site-based management committee. Unfortunately, my night classes made it difficult for me to attend a few key school events held in the evening, and only one third to one half of the parents in the school participated actively in PTA—and these were almost all European American parents living in the areas contiguous to the school.

I sent letters to the parents of every student asking them for interviews; a fair number gave me permission to talk to their kids, but only a few agreed to interviews themselves. African American parents were not among this group, and the absence of their voices is one major gap among many in this work. I did get to know Lila's mother (from PTA and back-to-school night) and Benny's mom (from the report card revision committee), but they didn't want to be interviewed.

In fact, many of the parents I got to know didn't agree to interviews. Sondra's mother told me one day that she thought it was a "privilege" to have me doing my research in the school, but she wouldn't talk to me on the record. Lauren's mother refused to be formally interviewed, but would ambush me in the parking lot and talk my ear off about what was bothering her about the school. Of the formal interviews I did with parents, some took place in a school conference room during the lunch hour, and some took place at the parents' houses. Some of the home interviews included the kids; some did not. Some parents seemed curious about what I was doing; others didn't. At the end of my interview with her, for example, I asked Mrs. Graham:

Jan:	Is there anything we didn't ask you about? That you want to talk about?
Mrs. Graham:	No, I don't reckon. I feel comfortable asking, though, questions and things. I feel like it's the only way you can get answers.
Jan:	Do you have any questions you want to ask us?
Mrs. Graham:	No. Oh no! [*Laughing*] I was going to ask you all what are you *really* doing? And have you enjoyed it?

Perhaps it's a measure of the differences in our standpoints that Mrs. Graham thought that people do research for the joy of it (although the question moves me, from a distance, as I think about my work: Perhaps pleasure, not just the researchers' but all the participants', would be a better criterion for judging research than most of the present philosophically inspired criteria). I answered Mrs. Graham:

> So far we've enjoyed it. We've been working mainly in the school....And, uh, we're trying to do a lot of different things. We're partly trying to bridge some gaps between Tech and the schools, because we don't really interact with the schools as much as we should, at least with the City. But we also are interested in things like parental involvement—so that's why I'm asking you all those questions about parental involvement. Thurber's an interesting school...because they are doing a lot of different kinds of things. The report cards are different. Uh, portfolios are somewhat different than other schools do....So, we, we're trying to understand better what's going on in the school, and we're also hoping that what we're doing will help teachers and maybe even parents a little bit.

"Sounds good," was Mrs. Graham's only reply.

Although I continued to do formal interviews with parents off and on over the two years, I found that recordings of conversations and discussions at meetings and other events were much more interesting and thought provoking. Parents, I think, saw me as partly or wholly aligned with the teachers, and despite my assurances of confidentiality, they were often circumspect. I was told by Mr. Watts, a number of teachers, and even some parents, for example, that one couple was especially critical of the school and constantly bad-mouthed it. In my interviews with them, however, they said nothing bad about the school and had only compliments about the teachers. Perhaps the teachers and Mr. Watts were simply wrong about this couple, but my suspicion is that they were not. I think these parents were critical of the school and were not reticent to air their views; after all, by many accounts they did so frequently and in public. Their measured comments to me illustrate, instead, the irrelevance of my work to them.

Sometimes in interviews one gets a sense that people are happy for an opportunity to talk about issues for which they lack a discussion forum. But these parents, at least a large group of them, did have forums and, as I showed in chaper 1, made their views known in public. They had little to gain from talking to me, and some probably saw me as aligned too closely to the principal. By contrast, the public meetings showed parents formulating their arguments for real audiences—teachers and other parents in this case, rather than researchers—and captured some of the emotional and expressive forms of speech suppressed in conventional interviews. I'm not suggesting we avoid interviews, but that we combine them with observations of parents' individual and collective encounters with the school. It seems likely, for example, that much of the perceived "passivity" of working-class parents vis-à-vis educators (e.g., Lareau, 1989) reflects their speech styles (as opposed to the speech styles of middle class parents) in interviews with middle-class researchers rather than their characteristic patterns of interaction. When acting in concert with one another, the working-class parents of Thurber students were anything but passive.

RESEARCH AT THE INTERSECTION OF KIDS AND ADULTS

When I first went into Mrs. Jumpers's room, I intended to stay just long enough to get to know the kids I'd be interviewing—a few days, perhaps—and then move to other classrooms. On my initial visit, after I introduced myself to the class, I sat in an empty chair near the computers in the back corner, where I hoped to be unobtrusive. This put me near the kids, or to be more exact, next to Lucy, who was sitting at the girls' table at the back of the room.

"Why do you wear that ponytail?" Lucy asked me after a minute.

"Well, my hair's so long that I need to tie it up or it blows in my eyes."

"It looks funny."

"Do you think it looks bad?"

"I don't know; it's different." We were silent for a few moments and then Lucy informed me: "I bumped my head."

"Oh, did you fall?"

"No, I was under a table and I stood up and hit it."

"I've done that."

"I have a cat named Sugar."

"Sugar?" I asked, not sure I heard the name right.

Lucy's voice was very soft so Mrs. Jumpers wouldn't hear us. "Yeah, Sugar, 'cause she's got brown spots on white, no, it's white and brown—like brown sugar and white sugar." I nodded that I was following. She told me Sugar was going to have kittens. "She's real fat; when she walks she goes like this from side to side," Lucy showed me with her hands. "If she has a white kitten, we're going to name her Snow White. And if Snow White has kittens, we're going to call them the seven dwarfs!"

A little later, when Mrs. Jumpers's attention was elsewhere, Lucy asked me where I taught. Virginia Tech, the university in Blacksburg, I explained. She asked if I had to get a substitute when I came to Thurber—the same question Mrs. Jumpers had asked—and I told her that school had ended for the college students. "That's not fair," she said. I agreed with her. "What are your students like?" I told her that they were mostly adults, grown-ups. I tried to explain that they didn't go to classes as she did. "Are people mean?" she asked.

"Well, some of them are, some aren't. Just like here."

As we whispered, I felt some complicity in the old student game of talking beneath the teacher's awareness. Unlike the high school and college students in whose classrooms I'd observed, the elementary school kids didn't ignore me. When I was nearby, they would include me in conversations—probably less from regard for my insights than to claim some autonomy for themselves within the room. Engaging me in the talk gave them some protection from Mrs. Jumpers (who would be less likely to scold them for talking to me than to each other). It also seemed to make them feel a little important.

In fact, I realized that first day that the kids were *anxious* to have me stay. Several clustered around me as the class broke for lunch and pleaded with me to come back in the afternoon. I did, and then at the end of the day another student asked me if I were going to be staying in *their* class. "Good!" she replied emphatically when I said I would.

It took me a couple of days to realize that part of the reason the kids wanted me in the room so badly was that they felt slighted by the fact that some of my graduate students and I had spent time in the other fifth-grade room but not in theirs. My second day in Mrs. Jumpers's room, a delegation of kids approached me at the end of the day and asked if I were coming back and specifically if I were going to be observing in the other fifth grade. They seemed desperate that I should stay in their room and *not* go to the other class; not wanting to disappoint them, I committed myself to return on a regular basis.

The kids' pleas were not the products of simple jealousy. They had realized, as I soon did, that their class was stigmatized in the eyes of the school. During one of my first days in the room, the special education aide, who was working with students labeled learning disabled (LD), stopped me in the middle of the room and said, "Have you been in this room before? I think she [Mrs. Jumpers] does a good job with children like this." I shrugged, astonished at her remarks that the kids could hear and even more irritated that she assumed I would participate in such a conversation. I became even more flustered when she continued by naming the kids "serviced" in the LD program and explained that this room and one of the third-grade classrooms had the most "LD kids" in them.[1]

I don't think she was saying anything the kids didn't already know. The public labeling of the class as the slower of the two fifth grades,

---

[1] At the end of the 1994 school year, I watched as the fourth-grade teachers allotted their students to the fifth-grade teachers for the following year: The children of parents who had complained during the year were placed in Mrs. Peel's room, and those labeled "emotionally disturbed" or considered discipline problems went to Mrs. Jumpers (except for some students who had to go to Mrs. Peel's room because they had conflicts with others already assigned to Mrs. Jumpers).

along with the fact that I hadn't come into the room until late April and had been in the other fifth grade as early as the previous fall, left the kids, who like all kids were sensitive to differential treatment and expectations, feeling slighted. Troubled that I might be reinforcing the negative labeling of the class, I spent as much time as possible there—16 days in the class during the last 6 weeks of the school year—in addition to going on three fieldtrips with the class.

RESEARCHER AS CONTEXT

Kids, like adults, impose meanings on research activities and on researchers. Many methodological strictures seem aimed at controlling these meanings and limiting research participants' abilities to impose them. Thorne (1993), in her 1970s observation-based work with fifth and sixth-grade kids, described how she carefully tried to create distance between herself and the kids she studied by refusing their attempts to cast her in recognizable roles such as aide or teacher. Except in cases where they seemed to be in physical danger she refused to intervene; instead she stood back and simply wrote down what she saw. Being a participant, she explained, entails an interactional engagement that would "run against the open-ended curiosity and witnessing that ethnography requires" (p. 16, cf. Rose, 1987). This attitude was probably typical of the era in which Thorne did her fieldwork. Sieber (1981) for example, said of his fieldwork in the early 1970s:

> In all the schools I was restricted to a considerable degree to the role of silent, relatively passive observer....The restrictions I encountered appear to be fairly typical in anthropological investigations of school life (Khleif, 1974; Wolcott, 1975). Khleif has pointed out that as compared with the normal anthropological fieldwork situation the school setting "lacks...avenues for participation" by the fieldworker, that studying schools is an "essentially observer's, not a participant's function," and that the anthropologist finally "remains more a stranger than a friend" (Khleif, 1964: 391). (Sieber, 1981, pp. 214–215)

My own early work in classroom observation research in the early 1980s followed the same approach: Sit quietly at the side or in a back corner, try to write down everything the teacher did, or focus on a few kids and try to record their behaviors. The ground rule was to avoid distracting or interacting with anyone: We were to be "objective" observers.

One problem with this strategy, aside from the fact that it precludes conversations with kids, is that people who spend a lot of time in surveillance-oriented places like classrooms get good at masking their actions. Even when we're looking right at someone it's often hard to see what they're doing. A convincing illustration comes from a study in New Zealand in which researchers attached microphones to individual students to record their private talk and then compared the transcripts with the observations of trained observers (one oberver per child):

> A comparison of the audio recordings and the observers' records revealed that fewer than a quarter of the private utterances recorded by the children's microphones were apparent to the observers. The simple finding that children's hidden classroom talk was far more prevalent than was apparent to the observers, who were each continuously watching one case-study child, reflects the children's expertise in hiding their private interactions. (Alton-Lee, Nuthall, & Patrick, 1993, p. 56)

Even if perfect surveillance were possible (a disturbing thought), the presence of an observer always has an impact on a situation, and an observer who refuses to exhibit any recognizable signs of being a normal person—talking, chatting, and so forth—makes the others present invent an intelligible role for him or her—spy, fool, asshole, whatever. By refusing to participate actively in the fashioning of an identity, an observer's presence becomes an uncontrolled disruption, possibly one of a greater magnitude than that caused by a reasonably interacting observer (Weick, 1985). In spite of Thorne's (1993) attempts to stay in the background and distance herself from the action, the kids seem to have found a role for her—that of a spy, scrutinizing and recording their activities. And although this invention of a purpose for the researcher may seem like an artifact of Thorne's nonparticipant observation strategy, researchers who do interview studies face the same dynamic, though they rarely investigate it. Researchers rarely talk to kids about their understanding of interviews, their reasons for participating, or their thoughts about the interviewers. Yet these processes must fundamentally shape how interviews unfold.

Being a reasonably interacting observer requires a certain openness. The fourth and fifth graders I worked with were curious about my personal and professional life. They asked whether I was married, whether I dated, what I did at work, whether I lived with my mother, how old I was. In keeping with the body-based perspective I explored in chapter 4, they spent a lot of time trying to make sense of me in bodily terms. The fifth graders had seen one of my graduate students and were skeptical that I could really be her teacher:

Lucy: She's too old to be your student though. She's older than you; she's older than you. She's about 50 years older than you.

Jan: How old do you think I am?

Helen: Uh, late 30s early 40s, somewhere in there.

Jan: That's good. I'm 37.

Lucy: But that lady looks like she's in her 60s.

Helen: We were right; we were right though. 'Cause we were telling
            Mrs. Jumpers that you were older than her.

My fieldnotes reveal that the fourth graders were more consoling:

Lauren asks me how old I am. "How old do you think I am?" I ask. "32,"
Hazel guesses. "35," Desiree guesses. I point upwards to give them a hint,
and finally Hazel guesses my age, 38. "That's two years older than my
dad," Desiree says. "Yeah, I'm really old," I say. "That's nothin'," Desiree
tells me, "my aunt is 40!" "You look 32," says Lauren. "Thank you," I say.

The ponytail I sported during most of the fieldwork placed me in an
ambiguous social category. It was the first thing Lucy had mentioned,
and many other students remarked on it. "You got long hair, Mr. Nespor.
When you gonna cut it?" Cindy would ask.

"I like it; don't cut it" Sybil would interject.

"Your hair is longer than mine," Cindy would point out. One day as I
was helping another student at a desk near hers, Cicily pulled out one
of my gray hairs. "You're gettin' old," she told me. "You've got gray hair."
Another day, as I sat down at lunch, Cicily looked up at me with mock
surprise and said, "I thought you were Mrs. Court."

"Do I look like Mrs. Court?" I asked.

"No, your hair is too long," she replied.

Mickey, who was sitting at the same table, asked, "Are you one of
them rough dudes?"

"What do you mean?" I was puzzled.

"In the movies the bad dudes always have ponytails." He struck a
karate pose (or as much of one as possible sitting down), and Mel piped
up, saying I looked like a biker.

He told me about going to the barber and seeing a bunch of motocycles
parked outside a nearby store. "My dad said it was a motorcycle team.
He knew their name, but I've forgotten it."

As this anecdote suggests, the hair defined me for some kids as a
not-quite-proper adult. I was pleased when Lila interviewed me for her
research on "how to get your parents to give you what you want" and
somewhat crushed when she described me in the report as "an old
unsivilised [sic] person."

As Pollard (1987) pointed out, doing research with kids, especially
collaborative or student research, represents "a deliberate attempt by
the researcher to overturn conventional adult–child relationships" that
emphasize separation (p. 101). In my fieldwork, the adult–child boundary was never overturned but instead served as a resource that the kids
manipulated. Knowledge of things childish and adult didn't define the
divide. "Don't you know anything!" Doug complained with exasperation
when I had to ask him to explain Power Rangers lore.

"You're not supposed to know about that; that's for kids," Tina told me, when I tried to talk to her about *Weinerville*, one of the television shows she liked.

Kids who wanted something from me—to borrow my camera or tape recorder, for example—would try to equalize our relationship by reassuring me of how responsible they were, how many grown-up things they did. But if I wouldn't do what they wanted, my adulthood was emphasized; they would warn me that if I didn't obey, they wouldn't like me anymore. Once, for example, when Felix became irritated with me because I wouldn't stop working with another student to edit one of his reports, he dramatically tore his paper into little pieces and dropped them one by one in the trash. "Felix," I scolded, "you're acting childish."

He laughed in my face. "I am a child!" The next day he asked me whether I had his story, suspecting, correctly, that I'd fished the pieces out of the garbage like a docile adult. Later, when I read Lila's research report on how to get your parents to give you what you want, I realized that many of the stratagems the kids used with me were similar to those they used with their parents.

And yet I seriously doubt they thought of me as they thought of their parents. The kids rarely worried about misbehaving in front of me, in spite of my best efforts to maintain control. They exploited moments of stolen time and transformed space. When the class split into small groups, they would plead to be allowed into hallway spaces, where they'd head for the stairs or the elevator alcove—somewhere that cut off sight lines from the classroom door. Fourth graders who were left in the room would rearrange desks and grab chairs they liked; the computer table chairs—which had wheels and allowed kids to spin around—were especially valued. Often I worried about what the teachers thought of me when they left me in charge of the room for a moment and the kids reclaimed it for their own purposes or rushed out to the bathrooms (cf. Best, 1983). Once, as I was left alone for a moment to watch the class, a fourth-grade girl snatched a Power Ranger card from a boy and ran from the room to the girls' bathroom with about six of her friends. Some boys chased after her. "Get them out of there!" I pleaded to the few remaining kids. I was petrified that the teacher would return to find I'd let the entire class escape into the girls' restroom.

On the one hand these plays for space, and the questions and comments about my physical appearance, reflected the kids' sensitivity to embodied meanings and bodily freedoms. But they were also a function of my willingness to answer the questions and laugh at the jibes. The kids seemed to know few adults, especially adult men from my social background, to talk to informally. Mr. Watts was distant, and although a retired man who worked as a volunteer in the library got along well with the kids, he was less accessible than I was and fit a more recognizable role. The kids were curious about me, and they could satisfy

their curiosity in frequent informal, conversational situations. To some
of the little girls I seemed to be a safe male outsider. One day before
school, for example, as I waited in the hall to see Mrs. Peel, Esmeralda
asked me why I wasn't there every day. I explained that I taught at the
university in Blacksburg and asked her if she'd ever been there. She
hadn't (most of the kids at Thurber had not, although the university is
only about 40 minutes away by car).

"Are you married?" Esmerelda asked me shyly.

"No, I'm not."

"Oh, I just thought you were," she said. "Do you have a girlfriend?"

"No," I answered.

"Oh, you're just playing," she smiled.

"Playing? I wish I were. Mostly I just work."

For some of the African American kids I was probably one of the
relatively few European American adults they had a chance to talk to
informally. My fieldnotes contain this account of of a busride to a
fieldtrip.

> Thurman asks me where I'm from and when I tell him Oklahoma, he tells
> me he was born in Cleveland, and lived in Chicago a while. I ask him where
> in Chicago, 'cause I went to school there. He thinks but can't remember.
> Anthony asks me if I live in a big house. Not really, I tell him. I ask him
> if he does, and he tells me that he and Benny, who's sitting on the other
> side of him, live in apartments. They told me about the big houses they'd
> like to have; then Anthony asks me what kind of bike I had when I was a
> kid. I don't know what it was called, so I try to describe it: one gear, big
> handlebars, small wheels, and thick tires. He says his father had a bike
> like that. They tell me about their bikes, and then Thurman tells Benny
> and me that he had a weird dream last night. In it he woke up, and his
> bed was outside, in his yard, and the ground around him was covered with
> snakes as far as he could see. Thurman turns back to me and asks me if
> I've ever been in California. Just for a few days, I tell him. He talks about
> visiting his sister in California during the summer and hearing a machine
> gun going off on the street; two women get shot. He says he doesn't think
> he'd want to live there.

I had scores of little conversations like these, and they reflected, I
think, the kids' use of me as a resource to learn about distant social
spaces. Of course, like Mr. Watts and the teachers, some of the kids had
had tangential experiences with my social worlds or were at least
conscious of my professional affiliations. Kids would ask me if I knew
such and such a person at Virginia Tech or would ask me a question
about the sports teams. And just as the principals' and some of the
teachers' experiences with college shaped their interactions with me, so
too did some of the kids' ideas about universities. Once, when I was
trying to raise the topic of testing and the gifted programs, Lucy told me
that she'd been tested by UVA [The University of Virginia]:

Lucy:	I took it from the UVA, I took tests from UVA and it was boring....See, one day I was in third grade and this big fat lady came in, and she said, "Come here Lucy, Earl." And we said okay, and then she went and got Olive. And we had to sit in this room, right here, in here, and we had to do tests. And then *all* we got afterward was a sucker. And then we went in fourth grade and had to do all these tests, and I said, "Why are we doing these stupid tests?"
Earl:	[*Joking*] 'Cause we're stupid?
Lucy:	And she said, "Well, cause UVA wants you to do it." And I said, "Well, I don't want to do it." And then she said, "Well, you don't have to if you don't want to." I said, "I'll just do it for the suckers." And then I went and, and then I went in fifth grade, and we had more tests, and I told my mom that they didn't give suckers anymore so I wanted to quit, so I quit.
Earl:	[*Incredulous*] You do tests for suckers?
Lucy:	[*Giggling*] Yes.
Jan:	. . . [To Earl] And you took those with Lucy?
Helen:	I took them, not in third grade.
Earl:	They were *booooorrrrring!*
Helen:	Very boring.
Earl:	Sit here for a year, and you'd get a headache just staring at the sheet of paper.
Lucy:	You sit there going like [*Mimics it with her body*].
Jan:	Did they tell you what they were for?
Earl:	Yeah.
	. . .
Lucy:	UVA!
Earl:	UVA!
Helen:	Well, if it said UVA, it must be good [*Tweaking me*].
Lucy:	I tested for the UVA.
Helen:	I've *been* to UVA.
Duane:	UNC? UN Luck. [Duane, a basketball fan (see chapter 5) was referring to the University of North Carolina, a college basketball power.]
Helen:	I'm going there!

Lucy: [Pointing to the meter on my recorder] That says UV.

Earl: That's VU!

Helen: Believe me, someone from Virginia Tech would not have a piece of equipment that said UVA.

Lucy: Why?

Helen: Because, Virginia Tech and UVA are sort of—they're not like this; they're sort of like eh! eh!

Lucy: They hate each other?

Helen: Yeah, there's a little bit of friction.

Lucy: Because somebody beat somebody?

Helen: No!...It's basically competition for students.

For Helen, making fun of my university was a way to tease me. In another interview, she asked me:

Helen: Did you read that article in the paper yesterday?

Jan: What?

Helen: Virginia Tech being second to last in graduating atheletes.

Jan: No I didn't, but it doesn't surprise me.

Helen: And UVA led the nation. In all three divisions, they led the nation, with 91%.

Jan: Doesn't surprise me.

Later in this interview, Helen got upset thinking about something another girl had said and suggested taking it out on me:

Helen: [Referring to a student not among the interview group members] I'm gonna hit her if she don't shut her mouth!

Jan: Calm down. I don't know what you're talking about, but calm down!

Neal: We're setting a good example.

Helen: Let's give him the wrong information; he's from Virginia Tech.

Jan: Sit down everybody.

Thinking about these anecdotes and interview fragments, I have difficulty placing myself in any of Fine's (1987) categories of adult researchers working with children: I was not "leader," "supervisor," "observer," nor "friend." I was simply a *context* for the kids. I was a marker for particular settings, situations, and activities that kids knew they could appropriate (at least in part) for their own uses. My presence and activity defined a certain space outside the constraints of the teachers, a space in which kids had relatively free rein to talk and interact. Once I'd begun interviewing kids in Mrs. Jumpers's class, for example, the kids would get up every time I stepped into the room, walk over to me, and ask, "Are you going to get us out of this?"

I was also a setting for informal interactions among kids. The group format of the interviews gave the kids, who had no playground time and short, quiet-enforced lunches, an opportunity to talk to each other loudly and informally and in cross-sex conversations. Helen, for example, often tried to insist on being in a discussion group with particular boys. And finally, the interviews themselves, which took place in a conference room in the library or in an empty office, were free, exploitable spaces where kids could physically do things they couldn't do elsewhere: move around, sit in office chairs, draw or write on chalkboards. But what did the kids think we were about in the interviews?

MEANINGS OF *RESEARCH*

Thorne (1993) described how at times some behavior or characteristic of the fifth and sixth graders she worked with, the girls especially, evoked memories from her own childhood, at which times she felt "more deeply inside their worlds" (p. 25). I can't make any such claims. I was nowhere near as smart or talkative when I was in fourth or fifth grade. I also treated adults with much more reverence and fear than these kids treated me. The kids were curious about what I did as an adult, recognized me as a relatively powerless specimen, and maneuvered me quite effectively. I had expected them to coopt me to some extent, but I'd hoped they could collaborate with me in thinking about the school. Thus, in the first interview with them, after explaining how I'd obtained permission from their parents and stressing that they could decline to participate, leave at any time, or refuse to answer questions they weren't comfortable with, I tried to explain what the research was about. It soon became evident, though, that the kids and I had very different ideas about the meaning of *research*:

> *Jan:*   We're interested in how kids learn in school and what they learn, and especially we're interested in what kind of things you read and you write. And interested in how you feel about your own experiences in school, whether or not you're learning; what you're learning; how you're learning. That kind of thing. Does that make any sense?

Lucy: You mean what, looking in encyclopedias about research? About research, they're looking in encyclopedias under our names?

Jan: They're going to look in encyclopedias under your names? Is that what you were asking? No, I don't think we're going to put you in an encyclopedia. This will be confidential. We're not going to put this under your name or tell anybody who said what. . . .

Lucy: I mean, do they, uh, like if they look up something...to research you have to look up something—what do they look up?

Jan: You're talking about our—the research we're doing? Well, this is a different kind of research than the research that you've done in the classroom? Is that what you're asking? We don't look things up in dictionaries, in encyclopedias. Does that make any sense? [They shook their heads No.] No! [Laughing] Well, let's see. Does anybody know what research is about? What kind of research do you do in the class? You go to the library, you look stuff up?

Earl: Yeah, we look up baseball players and stuff.

Jan: You look up baseball players?

Earl: Right now we are.

Jan: Yeah, you done any other kind of research?

Lucy: No.

Helen: Yeah, surveys.

Jan: . . . Okay, let me try to explain; this is a good question. So...you were saying, Helen, that you've done like surveys, where you write up the survey and then you give it to other students? What was that about?

Helen: Voting; this year we voted for president.

Jan: Oh, and then you've done the kind with encyclopedias. And have you done any other kind?

Lucy: Yeah.

Earl: We've reported on states.

Lucy: You had to look up things, and then you have to write, you have to write it, and then you have to read it to everybody.

Jan: You had to read it to everybody. That's a good thing too. Well, this kind of research...is a little bit different, in that—it's closer to the survey kind of stuff, but it's a little bit different. Surveys are good if you're asking people questions like "Who are you gonna vote for? This person or that person?" 'Cause then they can check one or the other. But if you wanted to find out *why* somebody was going to vote for Clinton or Bush, it'd be harder to do with a survey, right? You'd need to sit down with them and talk to them a little bit? So if I were going to find out how you all learned and how you felt about school, it'd be hard for me to do that on a survey. I could say, "Do you like school? Do you not like school?" And I kind of could do some of that, but it wouldn't be the same as sitting down with you and talking face to face, right? And by the same token, I can't go and look up what kids think of school in an encyclopedia, 'cause that's not in an encyclopedia; it's not in a lot of stuff that's been published. So what I'm kind of asking you all to do is help me out, collaborate with me, work with me here to find out—'cause you're the ones who have all the knowledge that I need. You're the ones that know what school's like for elementary school kids.

I'm not entirely sure what the kids made of my explanation. They immediately turned the conversation to my recording apparatus (which looked unfamiliar to them, especially the VU meter). I had to explain how the recorder worked, letting them say their names into the microphone, and replaying the recording for them. This process also raises some questions about kids' awareness of the nature of research. While we might assume that kids' casual encounters with audiotapes and portable cassette players would have familiarized them with "recording," I'm not so sure this is the case. Recall from the business-in-the-classroom activity in chapter two that kids' proficiency as consumers did not translate into competence as producers. The fact that kids buy tapes and listen to them doesn't mean they understand what recording is about or what it means that their words will be preserved and later transcribed. I did try to explain what I would do with the tapes:

Jan: Now, what we're going to do with this—is, uh, probably over the summer, take these tapes and transcribe them. And what that means is that we'll listen to them, and we'll type out what you say. We'll probably give you pseudonyms. That is, we'll let you think up fake names so that we don't use your real names, so that nobody knows who said what.

Lucy: Like "E.T. phone home."? [*Laughter*]

Helen: My name's legally changed; can I use my first name?

Jan: You can use any name you want, so long as it, you know, masks your identity....And we're going to transcribe them, and we're—you know, you think about what happens in school—I don't know, do you think teachers really know what's going on inside your head a lot of times?

All: No, uh-uh.

Helen: They can't read my mind; at least I hope they can't!

Jan: So in a way that's the purpose of this. We want to find out what kids know, to begin with—

Lucy: —I know what 2 + 2 is! [*Laughter*]

Jan: Okay.

Helen: Certain people might not know what that answer is, though.

Jan: Yeah, some would, and some might not. I mean, the thing about school is everybody knows something, but you know different kinds of things. And we want to find better ways that teachers and people who work in school can—work well with kids. To draw on what you already know, and draw on your strengths, and to help you to read and write better.

Lucy: Some old people think they know everything, and they can't teach children right.

Jan: That's right.

Lucy: Like Miss Pollard!

Jan: Miss Pollard?

          . . .

Neal: She would jerk me.

Earl: Some of them are good.

Helen: Trixie, who was it she made cry? She pulled somebody and made them cry.

Lucy: She popped Thurman's boil!

These unsolicited, spontaneous horror stories about teachers were a common feature in the talk of most of the kids I met. Did they reflect common experience? Did they emerge because the kids saw a chance to complain to an adult? Did the kids understand the functions of the tape and want to put their experiences down in the record? Here, though, they quickly returned to the topic of research and asked me:

Lucy: Well, what if the teachers sneak and listen to the tape.

Jan: No, no, we're not going to let anybody listen to it, so don't worry about that. But do remember that it is voluntary, so if you feel later on like you don't want to do it, you can quit. You don't have to.[2]

Lucy: You mean we're going to do it till June?

Jan: If you want. You can. Not every day.

Lucy: Do you go to different schools and do it?

---

[2]One student, Trixie, did opt out after a couple of group interviews, and during both years kids would excuse themselves from interviews or give me rain checks if they actually wanted to participate in something going on in class.

> *Jan*: No, we're doing it just in this one school. It takes so much time to do one school.
>
> *Earl*: Cool!

When I took the group out again the next day to talk, I began by asking them if they had any questions about why we were doing the research:

> *Lucy*: I know: Those people in the school want to know what we think. They have to do research on us (*Laughs*). To see if we, if we, if we—if we scream at the teacher or if we—
>
> *Earl*: Uh-uh. Teacher screams at us!
>
> *Jan*: No. I'm not here to do research on *you*. You're helping me do research on the school, okay?
>
> *Lucy*: We could do research on you!
>
> *Jan*: I didn't pick you out for any particular reason; you just were literally the only kids whose parents said okay when we asked. So I think you're a nice cross-section; you're all bright kids as far as I can tell [*They laugh*]. Very articulate, I could tell from last time. But, but I don't want you to feel like I'm putting you under the microscope, because I'm not. I think you have a lot of information about school, about what it's like for you from your perspective.
>
> *Lucy*: Gives me a headache.

It's possible the fifth graders, in spite of my explanations, didn't understand what I was doing as "research." The fourth graders, I think, had a better idea because I was able to enlist them as "researchers" on the class newsletter effort. Some of their projects were suggested by me, but many (usually the more successful ones) they thought up themselves. For some projects they had to take notes and then write articles on events. (One of the kids was unable to understand what I meant by notetaking until she associated it with the activities of the police detectives on the television series *Silk Stalkings*.) Most kids, however, fell in love with the tape recorder and wanted to do interviews. I would help them work out questions, let them practice, and then send them out. Many kids used interviewing as a way to explore school spaces—going into other classrooms—and some used interviewing as an opportunity to work outside direct adult surveillance. Once the interviews were done, I would transcribe the tapes and return the transcripts to the kids (with pseudonyms inserted) so they could write their stories or reports. The projects focused on such topics as kids' popular music preferences, dress preferences, feelings about the standardized tests they were made to take in the spring, fieldtrips, and so on.

Did the kids know what I was going to be writing about? At the time I was unsure myself, but even if I had been and had explained to the kids, could they have understood? Would any of them, even now (the oldest would be 15 now), be able to make sense of this text? They consented to work with me, but what they consented to was the embodied interaction, not the mobilization of these interactions in texts like this.

In any event, as the interview transcripts indicate, the kids didn't passively allow me to define the agenda in our interviews. More often than not, they ignored me and talked about their own interests, which in turn refocused mine. After all, the core of my initial proposal had emphasized collaboration and allowing participants to shape the research agenda. Although this idea didn't work well with teachers, the kids were much more comfortable articulating their interests. I eventually realized I should be taking their agendas seriously.

INTERVIEWS AND THE PRODUCTION
OF DISCOURSE

One reason the kids could take control of my conversations with them is that I often talked to them in groups or recorded their speech in ongoing activities. My original intent, I have to admit, had been to do conventional, one-on-one interviews focusing on schoolwork, but thanks to a misunderstanding, Mrs. Jumpers expected me to take groups of her fifth graders out for interviews, and after the first group interview, the kids also expected to talk in groups.

One-on-one interviews with kids pose complex methodological problems, some of which are reduced in group interviews, although the dynamics that take their place are equally problematic. Both Davies (1982) and Tammivaara and Enright (1986) warn that adult interviewers in one-on-one situations risk controlling interviews and eliciting from students what the kids think the interviewers want to hear. In group interviews, however, I found it impossible to control the direction of the talk; I could barely define issues to be discussed. The students used minimal or story-based "bridging" devices to make transitions from one topic to the next (Goffman, 1976; Newkirk & McLure, 1992). That is, they simply bounced off any element in the previous speaker's comments (a minimal bridge) or made thematic connections to the previous turn. One-on-one interviews, by contrast, usually function like conversations with text-based bridges, in which each speaker's turn is connected to a text—usually the interviewer's questions, which are in turn grounded in the texts of the researcher's academic discipline (Rose, 1987). Responses in these kinds of one-on-one interviews can be detached from the overall flow of the interview, coded, and combined with responses to the same questions asked in other interviews. Responses from collective discussions with minimal and story bridges, on the other hand, can be understood only in the context of the larger interview (cf. Briggs, 1986). As a consequence, when I quote from such interviews, I have to reproduce relatively long strips of conversation to make them intelligible.[3]

The group interviews also differed from one-on-one interviews in the variety of discourse forms they elicited. As Briggs (1986) argued, conventional one-on-one interviews shape speech into particular forms that are highly referential, require words to have discrete and unambiguous meanings, and presuppose shared understandings among interviewer and interviewee. Emotional, expressive, sarcastic, and ritual speech; poetry, singing, jokes, and so forth rarely appear in traditional interviews except as reported speech. In the two years I spent studying elementary school kids I found that when I interviewed them individually (as I did in the second year), they answered my questions with referential, segmentable, and presupposing forms. Only occasionally would they break out of the expected adult format. (After all, they were little kids and less experienced with interview forms than were adults; I had also interacted with them informally for a long time before the interviews.)

When I interviewed groups of kids, however, and especially when I recorded them talking among themselves, the speech events changed. I began to see rich verbal forms that the one-on-one interviews suppressed. In their casual conversation, the kids did not talk in turn but talked over each other, told jokes, imitated television characters, insulted each other ("Your mamma's so fat," one African American girl began as she delivered a snap to a tongue-tied European American boy, "she sat on George Washington's lap and a nickel popped out his nose"), made fun of me, asked me personal questions, asked each other personal questions, and so on. On the bus to one field trip, I let kids pass around a microphone; the tape they made had about an hour of singing and radio imitations. On another bus trip, a student grabbed the microphone and delivered an extemporaneous "news story." My point is that using conventional one-on-one interviews would have meant missing most of the kids' ways of expressing themselves; they might never have raised

---

[3]Schudson (1995), in a discussion on the history of using quotations in newspaper interviews, argued that they reflect a form of "impersonal surveillance." Although he was mainly concerned with their use in stories about powerful public officials, quotations do create an "anonymous surveillance" that lets people think they have gained insight into a class of people—children or parents or teachers. Readers must decide whether my quoting practices reinforce the dominant categories of adult perceptions of children or make them problematic, whether they simplify pictures to make them mobile and controllable or complicate and anchor them in time and space.

the same topics that arose in the other contexts. For example, many of my data on popular culture come from the fourth-graders' spontaneous conversations. Attempts to raise this issue in one-on-one conversations produced relatively short, stilted comments or expressions of amazement that I knew or want to know about such things.

The point, as Briggs (1986) argued, is not to abandon interviewing altogether but to change our understanding of it. Instead of imposing the conventional form received from the literature, we should first study the various ways of speaking and the speech events people participate in and try to model discussions with them on such events. There was ample evidence, for example, that many of the kids had understandings of an interview as a speech event very different from those presupposed in the research literature. For example, two fourth-grade girls, interviewing a classmate about his preferences for workmates, diverged from the questions and procedures I'd helped them develop to create a complex teasing game:

Trana: Mr. Wally, who do you like to sit with in groups?

Wally: Beavis.

Brenda: And who else?

Wally: Karl.

Brenda: Any girls or anything?

Wally: Uh-uh.

Brenda: Tell the truth.

Wally: I am.

Trana: And why do you like to sit with them? [*Pause*] Why do you like to sit with them!

Wally: Because Beavis goes nuts sometimes.

Trana: Why do you like nut people?

Wally: I don't know.

Brenda: He says, "I don't know."...Who do you like to sit with?

Wally: I done said it. Karl and Beavis.

Brenda: Friends that you really like?

Wally: That's all.

Trana: And why do you like to sit with them?

Wally: I just said, because they act like they're fools. And Beavis. I want to sit beside him because he goes "E-yah!"

Trana: Okay. What is your favorite subject?

Wally: Art.

Trana: Subject!

Brenda: Math, reading, spelling?

Wally: Math!

Trana: Why do you like math?

Wally: Because it's fun.

Trana: Why is it fun to you?

Wally: I don't know.

Brenda: You have to know.

Wally: I like math because you add and subtract, and you take away and stuff.

Brenda: Okay. We want you to say a girl.

Trana: Yeah. Who do you like to sit with at lunch?

Wally: [*Laughs*] Brenda. [*Giggling*]

Trana: Brenda and who?

Brenda: Is that the only girl?

Wally: Yes.

Trana: Ask him a question, Mrs. Brenda.

Brenda: [*Coldly*] Why do you like to sit with her at lunch?

Wally: I don't know. I don't know why I don't know.

Trana: You have to know a reason!

Brenda: To sit beside her!

Trana: Or is she your girlfriend?

Wally: Because she used to like me!

         [*Cry of outrage from Brenda*]

Trana: [*Almost laughing*] She used to like you, and you used to like her? You used to like her, and she used to like you?

Wally: [*Unclear*]

Brenda: That's not true! I don't like him.

The insistence that Wally tell the truth and name a girl and Trana's subsequent teasing of Brenda when she turned out to be that girl illustrate some of the kids' interpretations of one-on-one (or two-on-one) interviews as interrogations, perhaps modeled on adults' questionings of kids. The girls' remorseless demands for reasons bewildered poor Wally to the point that he could only reply to one query: "I don't know. I don't know why I don't know." Other kids saw one-on-one interviews with *me* as a game. For example, like many interviewers, I would ask kids before and after an interview whether they wanted to ask me anything. Doug responded at the end of an interview (quoted from in chapter 3) by firing back at me just about every question I'd asked him in the preceding hour, even making me draw a map of my neighborhood, as I'd asked him to do.

The interactive and social organization of the interview is thus a powerful influence on the kinds of discourse it elicits. But modeling interview practices on familiar discursive forms is more difficult than it at first seems. Group interviews do not necessarily allow interviewers to avoid the problems of the classic one-on-one interview organized around a set of discipline-based questions. In Davies' (1993) *Shards of Glass,* for example, groups of kids were *trained* to formulate their experiences in terms of a particular poststructuralist discourse. Although Davies considered this practice a means of allowing the kids to break free from the constraints of other discourses, it might also be seen, in Minh-Ha's (1991) terms, as the construction of a colonizing interdependency: "[T]he need for informants grows into a need for disciples. We have to train Insiders so that they may busy themselves with Our preoccupations, and make themselves useful by asking the right kind of Question and providing the right kind of Answer" (p. 68).

Group interviews thus are not a simple solution. I sometimes used one-on-one interviews, which need not be framed entirely around categories from academic discourses. Life history interviews, especially when conducted as a series of conversations over time, can allow the interviewee to define purposes for the interview and to control its directions (but see Nespor & Barylske, 1991). The interview in which I asked kids to talk about their activities in neighborhood space while drawing maps also allowed them some control, although recall Lila's difficulties in figuring out what I wanted. The maps themselves then became the structuring bridges shaping the conversational interaction.

MORE LOOSE ENDS

A broader consideration of some of the issues I've raised here would be worthwhile. Does participation in a research study influence teachers' or students' statuses within a school or neighborhood? Does it bring prestige or additional scrutiny? Does participation have any lasting consequences?

How is qualitative research on schools in the United States influenced by the institutional affiliations of researchers? What do kids and teachers think of educational researchers?

Because so much qualitative research in education is built around interviews, researchers should pay more attention to how kids' and teachers' understandings of interviews develop. How do these speech acts enter into their communicative repertoires? How do understandings of interviews shape the information they produce? How do kids, parents, and teachers understand research? How do these understandings develop over time?

One way to address some of these research-related questions might be to talk again to participants in studies and to study the ways research is published and consumed by other researchers, students, practitioners, and the public. There is curiously little systematic research along these lines, and yet such work seems a prerequisite to understand research praxis not as a theoretical posture or a writing style, but as actual social relations organized in time and space, producing texts that circulate and are interwoven with other practices in the intersections of social space.

References

Allen, J., & Pryke, M. (1994). The production of service space. *Environment and Planning D: Society and Space, 12,* 453–475.

Alton-Lee, A., Nuthall, G., & Patrick, J. (1993). Reframing classroom research: A lesson from the private world of children. *Harvard Educational Review, 63,* 50–84.

Amit-Talai, V., & Wulff, H. (Eds.). (1995). *Youth cultures.* New York: Routledge.

Appadurai, A. (1986). Commodities and the politics of value. In A. Appadurai (Ed.), *The social life of things: Commodities in cultural perspective* (pp. 3–63). Cambridge, U.K.: Cambridge University Press.

Appadurai, A. (1990). Disjuncture and difference in the global cultural economy. *Theory, Culture & Society, 7,* 295–310.

Appadurai, A. (1991). Global ethnoscapes. In R. Fox (Ed.), *Recapturing anthropology* (pp. 191–210). Santa Fe, NM: School of American Research Press.

Bacon-Smith, C. (1992). *Enterprising women: Television fandom and the creation of popular myth.* Philadelphia: University of Pennsylvania Press.

Bailey, D. (1980). *Improvisation: Its nature and practice in music.* Ashbourne, Derbyshire, U.K.: Moorland.

Bakhtin, M. (1968). *Rabelais and his world.* Cambridge, MA: MIT Press.

Ball, S. (1987). *The micropolitics of the school.* London: Methuen.

Barth, F. (1969). Introduction. In F. Barth (Ed.), *Ethnic groups and boundaries* (pp. 9–38). Boston, MA: Little, Brown.

Bateson, G. (1972). A theory of play and fantasy. In *Steps to an ecology of mind* (pp. 177–193). New York: Ballantine.

Baudrillard, J. (1981). *The mirror of production.* St. Louis, MO: Telos.

Baudrillard, J. (1983). *Simulations.* New York: Semiotext(e).

Beauregard, R. (1993). *Voices of decline: The postwar fate of US Cities.* Cambridge, MA: Blackwell.

Beauregard, R. (1995). If only the city could speak: The politics of representation. In H. Liggett & D. Perry (Eds.), *Spatial practices* (pp. 59–80). Thousand Oaks, CA: Sage.

Becker, H. (1963). *Outsiders.* New York: Free Press.

Becker, H. (1980). *Role and career problems of the Chicago school teacher.* New York: Arno Press. (Original work published 1951)

Becker, H. (1982). *Art worlds.* Berkeley & Los Angeles, CA: University of California Press.

Benjamin, W. (1978). *Reflections* (P. Demetz, Ed.). New York: Schocken Books.

Best, R. (1983). *We've all got scars.* Bloomington, IN: Indiana University Press.

Bishop, M. (1995, January 29). Street by street, block by block: How urban renewal uprooted Black Roanoke [Special section]. *Roanoke Times and World News,* pp. 1–12.

Booker, S. (1981). *Choices: Alternatives for Housing in Old Northwest Roanoke.* Roanoke, VA: Roanoke Valley Council of Community Service.

Bourdieu, P. (1977). *Outline of a theory of practice*. Cambridge, England: Cambridge University Press.

Bourdieu, P. (1984). *Distinction*. Cambridge, MA: Harvard University Press.

Bourdieu, P. (1985). The market of symbolic goods. *Poetics, 14*, 13–44.

Bourdieu, P. (1986). The forms of capital. In J. Richardson (Ed.), *Handbook of theory and and research for the sociology of education* (pp. 241–258). New York: Greenwood Press.

Brecht, B. (1976). Showing has to be shown. In J. Willett, R. Manheim, & E. Fried (Eds.), *Bertolt Brecht poems 1913–1956* (pp. 341–342). London: Methuen.

Briggs, C. (1986). *Learning how to ask*. Cambridge, England: Cambridge University Press.

Brooks, G. (1995, April 30). Teen-age infidels hanging out. *The New York Times Magazine*, pp. 44–49.

Brothers, T. (Ed.). (1992). *School reform: Business, education and government as partners*. New York: Conference Board.

Brown, J., Collins, A., & Deguid, P. (1989). Situated cognition and the culture of learning. *Educational Researcher, 18*, 32–42.

Brown, L. (1993, July 4). Old Northeast is back in town. *Roanoke Times & World News*, pp. D1, D4.

Buck-Morss, S. (1989). *The dialectics of seeing*. Cambridge, MA: MIT Press.

Butler, J. (1990). *Gender trouble*. New York: Routledge.

Cameron, D., Frazer, E., Harvey, P., Rampton, M., & Richardson, K. (1994). The relations between researcher and researched: Ethics, advocacy and empowerment. In D. Graddol, J. Maybin, & B. Stierer (Eds.), *Researching language and literacy in social context* (pp. 18–25). Clevedon, U.K.: Open University.

Campbell, A. (1984). *The girls in the gang*. Cambridge, MA: Blackwell.

Certeau, M., de. (1984). *The practice of everyday life*. Berkeley & Los Angeles, CA: University of California Press.

Chamberlin, J. (1982a, January 31). School board chief caught in dilemma on shake-up. *Roanoke Times & World News*, pp. A1, A14.

Chamberlin, J. (1982b, January 27). School demotion reasons too vague, attorneys say. *Roanoke Times & World News*, pp. A1, A12.

Chamberlin, J. (1982c, February 10). School board backs Tota on demotions. *Roanoke Times & World News*, pp. A1, A12.

Chamberlin, J. (1983, February 6). Unrest in Roanoke schools? *Roanoke Times & World News*, pp. A1, A12.

Chavkin, N. (1989). Debunking the myth about minority parents. *Educational Horizons, 67*, 119–123.

Children's Express. (1993). *Voices from the future: Our children tell us about violence in America*. New York: Crown.

Cochran-Smith, M., & Lytle, S. (1992). *Inside/outside*. New York: Teachers College Press.

Comer, J. (1984, May). Home/school relationships as they affect the academic success of children. *Education and Urban Society, 16*, 323–327.

Connell, R. (1987). *Gender and power*. Sydney, Australia: Allen & Unwin.

Corbin, A. (1986). *The fragrant and the foul: Odor and the French social imagination*. Cambridge, MA: Harvard University Press.

Crawford, M. (1992). The world in a shopping mall. In M. Sorkin (Ed.), *Variations on a theme park* (pp. 3–30). New York: Hill & Wang.

Cusick, P. (1973). *Inside high school*. New York: Holt, Rinehart, & Winston.

Davies, B. (1982). *Life in the classroom and playground*. London: Routledge & Kegan Paul.

Davies, B. (1993). *Shards of glass: Children reading and writing beyond gendered identities.* Cresskill, NJ: Hampton Press.

Davies, L. (1984). *Pupil power: Deviance and gender in school.* London: Falmer.

DeBell, J. (1993, August 15). Not everybody retires and moves to Florida. And where are the kids? *Roanoke Times & World News,* pp. A1, A8.

DeBell, J. (1994, January 2). If you can solve problems, you'll get a good job. *Roanoke Times & World News,* pp. A1, A4, A5.

Delamont, S., & Galton, M. (1987). Anxieties and anticipations—Pupils' views of transfer to secondary school. In A. Pollard (Ed.), *Children and their primary schools* (pp. 236–251). London: Falmer.

Denscombe, M. (1980). "Keeping 'em quiet": The significance of noise for the practical activity of teaching. In P. Woods (Ed.), *Teacher strategies* (pp. 61–83). London: Croom Helm.

Dimaggio, P. (1990). Cultural aspects of economic action and organization. In R. Friedland & A. Robinson (Eds.), *Beyond the marketplace: Rethinking economy and society* (pp. 113–136). New York: Aldine de Gruyter.

Dimaggio, P., & Powell, W. (1983). The iron cage revisited: Institutional isomorphism and collective rationality in organizational fields. *American Sociological Review, 48,* 147–160.

Ditton, J. (1979). *Controlology.* London: Macmillan.

Dorst, J. (1989). *The written suburb.* Philadelphia: University of Pennsylvania Press.

Duxbury, S. (1987). Childcare ideologies and resistance: The manipulative strategies of pre-school children. In A. Pollard (Ed.), *Children and their primary schools* (pp. 12–25). London: Falmer.

Dyson, A. (1993). *Social worlds of children learning to write.* New York: Teachers College Press.

Dyson, A. (1994). The Ninjas, the X-Men, and the Ladies: Playing with power and identity in an urban primary school. *Teachers College Record, 96,* 219–239.

Echols, F. (Producer). (1994, July 19). *Third Tuesday.* Roanoke, VA: WVTF.

Eckert, P. (1989). *Jocks and burnouts.* New York: Teachers College Press.

Edelsky, C. (1991). *With literacy and justice for all.* Philadelphia: Falmer.

Eder, D. (1990). Serious and playful disputes: Variation in conflict talk among female adolescents. In A. Grimshaw (Ed.), *Conflict talk* (pp. 67–84). New York: Cambridge University Press.

Eder, D. (1993). "Go get ya a French!": Romantic and sexual teasing among adolescent girls. In D. Tannen (Ed.), *Gender and conversational interaction* (pp. 17–31). New York: Oxford University Press.

Eder, D., Evans, C., & Parker, S. (1995). *School talk: Gender and adolescent culture.* New Brunswick, NJ: Rutgers University Press.

Edwards, R. (1979). *Contested terrain: The transformation of the workplace in the twentieth century.* New York: Basic Books.

Elias, N. (1978). *The history of manners.* (E. Jephcott, Trans.). New York: Pantheon Books. (Originally work published 1939)

Elias, N. (1983). *The court society.* New York: Pantheon Books.

Eliott, S. (1994, December 23). Advertising. *The New York Times,* p. D6.

Employment since '74: Yes, it has become a service economy. (1994, October). *Roanoker,* p. 15.

Epstein, J. (1995). School/family/community partnerships. *Phi Delta Kappan, 76,* 701–711.

Everhart, R. (1983). *Reading, writing, and resistance.* London: Routledge & Kegan Paul.

Fantasia, R. (1988). *Cultures of solidarity: Consciousness, action, and contemporary American workers.* Berkeley & Los Angeles: University of California Press.

Fantasia, R. (1995). From class consciousness to culture, action, and social organization. *Annual Review of Sociology, 21,* 269–287.

Fine, G. (1987). *With the boys.* Chicago, IL: The University of Chicago Press.

Fine, M. (1991). *Framing dropouts.* New York: Teachers College Press.

Fine, M. (1993). (Ap)parent involvement: Reflections on parents, power, and urban public schools. *Teachers College Record, 94*(4), 682–710.

First, J., Kellogg, J., Almeida, C., & Gray, R. (1991). *The good common school.* Boston, MA: National Coalition of Advocates for Students.

Fiske, J. (1989). *Understanding popular culture.* Boston: Unwin Human.

Fligstein, N. (1990). *The transformation of the American corporation.* Cambridge, MA: Harvard University Press.

Fligstein, N., & Freeland, R. (1995). Theoretical and comparative perspectives on corporate organization. *Annual Review of Sociology, 21,* 21–43.

Foucault, M. (1979). *Discipline and punish.* New York: Vintage.

Freidson, E. (1970). *Professional dominance.* New York: Atherton Press.

Frith, S., & Horne, H. (1987). *Art into pop.* London: Methuen.

Fullan, M. (with Stiegelbauer, S.). (1991). *The new meaning of educational change.* New York: Teachers College Press.

Gaines, D. (1991). *Teenage wasteland.* New York: Pantheon.

Gallimore, R. D. (1992). *Relationship between growth patterns and planning practices: A case study of the city of Roanoke.* Unpublished masters thesis, Department of Geography, Blacksburg, VA: Virginia Polytechnic Institute and State University.

General Accounting Office. (1994). *Elementary school children: Many change schools frequently, harming their education* (GAO/HEHS-94-95). Washington, DC: US General Accounting Office.

Gibboney, R. (1994). *The stone trumpet: A story of practical school reform 1960–1990.* Albany, NY: State University of New York Press.

Giddens, A. (1981). *A contemporary critique of historical materialism, Vol. 1: Power, property and the state.* Berkeley & Los Angeles, CA: University of California Press.

Giroux, H., & McLaren, P. (Eds.). (1994). *Between borders: Pedagogy and the politics of cultural studies.* New York: Routledge.

Giroux, H., & Simon, R. (Eds.). (1989). *Popular culture, schooling, and everyday life.* Granby, MA: Bergin & Garvey.

Goffman, E. (1976). Replies and responses. *Language in Society, 5,* 257–313.

Gold, B., & Miles, M. (1981). *Whose school is it anyway? Parent-teacher conflict over an innovative school.* New York: Praeger.

Goodson, I. (1991). Teachers' lives and educational research. In I. Goodson & R. Walker (Eds.), *Biography, identity and schooling: Episodes in educational research* (pp. 137–149). London: Falmer.

Goodson, I. (1993). The devil's bargain: Educational research and the teacher. *Education Policy Analysis Archives* [On-line serial]. *1*(3). Available at URL http://olam.ed.asu.edu/eppa/v1n3.html.

Goodson, I. (1994). Studying the teacher's life and work. *Teaching and Teacher Education, 10*(1), 29–37.

Gottdiener, M. (1995). *Postmodern semiotics.* Cambridge, MA: Blackwell.

Gramsci, A. (1971). *Selections from the prison notebooks* (Q. Hoare & G. Smith, Eds. & Trans.). New York: International.

Gregory, D. (1994). *Geographical imaginations.* Cambridge, MA: Blackwell.

Grossberg, L., Nelson, C., & Treichler, P. (Eds.). (1992). *Cultural studies.* New York: Routledge.

Hall, S. (1989). *Imaginary identification and politics.* Transcript of talk given at the Institute of Contemporary Arts, London.

Hanks, W. (1990). *Referential practice.* Chicago, IL: University of Chicago Press.

Haraway, D. (1988). Situated knowledges: The science question in feminism and the privilege of partial perspectives. *Feminist Studies, 14,* 575–599.

Haraway, D. (1991). The politics of postmodern bodies: Constitutions of self in immune system discourse. In *Simians, cyborgs, and women: The reinvention of nature* (pp. 203–230). New York: Routledge.

Hargreaves, A. (1981). Contrastive rhetoric and extremist talk: Teachers, hegemony and the educationist context. In L. Barton & S. Walker (Eds.), *Schools teachers & teaching* (pp. 303–329). Lewes, U.K.: Falmer.

Hargreaves, A. (1993). Individualism and individuality: Reinterpreting the teacher culture. In J. Little & M. McLaughlin (Eds.), *Teachers' work: Individuals, colleagues, and contexts* (pp. 51–76). New York: Teachers College Press.

Harvey, D. (1989). *The condition of postmodernity.* London: Blackwell.

Heath, S. B. (1983). *Ways with words.* Cambridge, U.K.: Cambridge University Press.

Heath, S. B., & Mangiola, L. (1991). *Children of promise: Literate activity in linguistically and culturally diverse classrooms.* Washington, DC: Naional Education Association.

Heath, S. B., & McLaughlin, M. (1993). Ethnicity and gender in theory and practice: The youth perspective. In S. B. Heath and M. McLaughlin (Eds.), *Identity and inner-city youth: Beyond ethnicity and gender* (pp. 13–35). New York: Teachers College Press.

Heath, S. B., & McLaughlin, M. (1994). Learning for anything everyday. *Journal of Curriculum Studies, 26,* 471–489.

Hodge, R., & Tripp, D. (1986). *Children and television: A semiotic approach.* London: Polity Press.

Holmes, R. (1995). *How young children perceive race.* Thousand Oaks, CA: Sage.

Hughes, L. (1988). "But that's not *really* mean": Competing in a cooperative mode. *Sex Roles, 9,* 669–687.

Hull, G. (1993). Hearing other voices: A critical assessment of popular views on literacy and work. *Harvard Educational Review, 63,* 20–49.

Hunter, M. (1984). Knowing, teaching, and supervising. In P. Hosford (Ed.), *Using what we know about teaching.* Alexandria, VA: Association for Supervision and Curriculum Development.

Jackobson, R. (1971). Shifters, verbal categories, and the Russian verb. In *Selected writings of Roman Jakobson 2* (pp. 130–147). The Hague, Netherlands: Mouton.

Jacobson, M., & Mazur, L. (1995). *Marketing madness.* Boulder, CO: Westview Press.

Jones, C. (1985, June 5). More than half of city teachers report sagging morale, poll says. *Roanoke Times & World News,* pp. A1, A10.

Jones, C. (1986a, October 15). Closing of 5 Older Roanoke schools proposed. *Roanoke Times & World News,* pp. A1, A4.

Jones, C. (1986b, December 3). Council asked to stay neutral on school closings. *Roanoke Times & World News,* pp. A1, A12

Jones, C. (1986c, December 10). "Keep neighborhood schools," city board told at final hearing. *Roanoke Times & World News,* p. B6.

Jones, C. (1986d, December 15). Tota says linking school closings, money "ridiculous." *Roanoke Times & World News,* pp. A1, A8.

Jones, C. (1987, January 14). Tota says no schools to close; bonds sought. *Roanoke Times & World News,* pp. A1, A7.

Katz, C. (1993). Growing girls/closing circles. In C. Katz & J. Monk (Eds.), *Full circles: Geographies of women over the life course* (pp. 88–106). London & New York: Routledge.

Katz, M. (1993). Reframing the "underclass" debate. In M. Katz (Ed.), *The "Underclass" debate: Views from history* (pp. 440–447). Princeton, NJ: Princeton University Press.

Kelly-Byrne, D. (1989). *A child's play life.* New York: Teachers College Press.

Kohn, A. (1993). *Punished by rewards.* Boston, MA: Houghton Mifflin.

Kondo, D. (1991). *Crafting selves.* Chicago, IL: University of Chicago Press.

Kopytoff, I. (1986). The cultural biography of things: Commoditization as process. In A. Appadurai (Ed.), *The social life of things* (pp. 64–91). Cambridge, England: Cambridge University Press.

Lareau, A. (1989). *Home advantage.* Philadelphia: Falmer.

Lash, S., & Urry, J. (1994). *Economies of signs and space.* Newbury Park, CA: Sage.

Latour, B. (1987). *Science in action.* Cambridge, MA: Harvard University Press.

Latour, B. (1988). The politics of explanation: An alternative. In S. Woolgar (Ed.), *Knowledge and reflexivity* (pp. 155–176). London: Sage.

Lave, J. (1988). *Cognition in practice.* Cambridge, England: Cambridge University Press.

Lave, J., & Wenger, E. (1991). *Situated learning.* Cambridge, U.K.: Cambridge University Press.

Layman, M. (1990a, September 20). 300 give to back merger. *Roanoke Times & World News,* pp.

Layman, M. (1990b, October 5). Eddy: States were exaggerated. *Roanoke Times & World News,* pp. B1, B2.

Layman, M. (1990c, October 30). Pro-merger forces raise $226,000. *Roanoke Times & World News,* pp. A1, A10.

Lefebvre, H. (1979). Space: Social product and use value. In J. Freiberg (Ed.), *Critical sociology* (pp. 285–295). New York: Irvington Publishers.

Lefebvre, H. (1991). *The production of space.* Cambridge, MA: Blackwell.

Lever, J. (1976). Sex differences in the games children play. *Social Problems, 23,* 478–487.

Lightfoot, S. (1978). *Worlds apart: Relationships between families and schools.* New York: Basic Books.

Lightfoot, S. (1981). Toward conflict and resolution: Relationships between families and schools. *Theory into Practice, 20,* 97–104.

Little, J. W. (1981). Norms of collegiality and experimentation: Workplace conditions of school success. *American Educational Research Journal, 19,* 325–340.

Lynch, K. (1979). The spatial world of the child. In *The child in the city: Today and tomorrow* (pp. 102–127). Toronto, Canada: University of Toronto Press.

Lynch, K. (Ed.). (1977). *Growing up in cities.* Cambridge, MA: MIT Press.

Mac an Ghaill, M. (1994). *The making of men.* Philadelphia: Open University Press.

Manegold, C. (1994, September 9). Study says schools must stress academics. *The New York Times,* p. A22.

Markus, T. (1993). *Buildings and power: Freedom and control in the origin of modern building types.* London: Routledge.

Martin, D. (1994, September 5). Super sellers. *Roanoke Times & World News,* pp. 1, 3.

Marx, K. (1967). *Capital* (Vol. 1). New York: International.

Massey, D. (1993). Power-geometry and a progressive sense of place. In J. Bird, B. Curtis, T. Putnam, G. Robertson, & L. Tickner (Eds.), *Mapping the futures* (pp. 59–69). London & New York: Routledge.

McDonald, M. (1971). *Teachers' messages for report cards.* Belmont, CA: Pitman Learning.

McLaughlin, M., Irby, M., & Langman, J. (1994). *Urban sanctuaries.* San Francisco: Jossey-Bass.

McLaughlin, M., & Talbert, J. (1993). How the world of students and teachers challenges policy coherence. In S. Fuhrman (Ed.), *Designing coherent educational policy* (pp. 220–249). San Francisco: Jossey-Bass.

Meyer, J. (1977). The effects of education as an institution. *American Journal of Sociology, 83*(1), 55–77.

Meyer, J., Boli, J., & Thomas, G. (1994). Ontology and rationalization in the Western cultural account. In R. Scott & J. Meyer (Eds.), *Institutional environments and organizations* (pp. 9–27). Thousand Oaks, CA: Sage.

Meyer, J., & Rowan, B. (1977). Institutionalized organizations: Formal structure as myth and ceremony. *American Journal of Sociology, 83*, 340–363.

Meyerowitz, J. (1985). *no sense of place.* New York: Oxford.

Miller, E. (1994). Letting talent flow: How schools can promote learning for the sheer love of it. *the Harvard Education Newsletter, 10*(2), 1–3, 8.

Minh-Ha, T. (1991). *When the moon waxes red.* New York: Routledge.

Mitchell, T. (1988). *Colonizing Egypt.* Cambridge, England: Cambridge University Press.

Moffett, J. (1988). *Storm in the mountains.* Carbondale & Edwardsville: Southern Illinois University Press.

Moll, L., & Gonzalez, N. (1994). Lessons from research with language minority children. *Journal of Reading Behavior, 26*, 439–456.

Moll, L., Tapia, J., & Whitmore, K. (1993). Living knowledge: the social distribution of cultural resources for thinking. In G. Salomon (Ed.), *Distributed cognitions* (pp. 139–163). Cambridge, England: Cambridge University Press.

Moore, H. (1994). *A passion for difference: Essays in anthropology and gender.* Bloomington: Indiana University Press.

Nespor, J. (1987a). Academic tasks in a high school English class. *Curriculum Inquiry, 17*, 203–228.

Nespor, J. (1987b). The role of beliefs in the practice of teaching. *Journal of Curriculum Studies, 19*, 317–328.

Nespor, J. (1990). Grades and knowledge in higher education. *Journal of Curriculum Studies, 22*, 545–556.

Nespor, J. (1994). *Knowledge in motion.* Philadelphia, PA: Falmer.

Nespor, J., & Barber, L. (1991). The rhetorical construction of "the teacher." *Harvard Educational Review, 61*, 417–433.

Nespor, J., & Barylske, J. (1991). Narrative discourse and teacher knowledge. *American Educational Research Journal, 28*, 805–823.

Newkirk, T. (with McLure, P.). (1992). *Listening in: Children talk about books (and other things).* Portsmouth, NH: Heinemann.

Newman, D., Griffin, P., & Cole, M. (1989). *The construction zone: Working for cognitive change in schools.* Cambridge, U.K.: Cambridge University Press.

Nias, J. (1989). *Primary teachers talking.* New York: Routledge.

Noble, D. (1994). Let them eat skills. *Review of Education / Pedagogy / Cultural Studies, 16*, 15–29.

Oakes, J. (1985). *Keeping track.* New Haven, CT: Yale University Press.

Office of Educational Research and Improvement. (1994) *What do student grades mean? Differences across schools* (Report OR 94-3401). Washington, DC: U.S. Department of Education.

Ogbu, J. (1974). *The next generation.* New York: Academic Press.

Orlans, H. (1967). Ethical problems and values in anthropological research. In *The use of social research in federal domestic programs* (Part IV; pp. 359–366). Washington, DC: U.S. Government Printing Office.

Pack: "Severed relations." (1980, February 7). *Roanoke Times & World News,* p. A12.

Pollard, A. (1987). Studying children's perspectives—A collaborative approach. In G. Walford (Ed.), *Doing sociology of education* (pp. 95–118). London: Falmer.

Poster, M. (1990). *The mode of information.* Chicago: University of Chicago Press.

Power Rangers workers' pay investigated. (1994, December 23). *Roanoke Times & World News,* p. A9.

Pred, A., & Watts, M. (1992). *Rethinking modernity.* New Brunswick, NJ: Rutgers University Press.

Radway, J. (1984). *Reading the romance.* Chapel Hill, NC: University of North Carolina Press.

Reay, D. (1991). Intersections of gender, race and class in the primary school. *British Journal of Sociology of Education, 12,* 163–182.

Robinson, J. (1923). *A mother's letters to a schoolmaster.* New York: Alfred A. Knopf.

Rogoff, B. (1994). Developing understanding of the idea of communities of learners. *Mind, Culture, and Activity, 1,* 209–229.

Rosaldo, R. (1989) *Culture and truth.* Boston, MA: Beacon.

Rose, D. (1987). *Black American street life: South Philadelphia, 1969–1971.* Philadelphia: University of Pennsylvania Press.

Rose, G. (1993). *Feminism and geography.* Minneapolis: University of Minnesota press.

Routman, R. (1991). *Invitations.* Portsmouth, NH: Heinemann.

Rugg, H., & Shumaker, A. (1928). *The child-centered school.* Yonkers-on-Hudson, NY: World Book.

Rusk, D. (1993). *Cities without suburbs.* Washington, DC: Woodrow Wilson Center Press.

Sarason, S. (1990). *The predictable failure of educational reform.* San Francisco, CA: Jossey-Bass.

Schudson, M. (1995). *The power of news.* Cambridge, MA: Harvard University Press.

Scott, J. (1985). *Weapons of the weak.* New Haven, CT: Yale University Press.

Scott, R., & Meyer, J. (Eds.). (1994). *Institutional environments and organizations.* Thousand Oaks, CA: Sage.

Sheff, D. (1993). *Game over: How Nintendo zapped an American industry, captured your dollars, and enslaved your children.* New York: Random House.

Sheldon, A. (1993). Pickle fights: Gendered talk in preschool disputes. In D. Tannen (Ed.), *Gender and conversational interaction* (pp. 83–109). New York: Oxford University Press.

Shilling, C. (1991). Social space, gender inequalities and educational differentiation. *British Journal of Sociology of Education, 12,* 23–44.

Shilling, C. (1993). *The body and social theory.* London: Sage.

Sibley, D. (1995). *Geographies of exclusion.* New York: Routledge.

Sieber, R. T. (1981). Many roles, many faces: Researching school–community relations in a heterogeneous American urban community. In D. Messerschmidt (Ed.), *Anthropologists at home in North America* (pp. 202–220). Cambridge, England: Cambridge University Press.

Silverstein, M. (1976). Shifters, linguistic categories, and cultural description. In K. Basso & H. Selby (Eds.), *Meaning in anthropology* (pp. 11–55). Albuquerque, NM: University of New Mexico Press.

Slater, D. (1987). On the wings of the sign: Commodity culture and social practice. *Media, Culture and Society, 9,* 457–480.

Smith, D. (1987). *The everyday world as problematic.* Boston: Northeastern University Press.

Smith, L., & Keith, P. (1971). *Anatomy of educational innovation.* New York: Wiley.

Smith, M., & Tardanico, R. (1987). Urban theory reconsidered: Production, reproduction and collective action. In M. Smith and J. Feagin (Eds.), *The capitalist city* (pp. 87–110). Cambridge, MA: Blackwell.

Soja, E. (1989). *Postmodern geographies.* London: Verso.

Stacey, J. (1990). On resistance, ambivalence and feminist theory: A response to Carol Gilligan. *Michigan Quarterly Review, 29,* 537–546.

Stack, C. (1991). Different voices, different visions: Gender, culture, and moral reasoning. In F. Ginsburg & A. Tsing (Eds.), *Uncertain terms: Negotiating gender in American culture* (pp. 19–27). Boston, MA: Beacon Press.

Stephens, S. (1995). Children and the politics of culture in "late capitalism." In S. Stephens (Ed.), *Children and the politics of culture* (pp. 3–48). Princeton, NJ: Princeton University Press.

Stern, D., Stone, J., Hopkins, C., McMillion, M., & Crain, R. (1994). *School-based enterprise: Productive learning in American high schools.* San Francisco, CA: Jossey-Bass.

Study finds Va. cities in decline. (1993, May 20). *Roanoke Times & World News,* p. C3.

Sturgeon, J. (1995, January 25). Job skills called lacking. *Roanoke Times & World News,* pp. B1, B7.

Tammivaara, J., & Enright, D. S. (1986). On eliciting information: Dialogues with child informants. *Anthropology and Education Quarterly, 17,* 218–238.

Thais assemble Power Rangers but can't afford them. (1994, December 17). *Roanoke Times & World News,* pp. A1, A4.

Tharp, R., & Gallimore, R. (1988). *Rousing minds to life.* Cambridge, England: Cambridge University Press.

Thompson, N. (1990, October 24). Teachers dodge merger stand. *Roanoke Times & World News,* pp. B1, B8.

Thompson, N. (1991, August 14). Committee makeup critized. *Roanoke Times & World News,* p. B4.

Thorne, B. (1993). *Gender play: Girls and boys in school.* New Brunswick, NJ: Rutgers University Press.

Turner, J. (1990a, October 30). Merger busing deceit charged. *Roanoke Times & World News,* pp. B1, B3.

Turner, J. (1990b, September 28). Merger foes swap charges. *Roanoke Times & World News,* pp. B1, B4.

Turner, J. (1990c, October 26). Merger foes blasted. *Roanoke Times & World News,* pp. B1, B3.

Turner, J. (1990d, October 24). Schools merger key. *Roanoke Times & World News,* p. B4.

Turner, J. (1990e, October 3). Teachers differ on merger. *Roanoke Times & World News,* pp. A1, A12.

Turner, J. (1993, June 25). Housing woes cross boundaries. *Roanoke Times & World News,* pp. B1, B3.

Turner, J. (1994a, January 20). Closing the gap by year 2000. *Roanoke Times & World News,* p. C4.

Turner, J. (1994b, May 11). O'Neil's opinions may have cost her board seat. *Roanoke Times & World News,* p. C1.

Turner, J. (1995, December 18). From fifth grade to the real world. *Roanoke Times & World News,* pp. C1, C3.

Upheaval in the city schools. (1982, January 27). *Roanoke Times & World News,* p. A8.

Varady, D., & Raffel, J. (1995). *Selling cities: Attracting homebuyers through schools and housing programs.* Albany, NY: State University of New York Press.

Wacquant, L. J. D. (1995). The ghetto, the state, and the new capitalist economy. In P. Kasinitz (Ed.), *Metropolis: Center and symbol of our times* (pp. 418–449). New York: New York University Press.

Wagner, L. (1994, January 21). New Century Council unveils draft of goals. *Roanoke Times & World News*, p. B1.

Waller, W. (1961). *The sociology of teaching.* New York: Russell & Russell.

Ward, C. (1978). *The child in the city.* New York: Pantheon.

Weick, K. (1976). Educational organizations as loosely coupled systems. *Administrative Science Quarterly, 21,* 1–19.

Weick, K. (1985). Systematic observational methods. In G. Lindzey & E. Aronson (Eds.), *Handbook of social psychology* (Vol. 1; 3rd ed.; pp. 567–634). New York: Random House.

Welker, R. (1991). Expertise and the teacher as expert: Rethinking a questionable metaphor. *American Educational Research Journal, 28,* 19–35.

White, C. (1982). *Roanoke: 1740–1982.* Roanoke, VA: Roanoke Valley Historical Society.

Whyte, J. (1983). *Beyond the Wendy house: Sex role stereotyping in the primary school.* York, U.K.: Longman.

Williamson, L. (1993, August 16). Everything is here except the job. *Roanoke Times & World News*, pp. A1, A5.

Willis, P. (1981). *Learning to labor.* New York: Columbia University Press.

Willis, P. (1990). *Common culture.* Boulder, CO: Westview Press.

Woods, P. (1978). Relating to schoolwork: Some pupil perceptions. *Educational Review, 30,* 167–175.

Yancy, D. (1990, November 11). Merger support fell off. *Roanoke Times & World News*, pp. A1, A2.

Yancy, D. (1993, October 11). Many familiar faces at the meeting. *Roanoke Times & World News*, pp. A1, A4.

Zukin, S. (1991). *Landscapes of power.* Berkeley, CA: University of California Press.

Zukin, S. (1995). *The cultures of cities.* London: Blackwell.

Author Index

Subject Index

A

Abstract space, 70, 76, 83, 91, 105, 107–108, 110, 121–122, 163, 165, 168, 191–192
  of corporate practice, 70
  as a distancing from the body, 121–122
  of finance, 76, 165
  housing patterns, 91, 105, 107–108, 110
  and popular culture, 191–192
African American community, 85–92
  desegregation of schools, 89–90
  effects of magnet schools, 90–91
  effects of urban renewal on, 86–89

B

Body meanings, *see also* Race
  farting, 129–130
  "freedom," 119–120
  gendering of, 131, 137
  grotesque canon, 130–131
  regulating the body, 127
    individualization, 128
    rationalization, 127–8
    socialization, 127
  spaces of the body vs. bodies in space, 121–122
Business–School partnership, 51–66, 69–80
  classrooms as competitive economies, 60–66, 69–80
  kids' attempts to make sense of, 69–80
  Teacher resistance to, 62–66
  corporate educational rhetorics, 51–54
  economic rationales for progressive pedagogy, 43–45
  simulating shopping malls, 54–60

C

Cicily, 81, 90–91, 95–105, 107, 116–117, 120–121, 132, 139–140, 152–153, 189–192, 222
  girls hit boys fight, 139–140
  neighborhood activities, 90–91, 95–105
  opinion on desk arrangements, 132
  roller skating, 120–121
  use of racial categories, 152–153
  x-chicks interview, 189–192
Circuits and organizational fields, 30–31
  parents', 31–36
    comparative, longitudinal view of schools, 31–35, 198
  teachers', 39–43
    parent–teacher communication, 42–43
    teacher disagreement over curriculum, 41–42
    teachers as repositories of pedagogical expertise, 39–40
    virtual pedagogy, 42, 197
Commodities and exchange, 174–180
  comic books, 175–176
  shopping, 165–166
  sport as spectacle, 179
  sports cards, 174–179

D

Desiree, 113–116, 132, 181, 189, 194, 222
  neighborhood activities, 113–116
  opinion on desk arrangments, 132
  theme park dreams, 194
Doug, 98, 100–105, 107, 116, 134, 153, 161, 166–167, 177, 185–187, 189–192, 222, 236
  baseball cards, 177
  neighborhood activities, 100–104
  on reputations of secondary schools, 161